Chris —

Best wishes for
your continued success
I'm confident you'll
be a star

Tom Hargreaves

Praise for
Innovating the Corporation

"While some may define *market leadership* in terms of attained market share, Kuczmarski, Middlebrooks, and Swaddling define it in terms of sustained innovation. Leadership is earned by being able to excite your customers. Only through innovation is a company able to . . . become the 'standards setter' that delivers the products that customers must consider when they make their purchases. This book speaks to corporate leaders who wish to obtain effective insight into the process of becoming market leaders. It presents frameworks and lessons to guide decisions that involve levels of risk and that create distinct benefits; there is no more strategic set of decisions than these. As the book states, 'It's all about risk and leadership.'"

> THOMAS P. HUSTAD
> Professor of Marketing and Kosin Fellow,
> Kelley School of Business, Indiana University,
> and Founder and Editor of *Journal of Product Innovation Management*

"The true power of this book lies in its wide applicability across Fortune 500 businesses struggling in the marketplace. Kuczmarski, Middlebrooks, and Swaddling bring to life a simple key to developing the innovation mind-set—*courage:* the courage to recognize the barriers to innovation cemented in corporate culture today; the courage to break down the myths that perpetuate new product failures; and, most importantly, the courage to make innovation a separate discipline with direct access to the CEO.

"This is a book about building *new wealth*, creating muscles in companies that for years have bulked up only on skills to steward existing wealth. With this book, courageous leaders can awaken the innovation that has been dormant in their companies for too long."

SCOTT LUTZ
President and CEO,
General Mills–DuPont Joint Venture

"*Innovating the Corporation* has many good points about innovation. The quote I feel is most important is 'Innovation is a team sport.' Teams make new products happen, especially 'continuous, predictable innovation,' as the authors point out. 'Rambo' types have no place in creating products for major corporations; they cannot motivate teams, and good teams make the difference."

JOHN MCMENNAMIN
Vice President,
Worldwide Nestlé/Disney Relations, Nestlé, Inc.

"The authors have identified an important issue facing today's large corporations; that is, how to create an environment that promotes innovation. The word *innovation* scares many employees because it implies taking risks. The authors provide step-by-step practical advice on how to establish a risk-supportive culture in large corporations that encourages employees to innovate. Employees need to feel encouraged and supported to take risks so they will innovate and create value. As the authors very clearly point out, 'innovation brings a new perceived benefit or value to a customer, employee, or shareholder.' Creating a risk-supportive culture is a win-win outcome for all constituents, and so is this book."

MARK E. ZMIJEWSKI
Deputy Dean of MBA Programs,
The University of Chicago Graduate School
of Business

Innovating the
CORPORATION

CREATING VALUE FOR CUSTOMERS AND SHAREHOLDERS

THOMAS KUCZMARSKI

ARTHUR MIDDLEBROOKS

JEFFREY SWADDLING

NTC Business Books

NTC/Contemporary Publishing Group

Library of Congress Cataloging-in-Publication Data

Kuczmarski, Thomas D.
    Innovating the corporation : creating value for customers and shareholders /
Thomas Kuczmarski, Arthur Middlebrooks, and Jeffrey Swaddling.
      p.   cm.
    Includes bibliographical references and index.
    ISBN 0-658-00304-6
    1. Organizational change—United States—Management.   2. Corporate
reorganizations—United States.   3. Creative ability in business—United States.
4. Technological innovations—United States—Management.   5. Employees—
Effect of technological innovations on—United States.   6. Industrial
management—United States.   I. Middlebrooks, Arthur.   II. Swaddling,
Jeffrey.   III. Title.
HD58.8 .K83   2000
658.4'063—dc21   00-34869
                                                             CIP

Interior design by Hespenheide Design

Published by NTC Business Books
A division of NTC/Contemporary Publishing Group, Inc.
4255 West Touhy Avenue, Lincolnwood (Chicago), Illinois 60712-1975 U.S.A.
Copyright © 2001 by Thomas Kuczmarski, Arthur Middlebrooks, and Jeffrey
Swaddling
Printed in the United States of America
International Standard Book Number: 0-658-00304-6
01 02 03 04 05 06 LB 18 17 16 15 14 13 12 11 10 9 8 7 6 5 4 3 2 1

To Susan Smith Kuczmarski,
a wonderful wife, mother, and partner,
and to my sons, John, James, and Thomas.

Tom

This book is dedicated with love to my wife, Patty,
to my son, Carter,
and to my parents, Jeanette and Burton.

Art

This book is lovingly dedicated to my wife, Amie—
the best friend, wife, mother, and partner I could ever imagine—
and to my children, David and Katelyn.

Jeff

CONTENTS

FOREWORD

During the past three decades, my experiences at Procter & Gamble, Kraft Foods, Johnson & Johnson, and General Mills have enabled me to see firsthand how to best innovate within a corporation. The concepts presented in this book match perfectly with my own perspective on what works and what doesn't. The seven Ps presented by the authors hit the bull's-eye for creating a corporate environment that can systematically and consistently innovate.

My own list of key criteria includes:

- Having support from senior management
- Having a depth and quality of understanding and insight into consumers
- Separating and protecting resources focused on breakthrough innovation
- Implementing a stage/gate development process
- Measuring progress
- Avoiding premature concept testing
- Rewarding milestones along the way
- Being open to ideas and proposals
- Balancing efforts against breakthrough innovation versus incremental innovation
- Having strong partnerships in the development process
- Starting early
- Maintaining some flexibility

The single most important factor is having support from *senior management*. Ideally, senior mangement would provide a motivating and challenging vision and have a day-to-day, hands-on role in creating an environment to foster innovative behavior. At a minimum, management must have a fundamental appreciation for the need for innovation and must provide strong, visible support for those who take on this challenge.

Having a *depth and quality of understanding and insight into consumers* is the second critical factor. Success is disproportionately tied to whether you have insights about consumers—and even better, what consumers will want in the future—that your competition does not have and how well your product addresses the consumers' needs, desires, and behaviors that you have identified.

It is quite important to *separate and protect resources focused on breakthrough* innovation. This allows you to create a different, customized environment more conducive to transformational innovation and to prevent resources from being drawn back into day-to-day activities.

No large company will be successful on a sustained basis without an overall development framework and a disciplined approach to project management and decision making. A *stage/gate development process* is the best vehicle for this, but it must be proactively practiced to realize full value from the tool. The key is to consider many ideas and projects in the early stages but actually execute only a few.

It is crucial that there be a means to *measure progress* so that you can determine whether you are really impacting the business with innovation. The ultimate measure is, obviously, consistent results in the marketplace. With experience, the expected value of projects in the latter stages of development can be estimated quantitatively to facilitate priority setting and gate decision making. It is foolish to do quantitative estimates of value for projects early in development, but those projects can be assessed *qualitatively* using principles of good development and innovation—and a good measure of experience.

Premature concept testing should be resisted. Using concept testing as the primary screening tool for new products is risky business. This type of research can be quite powerful if used at the right stage—near the middle of the process. But if used excessively or prematurely, it can easily thwart big innovation because it is biased toward close-in ideas. Frequently, you are testing how well concepts are written—not necessarily the power of the underlying ideas. Breakthrough innovations are almost always driven in early stages by the vision and passion of one person or a small group of people who seldom have consensus support from the entire organization.

Rewarding milestones along the way is crucial to achieving breakthrough innovation. Without encouragement at various stages and positive recognition of constructive failures, there will eventually be pull toward smaller, lower-risk projects that have a more certain chance to get to the marketplace. Of course, marketplace success should be disproportionately recognized.

Being open to ideas and proposals—particularly those from outside your organization—is a characteristic of highly innovative companies. Better yet, proactively seeking other ideas from every possible source will greatly increase chances of ongoing success.

Usually it is necessary to *balance efforts against breakthrough innovation versus the incremental innovation.* Getting the right mix is a matter of business strategy and can change over time, but incremental innovation will tend to dominate unless the balance is proactively managed.

It is critical to have *strong partnerships* among all the key development groups in the organization, particularly research and development, marketing, and consumer insights. An organizational model that relies on any one function to come up with and screen all ideas just won't work in today's environment.

An undervalued but important success factor is the need to *start early.* When possible, begin working on ideas with early stages long before these projects hit the current business agenda. Big innovation cannot be delivered on demand; time is a crucial asset in allowing ideas to mature.

Most companies tend to commit all resources to known, usually short-term projects, and thus cannot take advantage of big new ideas that emerge. Instead, companies need to *maintain some flexibility.* By *flexibility,* I don't mean idle resources, but resources that can be reassigned without risking the short-term business.

The number of items in your own list—whether it's seven or seven hundred—is simply a matter of preference. The only number that matters is the one on the bottom line. With this book, Kuczmarski, Middlebrooks, and Swaddling give you the formula for creating your own list to successfully innovating your corporation.

DANNY STRICKLAND

ACKNOWLEDGMENTS

This book is the result of over a decade of hard work and exciting dialogue with hundreds of colleagues, clients, and students from over one hundred innovative corporations. Our interactions with the managers and employees of our clients' organizations, as well as our spirited discussions and debates with other consulting colleagues and the hundreds of MBA students who have taken our classes at Northwestern's Kellogg Graduate School of Management and the University of Chicago Graduate School of Business, have helped us shape the thinking in this book. They have helped us understand how corporations become innovative. They have given us hope that our vision of a more innovative world in 2010 is not just a dream. Without the passion, energy, wisdom, and insights of these individuals, this project would not have been possible. To all of those we have worked with, we thank you!

In particular, we would like to thank the following individuals for their rich contributions and their outstanding thought leadership in creating and shaping the content of this book: John Berschied, former VP of Global R&D, S.C. Johnson & Son, Inc.; Carl Bochmann, Partner, Riverbend Engineering; and Danny Strickland, Senior Vice President of Innovation, Technology, and Quality, General Mills, Inc.

In addition to the individuals who helped shape our thinking for this book, several others were instrumental in helping us research, write, and edit the manuscript. Our special thanks to Kristen Hemingway for her time and effort in conducting secondary research for the book. Special thanks to Chris Rooney who contributed time and energy during the development of the first draft. Special thanks to Rich Hagle, for providing energy, guidance, structure, and invaluable editing suggestions and feedback during our entire writing process. We would also like to give extra special thanks to Adoleena A. Plunkett for the extraordinary time and effort she spent typing, editing, and proofreading to help produce a clean manuscript for our publisher.

Similarly, we wish to acknowledge our partners at NTC/ Contemporary Publishing: thanks to our editor, Danielle Egan-Miller, for her support and help in shaping the vision for this book; to Kristen Eberhard for her smooth management of the production; and to Denise Betts for her invaluable assistance and attention to detail.

Finally, we give heartfelt thanks to Susan Smith Kuczmarski, Patty Middlebrooks, and Amie Swaddling. Thank you for all of your work and encouragement during this process. We truly appreciate your sacrifices and selflessness.

To all, thank you for making this book possible!

INTRODUCTION

This book is about the innovation revolution—the force that is uprooting the risk-averse attitudes of corporations around the world. Corporate leaders at the top are now beginning to recognize that innovating their corporations is no longer a strategic decision or choice. It has become a basic business imperative for survival and a prerequisite for sustainable growth.

Innovation is the backbone of all newness. And newness is the watchword of the new millennium. New products, new services, new brands, and new companies; new approaches, processes, and delivery systems—all have exploded onto the scene during the last decade with a regularity that defies comparison with events of a century or more.

In the meantime, the large corporate culture just isn't what it used to be. Corporations are awakening to a new "parallel universe." The days of fat trimming and downsizing are gone. Instead of eliminating employees, the biggest challenge is attracting and keeping high-caliber talent. But the trend for many is clear. What used to be a lifetime employer has become a short-lived experience provider: go to a large corporation, gain some excellent experience for a few years, and then leave to start your own company.

In short, the shoe is on the other foot. Cost-cutting and reengineering strategies, even when necessary, ended up stifling creativity and suffocating innovation. Much of the philosophy of "low-cost" producer strategies, promulgated by consulting firms in the 1980s, wreaked havoc on corporate innovators whose budgets, teams, resources, and funding were cut mercilessly and often recklessly.

"Go forth (on your own) and innovate" became the new corporate creed. And it is what some of the most creative, innovative individuals did. They formed their own firms—small, vibrant companies that grew entire new industries and shook old ones to their foundations with new attitudes toward customers, agile approaches to creating new products, and a new mind-set that fostered virtual innovation communities. The result often was new competition that overtook the companies that had originally found the innovators expendable.

Thus, all the focus on squeezing out costs, looking to acquisitions as the key growth strategy, alienating innovative employees, and enshrining risk-averse leadership at the top has left many traditional corporations gasping for air. They are not only struggling with growth initiatives; they are struggling to survive.

And the proof is in. The solution to this pervasive problem is (as it was) innovation. Corporations that focus on frequent, consistent innovation beat out their competition in overall performance. The innovators enjoy higher stock prices, greater earnings growth, more satisfied customers, and valued employees who feel good about themselves and their accomplishments. Innovation increases shareholder, customer, and employee value. It can be the most compelling and riveting way to revitalize the corporate mind-set during the next decade.

Innovating the corporation means that your stock price will soar above that of your competitors', and your employees and customers will rally behind you and applaud your success. Why? Because they win too. Corporations that innovate successfully will be the ones with a market capitalization that exceeds their peers'. They'll keep the best people and secure a leadership model for future generations.

But hoping to innovate and actually creating sustainable innovation are two totally different things. Innovation isn't easy. It takes a huge amount of courage and brave leadership. We believe that corporations are sitting on a gold mine of future opportunity. By using innovation effectively, vast resources, very sharp and talented people, and core competencies can be pulled together to create new benefits for customers in the future.

Understandably, an approach for making one hundred thousand employees innovative is certainly different than an approach for an employee base of ten workers. Thus, this book is not for the small entrepreneurial inventor or start-up. There are many books on how to be creative and even more on process and culture. This book is targeted at corporate leaders and managers of Fortune 1000 companies and other large corporations around the world. It presents a systematic approach for building and infusing innovation into multibillion-dollar companies and inculcating them with the values and mind-set necessary for success.

Nevertheless, one person alone does not make an innovative company. Innovation is a job that goes well beyond the CEO. It does indeed require a village. Consequently, creating an innovation mind-set and a risk-free and risk-*freeing* environment requires participation by virtually everyone in the organization. The growth role of innovation needs to be articulated by employee after employee, and taking risks needs to be a commonplace practice that is the rule rather than the exception. It must be infused into the corporate bloodstream.

This book is aimed at helping twenty-eight million corporate employees. Our goal is to describe how to better marshal, stimulate, and energize these Fortune 1000 employees and managers to be brilliantly effective at innovation.

PART I

THE QUEST FOR INNOVATION

CHAPTER I

THE INNOVATION IMPERATIVE

The 1990s was the most remarkable period of U.S. economic growth in the twentieth century. America became the economic engine of the planet. Stock prices soared beyond our wildest imaginations. As recently as 1995, few would have believed that the Dow would exceed 11,000 and that the NASDAQ would crash through 5,000. An impossibility! That growth was fueled by innovation that created new products, services, processes, and business tools that changed the way people lived and worked. It made people more productive and more prosperous. It made stockholders wealthier and companies stronger. In addition to the tangible products and processes that have fueled corporate earnings, there has been the growth of an intangible spirit—the spirit of innovation. That spirit has become the new corporate growth strategy.

Innovation Must Go On

The future can remain vibrant and dynamic, with unparalleled growth, if the United States as a country and a society develops a passion for innovation. But not if it slips back into risk-averse, fail-safe approaches to managing growth. If that happens, it will rapidly lose the competitive edge, valuation successes, and national leadership it has enjoyed.

Evidence of the changes brought about by innovation-driven growth is everywhere. In addition to the explosion of the stock market to historic levels during the late 1990s (the Dow had never been over 4,000 before 1990), consider the following:

- *Measurement and planning.* During the last thirty or forty years, marketers' ability to measure results and target future strategies has undergone revolutionary changes in scope and precision. ZIP codes, introduced in the 1960s, made market segmentation commonplace shortly thereafter. Scanners were introduced into supermarkets during the 1970s, and, by the mid-1980s, manufacturers were marketing at the store level. By the mid-1990s, database marketing, including data warehousing and data mining, was becoming commonplace. Some marketers have replaced mass marketing with one-to-one models using more than one hundred psychographic variables.

- *Management and processes.* Total quality management, just-in-time management, and concurrent engineering are already old news. In early August 1999, Toyota announced that its new "virtual production line" would enable it to deliver a custom automobile within five days of receiving the order. DaimlerChrysler's response to this announcement was that it could now achieve the same in twelve days. General Motors said that its time was seventeen days. The remarkable thing is that all of these statements were made in the same century in which Henry Ford allegedly told customers they could have any color at all, so long as it was black. And more remarkable still, Toyota's capability can't really be considered a serious competitive advantage.

- *Motivation and people.* New methods of working and organizing work, including job sharing and telecommuting, as well as new approaches to rewarding both individuals and teams, have been contributing factors to productivity gains during the last decade of the century. In 1990, approximately four million people telecommuted. By the end of the decade, the number was reported to be more than twenty-one million.

Real sustainable growth has always been a key goal of business. And an increasingly high number of senior executives are "getting it." Although intelligent, frugal management of resources is a necessary component of success, radical downsizing and cost-cutting usually do not produce growth. As in the past, growth and prosperity depend on the continuation of innovation—the creation of new value through the development of new products and services. That means corporate leaders face an extraordinary challenge: if they wish to enjoy continued economic strength, they must surpass what a few years ago was an unsurpassable goal. And if they succeed, it will be because they have innovated, not downsized, their way to greater productivity, growth, and prosperity.

What Is Innovation?

Everyone should want to innovate. Many CEOs do. Investors certainly do. Employees want to. Customers benefit from it. Governments should encourage it. The economy will continue to thirst for it. But what is it?

Innovation brings a new perceived benefit or value to a customer, employee, or shareholder. The key words are *new perceived benefit*. The benefit may be functional, psychological, emotional, or financial. The range of benefits can be from minimal to massive. For example, a process innovation could bring a time-saving benefit to employees. A new videophone might bring functional, emotional, and psychological benefits to a customer. And a new innovative business launch might bring financial benefits to management and shareholders.

Furthermore, innovation does not exist in a risk-free zone, so while product and service improvements (e.g., line extensions, adaptations, and repositionings) are a part of the definition of innovation, they are only a part. Innovation must be defined as a portfolio of high and low risk-return endeavors and initiatives. Like a balanced stock portfolio, corporations should define innovation as *a portfolio of products, services, and processes all providing distinct benefits with varying degrees of risk and return.*

Simply put, innovation increases value to customers, employees, and shareholders. In traditional terms, it is "that which is newly introduced; a change." More to the point, innovation is the set of functional skills required to conceive and develop a new product or service and bring it to profitable realization. Innovation brings genuine newness to an organization's customers or constituencies. Further, it is a mind-set, an all-consuming attitude that drives the way managers think about business strategies, process, leadership, and structures. It is analogous to continuous process improvement in that it is an attitude that feeds on and sustains itself.

It should be easy to see that innovation thrives in an environment that uses analytical tools to measure and manage creative endeavors. Successful innovation is the result of the deliberate assessment of market demand and a company's internal strengths and abilities to meet those demands. Success is not the result of mysterious forces and impulses but rather the application of disciplined techniques. Like any skill, that discipline needs to be exercised to improve; the more it is used, the more it produces a greater ability and confidence, which in turn produces a higher than normal success rate, which ultimately reinforces the mind-set that produces such success.

Types of Innovation

Innovation, like genius, is an abstraction that can take many different shapes, forms, and manifestations. As illustrated in the following example, innovation is virtually boundless as long as a new benefit is realized and brought to fruition.

Technology tends to get all the attention, but planning (or strategy) is a tool that most consistently points the way to breakthrough new products. Wal-Mart is a classic example. While the company uses sophisticated buying procedures and just-in-time inventory tactics, it also outsmarts the competition through its choice of location and service and appeals to customers in unusual ways. For example, while virtually all companies actively discourage overnight parking in their parking lots, Wal-Mart actively encourages owners of recreational vehicles to use its parking lots for overnight parking—much to the chagrin of its competitors, which subsequently have had to scramble to show how "customer-friendly" they are.

Another example is Continental Airlines, long considered an also-ran in the airline industry. A February 9, 1999, *Wall Street Journal* article reported that the airline had become the leading operator in the New York City area. It had gained more than 3 percentage points in market share over an eighteen-month period—an enormous change. The airline simply made Newark Airport a hub, which enabled it to offer better and faster service to busy commuters. The strategy didn't involve a single new piece of technology, just more of what customers wanted. Like most manifestations of innovation, it was more a matter of attitude or approach, a way of being or looking at the world, than a matter of process.

Who Benefits from Innovation?

The short answer is everyone. The benefits that occur from innovation can be astounding. Exhibit 1.1 summarizes the benefits most commonly cited by companies that have engaged in and been rewarded by innovation.

Exhibit 1.1 Innovation Benefits

Shareholder Benefits	Customer Benefits	Employee Benefits	Company Benefits
• Increased market valuation • Superior stock appreciation • Higher dividends	• Customers with better satisfied needs and wants • Increased customer loyalty, satisfaction, and commitment	• Expanded employment opportunities • Energized, creative, and enthusiastic environment • Increased employee satisfaction	• Sustainable growth • Increased customer goodwill • Enhanced productivity • Increased margins and revenues • Position in new categories • Increased employee retention • Better marketing

First are shareholder benefits. Innovative approaches to markets and product development lead to market leadership and increased stock value. Microsoft's unusual success is reflected in smaller ways in hundreds of companies every day. The company built a dominant position in its industry in a variety of ways, and technological superiority was not the most important one. It developed innovative relationships with suppliers up and down the supply chain on one hand and provided extra value to consumers through aggressive marketing and distribution strategies on the other. The result was extraordinary value for stockholders.

One of Microsoft's chief competitors showed how just a single new product can make a rebound possible. In 1995, Apple Computer's stock sold for about $5 per share. The company had launched a number of product failures and the future was bleak. Then, four years later, its stock was over $100 per share. The turnaround was due to the introduction of the iMac, which was a computer user's delight: inexpensive, colorful, and friendly. The company had recaptured the magic of the original Mac in a product that followed a similarly innovative approach to products and customers.

The most tangible benefit that comes from innovation is increased stock price. Look at anyone's list of "best" companies. As a group, they have enjoyed an average annual increase of 70.5 percent in stock price versus an increase of 27.1 percent for the Standard and Poor's index (Exhibit 1.2). They sell to different markets with different propositions, using different types of employees with very different skill sets. But they share at least one characteristic: an innovative mind-set that drives an intense focus on a unique, essential core. Clearly, their ability to innovate successfully has resulted in significant increases in shareholder value. The financial community is looking for ways to assess a corporation's innovation potential or innovation readiness. There is economic benefit to be realized from innovation. So, the first benefit layer goes to shareholders in terms of market valuation, dividends, and stock price appreciation.

The second set of innovation benefits is realized by customers. When a new innovative approach, product, or service gives customers a new benefit, their lives are improved somehow. It might be a here-

**Exhibit 1.2 Innovative Corporations and
Their Valuations (1993–1998)**

Company	Return (%) 10-Year	5-Year
General Electric	39.1	34.2
Coca-Cola	1.3	26.1
Microsoft	114.6	68.9
Dell Computer	248.5	152.9
Berkshire Hathaway	52.2	33.8
Wal-Mart Stores	106.5	27.6
Southwest Airlines	38.4	6.6
Intel	69.0	50.6
Merck	41.3	37.0
Walt Disney	–8.5	16.9
Top ten average	**70.5**	**45.4**

Source: Dow Jones Interactive

and-now tangible benefit, such as a way to do business more profitably, or it might be more abstract, as in a sense of improved well-being. In either case, customers' "satisfaction quotient" goes up. When a customer finds your product or service outperforms competitive alternatives, or your delivery and service is faster and more reliable, you gain "loyalty points" with customers. Because it generally costs five to ten times more to attract a new customer than to sell to an existing one, a company's marketing becomes more effective and efficient.

The third group to benefit from innovation comprises employees and managers. Studies conducted by Kuczmarski & Associates show that four key motivators are most valued by people who want a career in innovation. They are: (1) a sense of pride and personal accomplishment; (2) peer recognition; (3) senior management exposure; and (4) career advancement. These compelling benefits mean higher self-esteem and a sense of success for everyone. As their security increases and their careers advance, loyalty to the corporation expands. Sounds like a win-win situation, doesn't it? Thus, innovation provides both expanded employment opportunities and increased employee satisfaction. Moreover, it energizes a group of people, making them more productive and personally enriched. Enthusiasm to come to work in the morning returns.

Finally, many company benefits accrue from innovation: more sustainable growth; increased margins; more effective and efficient marketing; more dynamic processes; stronger and more robust positions within categories; increased employee retention; positive public relations; and the ability to redefine the existing business and enter new markets, segments, and geographies.

Society as a whole also wins. Little more than fifty years ago, diabetes was a death sentence for thousands of people every year. For millions of others, it meant living on severely restricted terms. Today, with continuing advances in medicine, it is a mere inconvenience for many people who have it. Longer life and better quality of life: these are just two benefits of innovation.

What's Preventing Innovation?

> *It isn't as though no opportunity for innovation exists. While Procter & Gamble's Folgers and Philip Morris' Maxwell House toyed with new packaging, upstart Starbucks Corp. came along and revolutionized the coffee market.*
> Wall Street Journal, September 16, 1999

Imagine that. Two giant corporations, Procter & Gamble (P&G) and Philip Morris, with massive resources and market clout got sideswiped by an entrepreneur in Seattle, Washington. With nearly $100 billion in combined revenues and $10 billion in annual profits, these two Fortune 20 conglomerates had plenty of resources for innovation, if they had chosen to pursue it.

Insufficient resources are rarely the barrier to successful innovation. What if Howard Schultz, the current CEO of Starbucks, had been the president of the coffee divisions at either P&G or Philip Morris? Would he have successfully launched and expanded the Starbucks brand, product line, and new service experience? Or would he have been given several reasons why it wouldn't work, why another retail coffee concept couldn't succeed, why darker roasting was not what consumers wanted, and why coffee ice cream had no market potential? Probably the latter. Howard would most likely now be introducing new flavors of coffee in traditional packaging with "new and revitalized" graphics.

Innovation must be seen as a core business strategy. It requires the highest level of commitment and passion by the leaders at the top of an organization to make it work. It takes a willingness to dramatically change the company culture to one where individuals have high self-esteem and feel as if they have control to make decisions and take action. It requires an environment that encourages people to take risks.

So, why haven't large corporations been more consistently successful at innovation? What is holding them back? Why can't their culture seem to change to enable more people to innovate? The answer is relatively simple:

- Innovation is not being treated as a top priority.
- Management hasn't created a risk-taking culture or corporate mind-set.
- Employees are not encouraged and do not get paid to take risks.
- Adequate resources haven't been allocated for innovation.

The first challenge, then, is not to uncover new sources of funds that can fuel innovation but rather to discover new ways to change attitudes and mind-sets throughout a company. But is it possible for a large multibillion-dollar corporation to be innovative? Of course it is, and there are far more excellent examples than might be immediately apparent. From Lucent, Microsoft, and Dell to Schwab, Sony, and Southwest Airlines, corporate leaders who value the power of innovation insist on creating a culture that perpetuates and reinforces it.

The really good news is that any corporation can become effective at innovation and, within a two-year period, be an innovation power-house. This can occur, of course, after management (1) has agreed that innovation will serve as a fundamental growth strategy, and (2) has created a plan, process, and culture that work together as a system.

What if your company is one of those that believes acquisitions will better serve your growth strategy? What about it? Regardless of your business strategy, all corporations need to develop an internal capability to innovate. Saying your company doesn't need innovation would be the same as saying, "We're really an engineering and manufacturing-driven company, so we don't need any sales and marketing." An even better example may be leaders who ask, "Who needs this quality thing? Isn't quality something that every employee just needs to make part of his or her job?" Likewise, many corporate leaders have promulgated a similar belief regarding innovation: "Why can't everyone understand that it's their job to be innovative, to think of new solutions and new ways of doing things?"

Herein lies the key underlying problem preventing many corporations from excelling at innovation. Innovation must be viewed as a separate business discipline. It needs its own budget, measurements, dedicated people, distinct plan, unique rewards, and specific language to make it stand on its own. It's analogous to information technology. Virtually everyone within a corporation uses a computer. People interact and communicate through software and E-mail. Yet, there are also a dedicated resource base, separate budget, annual plan, and unique language that go along with the management, facilitation, upgrading, and maintenance of information technology.

The same is true for innovation. Everyone does need to be innovative every day. However, you can't just demand it in the same way you can tell everyone to take a computer course. People need to be trained, encouraged, and supported; others need to dedicate their full-time jobs to helping make it work for others. Innovation needs to be organized as a separate business function. It needs a separate leader—a chief innovation officer or vice president of innovation— who reports directly to the CEO. It needs a dedicated group of people who lead innovation teams, train others, measure progress, test concepts, lead discussions, and the like. Innovation needs to shine with its own power source. It needs its own set of "corporate batteries" to provide the energy, consistency, and light required to motivate several thousand employees within a corporation.

Risk and Leadership

Too many executives talk at cross-purposes. They say one thing and mean another. Or worse yet, they say one thing and reward another. Managers and employees walk a fine line between doing what they're told and second-guessing what they've heard. That's why the very first step in creating an innovative culture is being absolutely clear about its priority. All senior managers must reach consensus and buy into the strategic role that innovation is to play in future growth. They need to ask:

- What do we mean by innovation?
- How will we define it within the walls of our own company?
- Is it breakthrough innovation? Incremental innovation? Radical or discontinuous innovation?

Clarity in the role and priority of innovation sows the seeds for risk-taking. If this issue is not addressed clearly, completely, and concisely, the last thing employees will be willing to do is take risks.

Risk-taking is the essential ingredient for all innovation. Without it, companies allocate their resources against a known quantity like their existing product lines. But who wants to put their career or compensation at risk? So, the environment needs to become conducive to risk-taking. Every functional employee should be encouraged to take risks. It's a risk to hire a new employee, create an aggressive strategic plan, change an accounting method, champion a new product, initiate a new service, or change the dress code to casual. As General Electric's CEO, Jack Welch, has been heard to say, "Shake it, shake it, break it." The message is to shake up old patterns or behaviors, break old routines, and begin thinking differently.

For employees to feel a sense of freedom to take risks, two things need to happen. They need to have greater control over their decision making, and they can't be penalized for failure. Employees need to feel that they are in control rather then believing they are victims, helpless to control their decisions. This means that much more goal setting needs to be individually driven, as well as bottom-up rather than top-down. People need to have a sense of pride, a real sense of project ownership, to make it truly "theirs." When people try hard and genuinely attempt to make a new process, program, or product work, and it fails, just celebrate. That's right. Throw them a failure party to reinforce the corporate commitment to risk-taking.

In a similar vein, the way senior management behaves in a cross-functional team meeting can be either devastating or uplifting. When the team gets the sense that senior management is on their side, serving as their coach, sponsor, and advocate, you can feel the spirit in the room soar. On the other hand, in many meetings, you can watch the entire spirit and karma of an innovation team disintegrate and crumble. When a senior manager explains why this new product will "never be a success" and gives three reasons why it should be killed, the group's spirit is extinguished.

Senior managers need to adopt new behavioral norms and forms of communication. They must clarify their messages to other managers and employees. Recognizing their role as mentor versus "boss" is a key starting point for freeing up the corporate mind-set toward more risk-taking. And by the way, senior managers need to take some risks too. Unless they behave the way they want employees to, it will merely become a "do as I say not as I do" theatric.

Risk-taking opens up the mind. It expands the way you currently define a business. It instills self-confidence and bolsters personal self-worth. When an employee or team member has high self-esteem, his or her outputs, contributions, productivity, and overall value will be exponentially higher than before. *Disciplined freedom*, a term captured in Tom Kuczmarski's first book, *Managing New Products*, is described as: "A management style or culture that provides a balance whereby individuals have a sense of entrepreneurship and creativity and receive enough direction and control to guide their efforts."

Achieving this balance is a very delicate and difficult task for corporate leaders. Their natural tendency may be to take control; however, the goal should be to give control to others, support their taking of it.

So we return to our initial statement that the innovation priority must be clear to let risk-taking flourish. When a senior manager says,

"We need to focus on our strengths," does that mean the company should only launch line extensions? Should it keep marketing its current brands? What if leaders discover an opportunity that wouldn't leverage its strengths? The words and behavior of the people at the top usually get analyzed, interpreted, and discussed thoroughly. Management must be perfectly clear on the importance of innovation and what it means to corporate growth.

Innovation takes courage. Businesses have made it through the streamlining and pruning-back days. Now it is time for building up, expanding outward, and innovating across the organization.

Innovation can eventually become a core competency for a corporation. S.C. Johnson & Son, Inc., led by Fisk Johnson, is an outstanding example of an innovative company. As a consumer packaged goods company with household brand names that include Pledge, Windex, Glade, Raid, and others, millions of consumers use their products daily. Within the past four years, new products such as Glade Candle Scents, Windex Outdoor, and Pledge Grab-it have added hundreds of millions of revenues to its growth targets. Moreover, with Innovation Centers around the world, it is planning to stay in the innovation leadership position for the long term. While Fisk Johnson is a profound advocate of innovation, there is a sense of trust and risk-taking that permeates this more than $5 billion company. Innovation teams throughout the company are given permission to take risks and fail. Their key to success is matching technological advancements with customer wants and needs. Moreover, they've figured out how to do it consistently for decades, which has resulted in profitable growth and endeared an entire employee base to the family-owned corporation.

Don't let innovation lay dormant. Awaken it. What's required is stripping away some old behaviors to revitalize the culture in a way that breeds new mind-sets.

Everyone has a fear of failure and rejection. That's normal. But, usually, what people fear most is what they don't understand. Thus, the first step to overcoming fear is understanding at the most basic level. What if marketing and research and development people really took the time to get to know each other—actually spent time discovering each other's sources of motivation, fears, personal goals, and so on? What about finance, sales, and manufacturing people? Get to know people in other functional areas and learn their language; ask them to learn yours. Until everyone understands gross rating points, brand development index, run-on-press, fluorocarbons, and protein crystallization, progress on the innovation front will always be uneven and uncertain at best.

Why America Needs Corporate Innovation

While Internet start-ups and initial public offerings will continue to get loads of media attention and stock market coverage, large corporations need to take on the mantle of innovation leadership. Why? Because, to turn a phrase, size matters.

The Fortune 1000 corporations generate $6.8 trillion in revenues and employ 28.4 million people annually. The earnings performance of these companies dramatically influences stock price fluctuations from one day, one month, and one year to the next. The NASDAQ and NYSE are severely impacted when performance from these giants falls short of expectations. In short, these large corporations represent the bedrock of the national and global economy.

When you consider the potential impact of innovation from these thousand corporations on the world, it becomes almost incalculable—but not quite. Here are a few numbers. Approximately 30 percent of their total revenue—more than $2 trillion—comes from foreign markets. When one new product is launched globally, it can easily become a $100 million revenue generator within a couple of years. The sheer scale of the global marketplace provides enormous expansion opportunity for a new innovation.

Corporate America in 2010

The year is 2010. Managers have recognized their leadership role as mentors, coaches, and champions to marshal the massive resources of the corporation around the core strategy of innovating; that is, creating new approaches internally for doing business differently and new mind-sets for instilling trust. Corporations are pounding out innovative new products and services like never before and have regained their status as top jobs sought after by the best business schools. Employees are proud to be working for their employers. They feel well rewarded, personally satisfied, and highly valued. Employees now *want* to take risks. They know that failures are encouraged and all will learn from them.

When you walk into a corporation in the year 2010, here's what you'll see:

- A positive, fun, can-do-it attitude
- High energy levels among all employees
- Individuals who feel in control of and excited by their jobs
- People who work together as teams instead of alone
- Paychecks fluctuating greatly from one year to the next
- People with high self-esteem
- A lot happening
- Senior management offices in the middle of the workspace, glassed in with doors open
- The chief innovation officer's ten-year contract waiting to be renewed

It is possible to make this scenario a reality. This book's aim is to help corporations reach this state well before 2010.

CHAPTER 2

THE PROBLEM:
INNOVATION BARRIERS
AND MYTHS

If effective innovation can have such a positive impact on customers, stockholders, employees, and companies, why don't more companies focus on it and work to excel at it? After all, past "movements" that promised dramatic increases in financial performance spread rapidly and widely throughout the business community. In particular, the quality movement of the 1980s and the reengineering movement of the 1990s received widespread adoption.

Quality

In the 1980s, the threat of foreign competitors offering higher quality products propelled many companies to invest in quality improvement programs. These companies hired quality consultants, established vice presidents of quality, formed "quality circle" teams, sent employees through quality training, established and tracked quality metrics such as six sigma, and linked compensation and rewards to improvements in quality. National awards, such as the Malcolm Baldrige National Quality Award, were established. Associations that focused on quality, such as the Association for Productivity and Quality Control (APQC), were created. Companies publicly touted their focus on quality—Ford's advertising slogan was "Quality is Job #1." The quality movement even made its way into service industries, such as banking, automotive repair, airlines, and hotels, that previously had been thought to be "quality-proof." The entire nation rallied around the cry for quality. As a result, quality improved dramatically in many industries.

Reengineering

By the 1990s, companies had shifted their focus to reengineering, led by Michael Hammer, who pioneered the movement with his ground-breaking book *Reengineering the Corporation*. Reengineering—the radical redesign of a company's processes, organization, and culture to achieve a quantum leap in performance—promised simultaneous improvements in cost, cycle time, and customer service. The movement was a tidal wave that took most companies with it, regardless of their industry, size, or location. They set up reengineering committees, hired reengineering consultants, established reengineering priorities, measured reengineering results, and rewarded people based on their achievement of the stated goals. Many companies achieved significant bottom-line results from their reengineering efforts.

The Rise of Innovation

Certainly innovation has been receiving greater media attention these days. A flurry of business books, articles, studies, and news programs have focused on the topic. Even Hammer seems to have reengineered *himself* in an effort to become the innovation guru! Companies are beginning to publicly declare innovation as a top priority (for example, consumer products manufacturer Procter & Gamble's publicly stated top three priorities are "Stretch, Innovation, and Speed"), and more organizations are mentioning innovation in their annual reports as a core business strategy. One of the most effective "mentions" we have seen was on the front cover of the 1998 annual report for Capital One, a financial services firm. It captures the essence of the issue: There's no time for subtlety—innovate now!

THE INNOVATION IMPERATIVE

Change or die. That is the imperative of the Information Age. Back at the dawn of the century, Henry Ford's Model T ruled the road for almost twenty years before competitors made it obsolete. Now we see our competition in the rearview mirror in a matter of months. So our commitment to innovation is total. It's built into our strategy and into every associate, every department, every piece of technology, every process, and every test of new ideas. Our goal: be first to market, roll out at full speed, then move on. Rather than wait for the competition to obsolete our products, we do it ourselves. Capital One's strategy is working. The proof is in the profits and in the growth. Our innovation is constant. Half of what we now market did not exist six months ago. . . .

Reprinted by permission of Capital One Corp.

But innovation really isn't making much headway in terms of results. Many companies seem to be struggling to become more effective innovators. Regardless of industry or company size, the same barriers to innovation continue to surface. The fact is, the same barriers exist today that existed throughout the 1980s and the 1990s: it's too risky, it's too expensive, it's too impractical, and so on.

Barriers to Innovation

So, why are innovation results so disappointing? What prevents companies from becoming more effective at innovation? In our seminars, the top five barriers to innovation are:

1. Lack of priority
2. A risk-averse culture
3. Difficulty in measuring innovation
4. Overemphasis on short-term results
5. Lack of discipline

Because of these five barriers, companies fail to adequately embrace, cultivate, encourage, measure, reward, and carry out innovation.

Barrier #1—Lack of Priority

Take a walk down the halls of corporate America, and you often see "innovation" listed as a top priority on the corporate mission statement. These same companies will post a corporate values statement that says employees should "encourage risk-taking," "value new ideas," or "challenge past assumptions." But look beyond the carefully worded, professionally produced corporate mission and values statements. Four key areas reflect the *real* priorities.

Roles and Responsibilities

Who is responsible for innovation? How many different functional areas throughout the organization participate in innovation initiatives? Is responsibility for innovation housed in one or two departments, or does almost everyone in the company actively participate in and support these efforts? All too often people view innovation as someone else's job. Yet the companies whose leaders and employees believe this were often successful in getting quality or reengineering responsibilities distributed to everyone in the corporation. Unless innovation responsibility is distributed throughout a company, management is not really creating a risk-taking culture.

Orientation and Training Courses

Is every new employee exposed to innovation and educated on how he or she is expected to contribute to innovation success? Is innovation-oriented training provided for every relevant team? Are innovation team leaders given special training and attention? If innovation is indeed a top priority, then employees must be provided with the necessary skills to make it happen. And new employees should know from the outset the company's commitment to innovation.

Executive Time, Attention, and Communications

The focus of management's time and attention speaks volumes about the company's real priorities. What priorities does the executive team talk about? Where do they spend their time? Their written and spoken words can either reinforce their commitment to innovation or undermine it. People may at first be intimidated when the CEO shows up at the weekly meeting of an innovation team. But, over time, the CEO's action will demonstrate that the team's efforts are important, that they matter, and that the company is counting on them.

Budget and Human Resources

What activities get funded with company dollars and people resources? How much funding really goes toward innovation? An executive team may say innovation is an imperative, but take a look at the real measure—their pocketbook. One company we talked with established a five-year goal of $2 billion in incremental revenue that was expected to come from innovation. But when we scratched the surface, it became quite apparent that the company was not really committed to innovation at all: only two people had been assigned to fulfill that goal! At the "thirty-thousand-foot level," innovation looked great, but when it came to the serious business of allocating resources, the management team was overcome with astigmatism. And what became of the two lucky individuals? Surprise! They quickly became frustrated and left the company. While this example is a bit extreme, few corporations make the resource commitments necessary to achieve their innovation goals.

Barrier #2—A Risk-Averse Culture

Each year we conduct dozens of innovation seminars, meetings, and training classes with middle and senior managers across a broad range of industries. Without fail, the most frequent barrier to innovation that surfaces is risk aversion. Most companies tell their employees in all kinds of implicit ways that they simply will not tolerate failure.

The challenge of balancing the need for success with the need to accept risk can be daunting. The executive vice president of Intuit, makers of Quicken software, frames this issue quite succinctly:

Innovation is a risky business, and failure is commonplace. Rewarding success is easy, but we think that rewarding intelligent failure is more important. We don't judge people strictly by results; we try to judge them by the quality of their efforts. We want people to take intelligent business risks without also risking their compensation or their careers.

Harvard Business Review, November-December 1995

Again, many companies say they encourage risk-taking. In reality, their actions may suggest quite the opposite. You must dig deep to discover a company's actual willingness to accept innovation risks.

Criteria for Promotion

How do people get promoted? Are they promoted for attempting new things or for avoiding failures? The vice president of human resources at one large consumer products company we encountered openly admitted that people in his company had been traditionally promoted for not failing. He described how people were encouraged to support the status quo, wait until their boss failed in some area, and then step in and take over the boss's responsibilities. In this company, to attempt an innovation initiative and fail was a surefire way to stall your career.

Over many years, this company had fostered a culture that was competitive, not collaborative, and stifled risk-taking behavior. There were two additional consequences: backbiting and sandbagging. After all, if someone else's failure was the key to your promotion, what would you do? Support those forces that encouraged failure or diminished success.

Measurement, Compensation, and Bonus Systems

How are people compensated? To what extent are salary increases and bonuses linked to innovation? First, innovation is difficult to measure (see Barrier #3), making compensating for it difficult. Second, compensating people for innovation successes could result in midlevel employees receiving higher compensation than some executives. As a result, few companies make a serious attempt to link innovation and compensation. What they fundamentally state through their compensation system is that the company does not offer a significant reward for taking risks. So, why should anyone do it?

Innovation Career Paths

How do people get to the top—by taking risks or avoiding them? Does a "stint" in innovation help or stall a career? Are people expected to stay in certain positions for such a brief time that they are not encouraged to take bigger, longer-term risks ("Just don't screw anything up")? In many companies we have visited, the average tenure of a midlevel marketing person in any one position is eighteen months. After eighteen months, these people are moved to another category, division, or country to continue their climb up the corporate ladder. Unfortunately, it takes more than eighteen months to uncover, develop, test, launch, and measure the outcome of most significant innovations. It's no wonder that companies with this type of career track find a huge void in the area of breakthrough innovations.

Executive Recognition

What gets publicly rewarded and recognized? When was the last party held for a team that "pulled the plug" on a failed innovation effort? What happened to team members who were part of a failed innovation effort? In particular, the way in which executives handle failed innovation efforts offers important insights into the company's risk tolerance. Often, failures are covered up. In other cases, team members are punished by being fired or sent off to undesirable positions. Some team members are even left with a "black mark" on their employee records that follows them wherever they go in the company.

Make no mistake: we are not suggesting that every failure be tolerated and even celebrated. Rather, teams should be commended when they did what was within their power to mitigate risks, followed an effective process, kept executives informed, identified potential issues early, and ultimately enhanced the organization's capabilities for the future. This suggests one additional question: how much effort is spent on learning from failures?

When you ask questions and investigate these areas, you can quickly uncover whether a company really promotes risk-taking or just gives it lip service.

Barrier #3—Difficulty in Measuring Innovation

A third barrier to innovation effectiveness is the inherent difficulty of measuring innovation results. Innovation requires a "batting average" mentality. Studies continue to show that even the best innovators are only successful 60 percent to 70 percent of the time. Because innovation results are inherently unpredictable, companies often feel like they can't depend on it. If they pour money into innovation efforts, they don't know what will happen. As a result, similar to advertising spending, innovation is often the first thing to get cut when times are lean.

Companies often believe that it is much easier and more reliable to grow through acquisitions and investments in their current business than through internal innovation. Consider the regulated utility industry, where companies are guaranteed a predetermined (though low) rate of return for certain types of investments. Is there any question as to why the utility industry has a particularly difficult time embracing innovation when it compares guaranteed returns from current businesses against uncertain returns from innovation?

Innovation measurement is a serious topic. Without appropriate and helpful measures, companies tend to underinvest in innovation activities. They devote too few dollars and people, they stretch people over too many projects, and they do not devote high-performing people with the appropriate skills. Especially in today's reengineered and downsized corporations, drumming up support for innovation can be a significant challenge. In many cases, the dollar resources may be available but sufficient people resources may not. Of course, there may be opportunities to get a bigger bang for current innovation bucks through improved processes, better organization and management of efforts, enhanced employee training, better portfolio management, and the like. However, for innovation to take off, most companies must divert resources away from other valuable activities. As an old saying goes, "Picking between good and bad is easy. Picking between good and better is the real challenge." The root cause of this barrier is a lack of innovation measures.

Why is innovation so difficult to measure?

Organization-wide Impact
Innovation activities tend to be dispersed across an organization; they don't fit nicely into one functional area. As a result, it's difficult to track them, let alone identify who is doing what or how much time they are spending. Furthermore, many innovation activities, especially those in the early stages of a product development process, cannot be allocated to a specific product or project. In particular, market research and technical research and development work performed early in the process may uncover and spawn many (or few) innovation efforts.

Inadequate Accounting Systems
Take a look at an income statement, balance sheet, and cash flow statement for any company. The closest thing to innovation is a line item called "R&D" that occasionally shows up on an income statement. Although research and development may be correlated with innovation, it simply measures dollars spent for certain activities, not revenues or profits realized. In short, generally accepted accounting principles (GAAP) offer little help for innovation. Furthermore, today's complicated accounting systems are not set up to track the revenues, profits, and costs associated with innovation. These systems deal much more effectively with existing products, businesses, and departments.

Lack of Ownership
No one person typically owns a profit and loss statement for innovation. Accountability in most companies centers around a business unit or department. And most companies have not assigned one individual to measure and be accountable for innovation results. Of course, this begs the question: should organizations have an innovation owner—a chief innovation officer (CIO) or vice president of innovation? We address that question in Chapter 4.

Focus on Outcomes Measurement
Today, even those companies that do measure innovation only measure "after-the-fact" outcomes of their efforts: the success rate of innovations, total revenues and profits generated from innovation, and

the like. Companies need the ability to more accurately measure where they stand with regard to innovation at any given time, what their pipeline of activity looks like, and the returns that can be expected. Although there are numerous "go/no-go" stages in the development process, innovation is not a simple yes or no proposition. A product or idea may change shape throughout its development. That's why measurement along the way is essential.

The Extended Time Required

The outcomes and success of some company activities can be measured fairly quickly. For example, ask the vice president of customer service to assess the impact of having hired additional employees for the customer service call center. He or she will be able to quickly show you how average customer wait times have declined. But most innovation questions—typically the most important ones—are not so straightforward. Suppose a company launches a breakthrough new product into the market, and the product is performing below expectations. A logical question would be: why are the results disappointing, and will they improve? This question isn't a simple yes or no, go or no go; it is complex and requires further diagnosis:

- Are the forecasting methods accurate?
- Is the new product cannibalizing existing products more than expected?
- Is the market more competitive than anticipated?
- Is the sales force properly trained and motivated to introduce the new product?
- Did marketing communications and promotions motivate sufficient numbers of people to try the new product?
- Is the product performing at the expected quality level?
- Is the market still in its earliest stage where only a small minority of customers, the early adopters, are currently purchasing the product?

This company may not be able to accurately assess the true impact of its innovation and whether or not it was really a success for several years.

Barrier #4—Overemphasis on Short-Term Results

The fourth barrier to innovation is a lack of patience. Many corporate activities can have a positive short-term, bottom-line impact—for example, acquisitions, plant closings, layoffs, sales promotions—but not innovation. Unlike quality and reengineering teams, which often uncover "quick-hit" opportunities, few significant innovation efforts fall into this category. To make matters worse, the financial community measures performance in ninety-day increments! Innovation is not a short-term fix.

Over the past decade, much of the innovation literature has focused on speed-to-market and cycle time reduction. Indeed, these are worthy pursuits. However, executives can get two false impressions:

- Innovation can be sped up to show significant results within the ninety-day financial market window.
- Speeding up innovation is always a good thing.

In many cases, speed kills! Especially when dealing with breakthrough innovations, speeding up the process often results in speeding a failure to market. Speed can cause companies to suboptimize their innovations by not allowing adequate time to refine them and properly introduce them into the market.

The Quick Fix Syndrome

Because of a lack of realism in the face of pressure for a quick fix, many companies simply choose—or put themselves in the position of having to rely solely on—acquisitions as their primary growth mode by default. One industrial products company boldly promised Wall Street that it would double its business in five years (i.e., grow from $400 million to $800 million), despite the fact that its long-term historical annual growth rate had been 7 percent. The new goal required the company to grow at 15 percent annually. Shortly after the public announcement, reality began to set in. The executive team decided to take a closer look at how they were going to accomplish their goal. To no one's surprise, the existing business could only grow at (guess what?) roughly 7 percent. In looking at the other 8 percent of the growth goal, two options surfaced: innovation and acquisitions. The executives realized that even if they immediately vamped up innovation efforts, innovation would only start to make a significant impact on revenue after three years. Too late to make a serious dent in their goal. Almost by default, the bulk of the growth goal would need to come from acquisitions. The most positive part of this story was that the team was realistic enough to see that they could not innovate to reach an unrealistic goal by force-feeding a program to their company or by relying on a "silver bullet" (see the next section).

The Search for the Big Idea Syndrome

Another result of lack of patience is the "search for the big idea syndrome." The thought process goes like this: if only the company can place the right innovation "bets" and focus all of its resources on them, then its problems will be solved. All it needs is a few big "hits" and the growth goal will be met. Breakthrough innovation becomes a silver bullet that will rescue the company.

Obviously, setting priorities is a key ingredient for successful innovation. Some companies probably are focused on too many small innovations. In such cases, limited resources become spread over too many initiatives, and no substantial progress is made toward anything. Lots of little line extensions are launched that offer only minor value to customers. However, the search for the big idea syndrome swings the pendulum to the opposite side. Companies with this mindset hope for a few big breakthroughs that will make managers look like stars and cover over any mistakes along the way. In reality, companies need a portfolio of innovations that support different objectives. Some innovations will represent major breakthroughs in the market, and others will have less impact but still serve important roles. A portfolio approach to investing in the stock market has been widely understood and applauded for years: the notion of investing all of your money in a few stocks is rejected out of hand as overly risky and unwise. For some reason, a portfolio approach to innovation is not nearly as well understood or applied.

Barrier #5—Lack of Discipline

Innovation is a discipline. It takes ongoing resource commitment and ongoing management time and attention—and continuous care and feeding. It is not something that can be started today at a moment's notice, then cut off tomorrow, and restarted at will in the future when the business turns around. After all, if innovation were that easy, why would it be so difficult to find companies that have maintained a track record for successful innovation over a long period of time? Innovation takes hard work.

Everyone has heard the compelling arguments about why discipline is bad for innovation:

- "You will stifle the team's creativity."
- "An innovation process will slow things down."
- "Innovation can't be planned. It just happens."
- "I don't care what you have to do, just get it out in the market. We'll fix it later if we need to."
- "Our company has an aversion to process."
- "You can't train people to be innovative. They either are or they aren't."

At the root of these excuses is a desire to avoid the discipline that innovation demands. Short cuts simply do not work—not systematically and not over time. An executive will occasionally get lucky by short-changing the process and pushing through a pet idea to get it to market faster. But in the long run, this approach will fail.

The Challenge of Aligning Innovation with Business Strategy

Innovation also requires a ruthless alignment with the company's business strategy. In many companies, when we ask leaders to show us their innovation strategy, they bring out a long list of projects. A list of innovation projects does not make a strategy! An innovation strategy bridges the gap between the business strategy and the efforts of individual innovation teams. It forces alignment to make sure people are focused on the right areas. Nothing is more frustrating for an innovation team than to make progress for several months (or years), and then be told their project has been canceled because it does not fit the corporation's business direction.

The difficult part of aligning innovation with the corporate business strategy is that it forces people to do things they do not normally like to do:

- They must say no to many potentially appealing opportunities. Otherwise, any opportunity looks like a good opportunity.
- They must put their money where their mouths are and align company resources with the innovation goals. Otherwise, executives set high expectations without dedicating the necessary resources.
- They must determine how much risk they are willing to take to achieve their goals. Otherwise, expectations can be established that goals will be attained without any failures.
- They must identify the hurdle rates that must be overcome *prior* to launching an innovation. Otherwise, managers can justify any innovation by making up their own hurdle rates or by labeling it "strategic."

Whether leaders like it or not, innovation needs continuous commitment and a close fit with the company's goals.

Innovation Myths

The five innovation barriers exist, in large part, due to misunderstandings surrounding innovation. Frankly, there is a lot of bad information out there. One of the battles that any individual or company faces in trying to make innovation a top priority is that much of the literature, seminars, and war stories perpetuate myths about innovation that can point people in the wrong direction.

For example, there's the myth of the solo geniuses—Thomas Edison types working alone in their garages. Then there is the visionary CEO who overcame all odds to build an empire. Bill Gates and Steve Jobs were the subjects of a recent movie using that theme. These stories can give the wrong impression, that innovation is a fleeting thing, difficult to capture and replicate within a large company.

On the flip side, some companies find comfort in a detailed innovation process. They believe innovation can be totally systematized. If a company follows the right innovation process, then results will automatically be good. A former student who works for a supplier to the major automobile manufacturers brought in two binders that were devoted to just one stage of his company's ten-stage process! Although on one hand innovation isn't simply the province of mad geniuses, on the other hand it is not simply a mindlessly mechanical process.

Playing out some of these myths to their logical conclusion would suggest companies take absurd actions to increase their innovation effectiveness, such as replacing the bulk of their workforce with new (different) employees or automating the innovation process so that human intervention is no longer required. Nothing could be further from the truth. Some of the most common and damaging innovation myths we have encountered and their corollary realities are listed in Exhibit 2.1.

Exhibit 2.1 Innovation Myths and Realities

Myth		Reality
1. Individuals drive innovation.	⟶	Innovation is a team sport.
2. Innovation begins with brainstorming sessions.	⟶	Innovation begins with a thorough understanding of the customer.
3. Innovation requires "creative" people.	⟶	Innovation requires effective problem solvers called "creators."
4. An innovation process will give you the results you need.	⟶	An innovation process is only one tool or enabler for effective innovation.

Myth #1: Individuals Drive Innovation.
Reality: Innovation Is a Team Sport.

From the outset, many companies have a flawed view of who needs to drive innovation. They assume that innovation is primarily driven by individuals who work fairly independently from others. Some companies seem to envision Rambo as the ideal innovator—one person who single-handedly comes up with ideas, sets an aggressive goal, executes a plan, and destroys all internal obstacles that keep ideas from getting to market. Rambo may be the CEO or a midlevel manager charged with an innovation initiative. The belief is that Rambo will make innovation happen come hell or high water. Other companies have a vision that the mad scientist is the ideal innovator—a technical person who goes off into a closet, thinks brilliant thoughts, tinkers around with various inventions, and eventually has a stroke of brilliance that will transform the company.

Companies that buy into a vision of the individual innovator eventually become disenchanted because the results are highly unpredictable and haphazard. Yes, the occasional Rambo or mad scientist will come along and even be successful—once or twice. But more often than not Rambo dies on the battlefield and the mad scientist comes up with a new gadget that flops in the market because no one really needed it in the first place. Continuous, predictable innovation requires effective teamwork—people with complementary skill sets who can see the customers' problems from different perspectives, bring in alternative solutions, build momentum and excitement throughout the organization, and orchestrate an effective launch. Later in the book we discuss the characteristics of these effective innovation "platoons."

Myth #2: Innovation Begins with Brainstorming Sessions.
Reality: Innovation Begins with a Thorough Understanding of the Customer.

Studies show that this myth is rampant. In conducting innovation research during the past five years, we have collected over five hundred examples of innovation processes within companies. In analyzing them, we find that over 80 percent start with a step titled Ideation,

Idea Generation, Brainstorming, or something similar. The natural question we ask is, "Where does the customer fit into your process?" The typical answers are:

- "The sales force knows the customer."
- "The market research department has conducted extensive quantitative research, and they have uncovered our customers' top needs."
- "Customers don't know what they want."

The response many companies come up with when faced with an empty innovation funnel is to hold a brainstorming session. Hire an outside moderator, invite creative people, and the answers will come—all in less than a week! Brainstorming sessions are looked to as the quick fix, and they perpetuate the belief that innovation is just a creative exercise that doesn't really require hard work. It ultimately suggests that a group of smart people can sit around a room, brainstorm ideas, and come up with great innovations, uninhibited by the customer. The problem is, who represents the customer? Where is the customer's voice in the whole process? In very few cases does the team sitting around a brainstorming session really represent the target customers to be served.

In nearly every case where we have witnessed a company take this approach, it has been a waste of time and money. Everyone has fun during the session, ideas are posted on flip charts all around the room, and people leave feeling like they have contributed. But now what? How do you determine which, if any, of the ideas should be pursued? Did the brainstorming even go in the right direction? Without a solid understanding of customers' lives, routines, problems, frustrations, hopes, fears, and the like, you are left without an effective filter to apply against your ideas. People resort to "voting" with colored stickers, and the ideas with the most votes win.

Myth #3: Innovation Requires "Creative" People.
Reality: Innovation Requires Effective Problem Solvers Called "Creators."

This innovation myth suggests that only certain types of people can be effective innovators. It goes something like this: "The reason we don't have enough innovation is that we have been expecting it from the wrong people. What we really need are more 'creative' types to think outside the box and bring a fresh perspective." Some companies have gone so far as to change their hiring profile to make sure they select more "creative" people for the organization. The goal is certainly a worthy one—try to break out of the traditional ways of thinking. The method, however, does not tend to have a significant impact.

One of the exercises we conduct at innovation seminars is to ask the question: "How many of you would consider yourselves very creative people?" Without fail, approximately 10 percent of the audience raises their hands. Very few people believe they are creative. At this point, we could end the seminar and ask everyone to go home. However, we ask a follow-up question: "How many of you would consider yourselves very good problem solvers?" Almost all of the hands in the room go up. The good news is, to be effective innovators, companies do not need a whole host of creative people. What they need are people who take the time to really understand customers' problems (as described for Myth #2) and then develop solutions to those problems. There are countless examples all around of the truth of these statements. For instance, the Portable Auto Office by Rubbermaid was the direct result of looking at the problems people—businesspeople who spent a good deal of their time in a car—had and determining what would solve their problem(s). The result was a wildly successful product that filled a real need and produced a considerable profit.

Rather than looking for an adjective (*creative* people), companies need to look for a noun—*creators*. People are born to create. To get innovation flowing, what organizations really need to do is channel that inborn ability in the appropriate direction—toward customer needs.

Myth #4: An Innovation Process Will Give You the Results You Need.

Reality: An Innovation Process Is Only One Tool or Enabler for Effective Innovation.

One widely held belief is that an innovation process, in and of itself, will deliver the desired results. A process often gives corporations a false sense of security that innovation can be formulaic, almost automated. We have witnessed many companies embark on an effort to benchmark the "best practice" processes used, develop their own systematic and staged innovation process, document the process in a thick manual, and then train people on the process. After completing such an effort, these companies expect innovations to begin flowing out of the process. All they will have to do is sit back and pick the best ones.

Unfortunately, innovation is both process and people dependent. One without the other is ineffective and unpredictable. A solid process can do terrific things for a company—create a common language, ensure the proper sequence of activities, and involve management at the appropriate points. The process is a tool that frees people up to focus on customer needs and solutions to those needs instead of worrying about what steps to take and how to navigate the internal politics. But the process itself is not the ultimate answer.

Most companies have bought into at least one of these innovation myths. The impact is corrupting. By buying into a myth, employees get and send the wrong messages about innovation. They innocently set the wrong priorities, model the wrong behaviors, and take the wrong actions. Innovating the corporation demands that executives and employees alike have an informed and accurate picture of the ingredients for successful innovation.

What Next?

The list of innovation barriers and myths just described can appear overwhelming. In addition, they are often intertwined and difficult to separate out. The logical questions are: "Which barriers should we focus on first?" and "How do we get started?"

In reality, a company cannot start knocking down barriers unless it is willing to be vulnerable, submit to some self-diagnosis, and identify where it is starting from. The innovation myths often lull companies into a false sense of security and accomplishment. People often believe they are already doing the right things.

Conducting an innovation summit and diagnostic audit as outlined in Chapters 4 and 5, respectively, can be a great place to start.

Companies that are committed to making innovation a top priority can in fact make it happen. Perhaps they cannot change the entire company overnight, but they can adopt a comprehensive framework, set up some innovation platoons, and begin delivering results. And results are the most powerful motivators for changing a company's approach to innovation. Chapter 3 outlines our framework for breaking down the nebulous concept of innovation into specific areas that can be focused on and executed to generate results.

THE GUARANTEED
INNOVATION SYSTEM

To this point, we have explored the forces that contribute to making innovation so important to corporations and the major barriers to good performance. So, how does a company actually become innovative? How can it overcome the major innovation obstacles? How can it position itself to develop a valuable portfolio of new offerings? Most companies have tried many things in the past to help find more "big" ideas and improve innovation success rates. In fact, U.S. corporations collectively spent more than $2 billion on innovation consulting services over the last five years, designing processes and conducting brainstorming sessions to find the next big winners. Despite all these efforts, however, corporations still aren't seeing the results they are looking for. How do successful companies innovate?

The simple answer to this question is that successful companies view innovation as a system, not as random projects, process steps, or creativity exercises. A system is defined as a group of interacting, interrelated, or interdependent elements forming a complex whole. All elements are needed. When a company is missing one or more parts of a Guaranteed Innovation (GI) system, its efforts will be diminished. Its programs won't function as efficiently and effectively as they might, and innovation success will be sporadic. Until every element of a GI system is in place and functioning within a corporation, it will experience inconsistent new product and service results at best.

Successful companies put all the components of a GI system in place and measure the performance of each component over time to make sure that everything is working properly. They monitor components and make required changes, repairs, and even complete overhauls, in some cases, to keep their "innovation machine" running smoothly. When a GI system is complete and functioning as it should, however, the effects of breakthrough innovations are consistent.

Most companies have some of the required components of a GI system, but very few have them all. Unfortunately, "almost all" doesn't lead to successful innovation. If an organization is missing even one key ingredient, the system doesn't work and innovation results cannot be maximized. Similarly, knowing which components need to be revised or repaired and making the necessary corrections are critical to maximizing innovation effectiveness.

An Overview of the Guaranteed Innovation System

The GI system components are universal and relevant to organizations in every industry in both consumer and business-to-business environments. They are relevant to product- and service-oriented companies, as well as to for-profit and not-for-profit organizations alike. And although the scale and formality of the components may be different for different companies, the guiding principles of the GI system are relevant to all large corporations. While the overall structure and guiding principles of each component of the GI system must be standard in successful companies, the specific design and execution of the components can and should be tailored to meet the needs of different organizational structures and cultures. The seven required components of a GI system are shown in Exhibit 3.1.

Exhibit 3.1 The Seven Components of a Guaranteed Innovation System

---

1. **Priority.** Establishment of senior management champions who believe in, reward, and consistently commit resources to innovation and a system to support it
2. **Policy.** Strategy to guide innovation efforts
3. **Platoons.** Dedicated, cross-functional innovation teams
4. **Process.** Formal yet flexible staged innovation development process
5. **Problem orientation.** Focus on solving breakthrough problems to maximize innovation value
6. **Platforms.** Breakthrough technology development programs
7. **Payback metrics.** Measures to gauge innovation success and monitor GI system and platoon health

---

Visualizing the GI System

The dynamics of a GI system can be understood best by visualizing a funnel. As Exhibit 3.2 shows, priority, policy, platoons, and process are the forces that help shape and manage the funnel. Problem orientation, platforms, and payback metrics are the "fuels" that keep the system running, and they help to gauge the efficiency and the overall health of the GI system and its outputs, a diverse portfolio of valuable innovations.

The secret of successfully innovating your corporation is to design a funnel that meets the specific needs of your organization and then ensure that the right amount of fuels run through it. If the funnel is too wide or too long, or if too little fuel is available (that is, if too few problems and technology platforms are being discovered), the funnel

Exhibit 3.2 The Guaranteed Innovation System

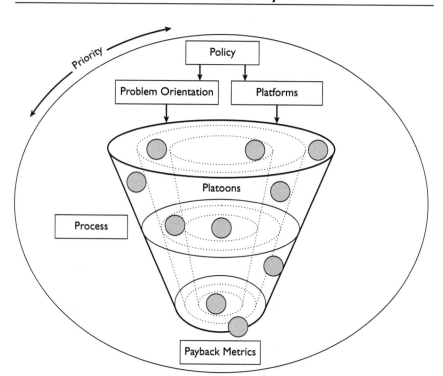

will dry up. Innovation efforts will not be maximized. Conversely, if the funnel is too narrow or too short, or if too much fuel runs through it too quickly, the funnel will overflow or spring a leak.

By understanding the ideal GI system design and the amount and types of fuel the system will hold and use, corporations can assemble and allocate their innovation resources properly and maximize the efficiency and effectiveness of their GI system and results. These topics are the focus of the remainder of this book.

Specifically, Chapter 4 addresses the issue of innovation priority and the factors an organization should consider when identifying senior management champions, setting up a GI system and rewards, and fostering an innovation mind-set within the corporation. A description of the key roles, responsibilities, and attitudes that innovation champions in successful organizations must assume is also presented. Chapter 5 explores the concept of innovation policy and the role that policy plays as a blueprint for innovation design research and scope. Chapter 6 looks at the concept of innovation platoons, the cross-functional teams that manage projects through the process. Characteristics of effective platoon leaders and members are outlined. Chapter 7 discusses the characteristics of an effective staged development process. Chapters 8 and 9 examine two types of innovation fuel: customer problems and technology platforms. Techniques and key principles for planning and executing "best of class" exploratory customer and technology platform research are described. Finally, Chapter 10 defines the major innovation payback metrics, the last innovation fuel, and explores how these metrics are used to assess the efficiency and effectiveness of innovation, the GI system, and platoons.

Understanding the Seven Components

Before we get into more details of each component of the Guaranteed Innovation system, let's define each one a bit more clearly and describe the specific role that each component plays in generating successful innovations.

Component One: Priority

The first component of a GI system is priority. For the purposes of this book, *priority* is defined as the identification of innovation champions and the commitment by those champions to foster an innovation mind-set and institute a GI system and rewards in their organization. Innovation champions can come from anywhere within an organization, though they are typically senior leaders with the authority to make structural changes, create new processes, and allocate resources for a company or business unit. Innovation champions are responsible for setting up the GI system, developing innovation policy, and ensuring that innovation participants and platoons are given the resources and support they need to carry out high-priority initiatives. If the champions are not senior leaders or do not have the authority to make changes like these directly, they must be given indirect authority from management to make required structural or resource allocation decisions. Without the participation or support of senior management champions within an organization, the GI system concept cannot be implemented.

The importance of establishing innovation as a high priority within a corporation cannot be overemphasized. Without intense commitment, employees cannot—or are reluctant to—take the steps and risks necessary to implement the GI system and make innovation happen. Innovation research supports this concept. The *Journal of Business Strategy* reported that pioneer consulting firm Arthur D. Little, Inc., in its 1998 Global Innovation Study, identified priority for innovation from upper management as one of four characteristics of successful innovators. A high priority for innovation motivates employees and paves the way for a corporate culture and mind-set that make innovation successful.

An innovation priority and "no-blame" culture at 3M have helped fuel its reputation for innovation success over the years. William McKnight, former president of 3M, believed that employees must feel the support for innovation from senior management and have the freedom to fail in order for innovation to succeed. As reported in *Marketing*, McKnight, in 1941, explained, "Management that is destructively critical when mistakes are made kills initiative, and it is essential that we have people with initiative if we are to continue to grow." Similarly, at Kimberly-Clark, CEO Wayne Sanders preaches the value of having a tangible management priority for innovation. Kimberly-Clark not only rewards employees for successful new ideas, but it promises never to punish employees who experiment and fail. The origin of one of the firm's profitable new products, a dignified incontinence garment, was a new product failure as Kotex Personals, a form of disposable underwear for menstruating women.

In addition to senior management champions, most successful corporations have a GI system owner to manage and guide innovation initiatives within the company or division. This individual is responsible for managing the innovation platoons, and for ensuring that the right amount of customer problem and technology platform research is being conducted and that development projects are moving through the innovation funnel efficiently and effectively.

Component Two: Policy

Once companies establish a priority for innovation, attention should turn to developing an innovation policy. Like priority, innovation policy helps shape the GI system funnel by providing additional guidelines for the scope and direction of innovation initiatives. Innovation policy serves as the game plan to guide development projects. It helps determine the future requirements for success and the goals to be reached using innovation, including:

- The resource strategy, which outlines the financial and human resource requirements for successful innovation
- The financial growth gap that innovations are expected to fill over the next five years
- The vision and strategic roles that innovations must satisfy
- The screening criteria to be used for moving ideas and concepts through the development process

Without an innovation policy, it is very difficult for the GI system champion and platoons to know how to proceed. Additionally, companies without a well-articulated strategy often support too few or too many projects. The result is underutilized or wasted innovation resources and the potential for misdirected and demotivated platoon members. Innovation policy outputs provide the needed focus for innovation platoons and help take the uncertainty out of what they are striving to achieve.

The financial growth gap helps determine the breadth of innovation research a corporation must undertake. A large gap usually dictates a broad research scope. Organizations with large growth gaps often need to focus on identifying breakthrough innovations inside and outside of their current markets or categories. Similarly, the innovation vision and strategic roles provide innovation platoons with qualitative benchmarks to guide problem exploration and development. They add specificity to the growth gap by defining "what's in" and "what's out" from an innovation perspective. Lastly, screening criteria help platoons separate the winners from the losers during customer problem identification, idea generation, concept development, and market testing. The criteria provide metrics across a variety of categories to help teams understand the relative attractiveness of various initiatives. While innovation policy setting definitely takes time, companies that create policies and then stick to them enjoy far greater innovation results.

Successful companies like Intel, Netscape, Sony, 3M, and Gillette all rely on strong innovation policies to provide direction for the development of new offerings. For decades, Gillette has been a model of strong innovation policy setting and commitment. In the late 1960s, Gillette's policy included a firm desire for breakthrough new offerings inside and outside of the company's core business of shaving products. In 1967, shortly after Gillette acquired Braun AG, investors advised the company to sell Braun's appliance divisions and focus on the more profitable shaver division. However, Coleman Mockler, Gillette's chairman, supported Gillette's innovation policy goals by making heavy capital and research investments in the small-appliance market. Mockler's bet eventually paid off. In 1996, Braun had become a $1.7 billion business with leadership in the oral care, epilator, hair dryer, and handheld blender markets.

Not surprisingly, companies that don't create a clear policy aren't nearly as successful. In one major consumer packaged goods company with which we worked recently, lack of a corporate innovation policy resulted in many more projects being pursued than the company could support. The company never saw a project it didn't like! As a result, employees who were assigned to many project teams had very little commitment to the assignments they were working on. Furthermore, because resources were stretched too thin, too little attention was given to each project, and many valuable initiatives were delayed or abandoned. This sequence of events illustrates a path that is often followed: a lack of policy equals a lack of focus in definition, which translates into a lack of commitment and direction, which results in some degree of suboptimization.

Component Three: Platoons

Innovation platoons are the special teams that manage the innovation research and discovery processes. With a well-articulated policy in place, platoons explore and identify problems and platforms in an effort to provide a solid foundation for new ideas, concepts, and technologies. While the specific characteristics and membership of innovation platoons vary from company to company and industry to industry, there are a few common elements of all well-functioning platoons, including:

- Cross-functional representation
- Dedicated team leaders and core team members
- Individual and team rewards that recognize performance

Platoons members should represent a mix of different functional areas to provide a cross section of expertise, perspective, and experience. No one functional area is more important than another. On average, the most effective innovation platoons have between five and seven members.

Although the amount of time each team member allocates to a platoon differs somewhat from project to project, platoon leaders and core members should generally dedicate between 50 percent and 100 percent of their time to the innovation initiative. Anything less than 50 percent becomes a recipe for failure. Part-time involvement from platoon leaders and core team members simply doesn't work.

Financial and nonfinancial rewards that recognize performance on a platoon are critical for effective innovation teams. Rewards come in different shapes and sizes, but they must be given in some form. Furthermore, these rewards should be based on performance; that is, they should recognize platoon members according to the actual market performance of the innovations they develop and/or deliver.

The formation of innovation platoons, like the establishment of priority and policy, is critical to effective innovation. Specifically, platoons manage the GI system projects and ensure that they proceed efficiently and effectively. The productivity and performance of these platoons, in large part, make or break innovation success in an organization. It is important for companies to take adequate time to determine the right mix of team members, the appropriate platoon leader, and the skills required of participants from each functional area on a specific project.

The use of innovation platoons at Chrysler helps to minimize miscommunication during the innovation process. Chrysler's vehicle deployment innovation teams include dedicated employees from marketing, design, engineering, purchasing, manufacturing, product planning, and finance. This dedication and diversity provide the platoons with a broad knowledge base and promote the sharing of ideas throughout the project, resulting in a greater number of innovation successes.

Motorcycle manufacturer Harley-Davidson also has an impressive history of commitment to innovation platoons. Major innovation initiatives at Harley draw on employees from engineering, purchasing, manufacturing, and marketing, who are dedicated to their projects full-time from the initial conceptual stages of design and development through delivery. Platoon members are often located in a single building to enhance communication and coordination. This platoon approach to innovation has positioned Harley to realize its goal of producing and selling more than two hundred thousand motorcycles a year by 2003.

Component Four: Process

After the right innovation policy and platoons are in place, the platoons should work together, or with a dedicated task force, to design and implement a staged development process. A *staged development process* is a tool to manage innovations as they move through various phases of development, from problems and ideas to concepts and launches. An innovation process reduces development cycle time and increases the probability of launching successful offerings by serving as a checklist for innovation platoons. There are six major stages in the GI innovation process, which are discussed in detail in Chapter 7:

- Problem identification
- Problem development and ideation
- Conceptualization
- Development
- Testing
- Launch

A staged development process is critical to innovation success because it provides platoons with a structure to guide them as they identify, shape, and prioritize initiatives. A staged process also enables objective decision points to be built into the process and allows for adjustment after each step. Most important, though, a staged process allows corporations to monitor the inputs and outputs of the GI system and track the number of innovations under development at any time in each stage. Then, depending on the innovation goals an organization has established, it can quickly determine whether the right number of projects are being undertaken and the right amount of resources are being applied to the projects.

For example, assume an organization is expecting two successful new innovations to be launched in a single year. If the company expects a 50 percent success rate, this means that it would have to launch four products or services into the marketplace to get two successful ones. Four launched innovations might require six to eight products in test market, eight to ten developed concepts, twenty-five to thirty new ideas, and so on. The value of this step-function progression is that it enables the organization to measure and monitor the projects in the "funnel" at each stage. This funnel flow tracking (Exhibit 3.3) helps companies project how many new products and services they can expect to launch and when.

Exhibit 3.3 Innovation New Product Project Funnel

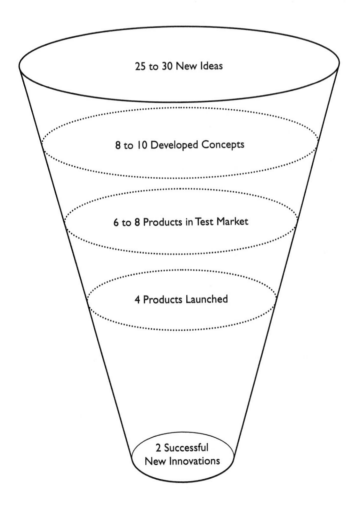

25 to 30 New Ideas

8 to 10 Developed Concepts

6 to 8 Products in Test Market

4 Products Launched

2 Successful
New Innovations

Many large corporations, including IBM, Procter & Gamble, 3M, Corning, and General Motors, have successfully implemented staged innovation processes. In fact, Corning has made the process mandatory for nearly all of its major innovation platform projects. Corning managers believe that the process reduces development time, allows quick identification of projects that should be terminated, and increases the ratio of projects that make it through the launch stage into the marketplace.

However, while staged development processes have been broadly implemented in large corporations, research suggests that they are still not understood or applied consistently. A 1998 innovation study by Kuczmarski & Associates revealed that although 59 percent of companies had formal innovation processes in place, less than 15 percent were wholly understood or consistently applied. Additionally, even in companies in which processes are being implemented successfully, the front end of the process—often called the "fuzzy front end"—is often missing or poorly defined. This lack of discipline and attention to process and the fuzzy front end contributed to alarmingly low innovation success rates in the United States in the 1990s. For example, the success rate for product introduction in the packaged goods industry fell below 30 percent.

Component Five: Problem Orientation

Once GI system platoons and process are defined, organizations should turn their attention to collecting the fuels that generate new breakthrough ideas and concepts—problems and technology platforms. Problems, the first of the fuels, are at the heart of breakthrough innovation. Companies that develop products and services that solve breakthrough customer needs will most likely be breakthrough themselves. But identifying breakthrough customer needs is challenging. It requires a disciplined research approach in which innovation platoons use a unique mix of qualitative and quantitative research techniques to explore and identify customers' most intense problems and needs.

The approach begins very broadly by identifying customers' life issues and then—through iterative waves of qualitative and quantitative focus groups, in-depth interviews, observational interviews, projective interviews, lead user groups, and surveys—gets progressively deeper and more detailed until the customer problems and needs are extremely detailed and well understood. These problems then provide a focus for idea generation and breakthrough new product and service concept development.

There are also many different types of customer needs, from observable and explicit needs to tacit and latent needs. All types of customer needs are valuable and important to understand. Any one of the types could lead to breakthrough innovations. However, the processes for identifying different types of needs are quite different. Ensuring that the innovation platoons understand these tools and that they have the right mix of skills and expertise to unearth the different customer need types is critical to maximizing GI system results.

Companies with a strong problem orientation create innovations that customers truly value. For example, during Boeing's development of the 777, engineers from Boeing worked closely with engineers, pilots, and flight attendants from United Airlines to ensure that the airplane addressed their key functionality and comfort problems and needs. Boeing also included parts suppliers from General Electric and other companies to ensure that the 777 would be highly compatible with them as well.

Similarly, Nokia's strong problem orientation in 1997 led to the development of its innovative 6100 series of cellular phones. Customers told Nokia they were frustrated with their current mobile phones, which weren't very easy to use, only came in a single design, and didn't last as long as they would like on a single charge. Nokia's answer was a phone with a simple interface, a range of colors and ring tones, and long standby and talk times. Through customer-centered design and development, Nokia was able to enter a market dominated by Motorola and make significant inroads.

Unfortunately, examples of problem orientation aren't all positive ones. Notable innovation failures like Miller Clear Beer and Lotus 1-2-3 computer software resulted from a lack of understanding of customers and their problems. Miller Clear Beer was introduced as part of the "clear craze" that swept the United States in 1992. The product failed because it didn't offer a meaningful benefit to con-sumers. Similarly, the failure of the Lotus 1-2-3 spreadsheet was par-tially a result of Lotus's failure to satisfy customer needs with regard to features—including program speed—and quality. In both of these very different cases, there was an insufficient amount of research about what was important to customers.

Component Six: Platforms

In addition to identifying customer needs as the source of potential ideas, innovative companies focus on identifying core technologies or technical expertise that may be leveraged in developing breakthrough innovations. Developing technology platforms can allow a company to have proprietary, new-to-the-world technologies and benefits that can be used as a launching pad for a variety of new offerings. Alternatively, innovative technologies can be used as an ingredient in the formation of a breakthrough innovation that solves an important customer problem or need.

For example, microencapsulation, a core platform technology at 3M, has made products as diverse as timed-release medication and Post-it notes possible. This know-how can be applied to a spectrum of innova-tions. Technology platforms like microencapsulation and others can be used to gain competitive advantage protection. The platforms may give an innovation a few extra months of uniqueness before the competition is able to copy it. This is important in maximizing GI system results.

Also, although some technology platforms should be developed in an internal vacuum, arising from the creativity and inspiration of company scientists and engineers, other platforms should arise from customer needs research, which routinely identifies technical "hot spots" that customers directly or indirectly envision for the future.

Once core technology platforms and new technical skill areas have been identified for innovation efforts, adequate investments and appropriate technical talent must be secured. The challenge is to accurately identify the technologies that can best be exploited and pro-vide support to the new products under development that leverage these technologies.

What Platforms Can Do

Gillette's enthusiasm for innovation platforms has fueled its global leadership in shaving technologies. From the 1970s (when Gillette began working on its sensor technology for razors) to the 1990s (when the company introduced its multimillion-dollar Mach III platform), top management at Gillette has been consistently committed to technical innovation. Gordon McKibben, author of *Cutting Edge*, a book that chronicles the history of Gillette, explains, "Gillette's market dominance is based on its technical prowess . . . A lot of people think of Gillette as a marketing company, but Gillette thinks of itself as a technology company."

3M's focus on technology platforms is equally impressive. The company discovers new platforms through leveraging the creative potential of its staff. Employees at 3M are allowed to spend 15 percent of their work time experimenting with and searching for new technical innovations. Using a combination of individual inspiration and customer problem insight research, 3M staffers have discovered the breakthrough platforms driving products like Post-it notes and Scotch tape.

While technology platforms are critically important to successful innovation, the assets required to transform technologies into commercial innovations don't always need to be developed internally. When Microsoft fully realized the importance of offering access to the Internet, it was nearly a year behind Netscape in getting a technically competitive browser to market. By entering into a strategic alliance with America Online, the largest on-line service provider in the United States, Microsoft quickly gained access to a distribution channel that encouraged rapid adoption of its product. Through this partnership, Microsoft has narrowed Netscape's lead in the browser market.

Component Seven: Payback Metrics

The final component of a GI system is payback metrics. While senior management manages the system design and policy, and platoons manage the projects in the funnel, the only way that success and performance can truly be assessed and measured is with effective metrics. Two categories of payback metrics should be considered:

- *Outcome metrics.* These metrics describe how effectively the corporation is innovating from a financial perspective, including resource investment returns, innovation success rates, survival rates, and the overall return on innovation.
- *System metrics.* These metrics describe how well the innovation process and portfolio are being managed, including the balance of projects in each step of the process pipeline and the innovation portfolio mix.

Specific innovation payback metrics are described in detail in Chapter 10. The relevant point here is the need to measure and reward tangible innovation results versus innovation policy objectives. The exact metrics used should be tailored to an individual company's own specific innovation goals and stage of development. However, several key principles can be adopted by most organizations. Additionally, one common return measure—return on innovation—should be used by all companies.

Return on innovation should be tracked over time and measured to determine the yields that have been generated from an organization's innovation investments. In addition, progress should be measured against stated innovation goals, and innovation participants should be measured and rewarded against innovation performance relative to the outputs or satisfaction levels achieved.

Very few companies measure innovation results. Even fewer companies measure results effectively. Arthur D. Little's 1998 Global Innovation Study identified lack of innovation performance and system measurement as one of four characteristics that separated successful innovators from the rest. Examples of companies that use metrics effectively to drive innovation performance do exist. Management at AlliedSignal believes that metrics are critical to the evaluation and improvement of innovation efforts in the company. Payback metrics at AlliedSignal have helped reduce development cycle times, guided developers to consider intellectual property issues sooner, and focused innovation initiatives on specific types of ideas (e.g., breakthrough ideas with long-term potential).

Creating Shareholder and Customer Value

The seven components of the GI system are each important elements of a successful innovation program in large corporations. Furthermore, each of the elements is required to make innovation happen. Similar to a fixed menu in an expensive restaurant, where everything is priced together as a single meal, GI system components cannot be chosen individually. They are not like items on a fast-food restaurant menu. They must all be in place and working together for shareholder and customer value to be maximized.

Although the GI system model may sound complex and challenging to implement, the truth is that any corporation can implement this system with some modest time, personnel, and financial commitments. While there are seven required components, corporations should view GI system implementation as a series of smaller stages. Beginning with priority and policy; moving to platoons and process; and ending with problems, platforms, and payback metrics, the GI system will gradually transform an organization. The key word is *gradually*.

DESIGNING THE SYSTEM

PRIORITY

Priority means precedence in time, order, and importance. If innovation is a priority for a corporation, that means it precedes something else. In effect, management is choosing to elevate the role, value, and significance of innovation above those of other initiatives and investments. Priority means that innovation ends up moving toward the top of the to-do list.

Priority also involves sacrifice and requires saying no. By saying yes to innovation, managers are, de facto, positioning other activities and tasks on a lower rung of the importance ladder. The key reason priority is the first component (or P) of our Guaranteed Innovation system is because making a choice drives attitude and mind-set. When innovation has gained "priority seating" status among all functional managers, resources get allocated in a way that speeds up results. Innovation success, then, is all about making a conscious choice and a deliberate decision to put innovation ahead of other resource-needy growth strategies, programs, and investments.

Choice is the operative word. Too often, management avoids making the decision to prioritize and, even more frequently, doesn't clearly or consistently communicate the decision that's made. The reason the priority-setting choice for innovation doesn't get made is simple: who likes to deal with rejection? By placing innovation at the head of the pack, other initiatives get relegated to a lower priority or perhaps do not even make the list. But that's exactly what priority is all about. Innovation needs attention, focus, and commitment. Making people innovative within a large corporation requires a commonly agreed-upon set of expectations and attitudes toward risk-taking. Putting innovation first makes it possible to create a culture that tells everyone that risk-taking is a good thing and that failures are just a natural part of being innovative. Durk Jager, the former CEO of Procter & Gamble, is a good example of someone who understands the importance of innovation leadership. He states in a 1999 *Fortune* article: "You will find that there are people who have the ability and the want and the desire to be rebels . . . our job is to emancipate them." He has set very aggressive growth goals that were expected to be filled by new products, new services, new solutions, and new approaches.

Jager is truly seeking to innovate his corporation and have everyone be innovative on an ongoing, daily basis. He may not have our other GI system components in place, but he certainly has mastered priority. Procter & Gamble has identified innovation as one of the top three strategic drivers for the entire corporation during the next five years. It has established three goals: "Stretch, Innovation, and Speed." Constrained in the past by taking too long and analyzing and testing new products to death, speed to market is an essential Procter & Gamble goal for growth. Moreover, stretch and innovation are intended to apply to every single employee. That is, each staffer is to set and exceed stretch goals and be innovative on an ongoing basis. According to Jager: "The core business is innovation. If we innovate well, we will ultimately win. If we innovate poorly, we won't win."

If innovation truly becomes a core competency of the corporation, growth power is unleashed. But a certain degree of passion and zeal needs to accompany the announcement of innovation as a priority. Without it, the ever-so-important emotional element will be missing. To convert a risk-averse culture into an "innovation factory," management needs to fervently convey its commitment to innovation. Fever-pitch messages need to be delivered to cut through the many other initiatives and disguised messages that employees receive every day.

So, priority is a call to action. It establishes a mind-set, an attitude and understanding, that says: "Listen, innovation is not the management fad of the month. Rather, it will be the new way of doing business and serves as the core growth strategy of the company." Priority not only describes the speed, magnitude, and breadth of innovation throughout a corporation, it sets the stage for empowering employees. An innovation culture will offer a new sense of freedom; that is, an ability to actually try new things, make more decisions autonomously, and create new solutions—without fear. The corporate risk-aversion syndrome will begin to disappear as priority comes into full focus.

Newness Versus Sameness

First and foremost, by innovating the corporation, you need to create a culture that values "newness" over "sameness." Historically, the divisions or business units that receive the bulk of the talent, capital, budget dollars, management attention, and rewards are those that generate most of the revenues and profits from existing products and services. The misguided strategy has been to invest a high percentage of resources against proved entities that will yield high profits and returns.

Therefore, the newness innovator is told that there just aren't enough resources left to give him or her what is needed to create and commercialize new products and services. Sound familiar? In contrast, innovating the corporation means putting newness at the top of the allocating-resources heap. There is no substitute for senior management's commitment to innovation. Every verbal message articulated and facial expression made by each senior manager communicates a clear-cut level of belief or disbelief in innovation.

Here's the key point: senior managers need to first decide whether or not innovation is a critical component of their corporation's growth strategy. If it is, then innovation must be elevated to the top of the priority list. All statements, actions, and behaviors by senior executives need to be consistent and congruent with each other. The number one way to stifle innovation within a corporation is to have the CEO, chief operating officer (COO), and divisional president conveying different points of view on the role of innovation. All senior managers must be on the same page. This is where sameness is better than newness! Innovation must receive recognition and internal stature as the "place to be." The goal is to ultimately build an environment where innovation is a state of mind—regardless of the department or division that one is stationed in. Corporate leaders begin to put a positive spin on the innovation mind-set when they define newness as an essential part of employees' performance, the company's stock price, and customers' satisfaction levels.

ACT Begets Priority

To make it easy to remember how to achieve innovation as a priority and provide a framework for making priority come to life, we have come up with ACT. Innovation must reside in both the hearts and minds of all employees. That's why priority is the catalyst for linking all of the other Ps into an overall system that works. To make priority real, management has to act. Words alone do not a priority make. ACT stands for Attitude, Champions, and Taking risks.

Attitude. A mind-set or mental orientation that gravitates toward innovation, risk-taking, and newness.
Champions. Strong believers in innovation who serve as spokespersons, leaders, and coaches. They must include managers across all levels and functions.
Taking risks. Permission to fail; allowance and leeway given to individuals and teams to explore, create, and develop new ideas, solutions, products, and services. Risk can be defined as the probability of success or failure given certain assumptions and investments.

The key to igniting priority throughout a company is ensuring that the right attitudes are cultivated, accountability is clear, champions are nurtured, and risk-taking is reinforced and celebrated. It's the interconnectedness of all three that generates the enthusiasm, excitement, and exuberance needed to get the internal innovation engines revved up and started.

Attitude

The ad copy for the 1999 Special Olympics captures perfectly the first step in creating priority within corporations. "It's All About Attitude" is the theme for bringing seven thousand special athletes together to make many dreams happen (Exhibit 4.1). It should also be the national theme for stimulating innovation. Companies like Pfizer, Charles Schwab, Gillette, Lucent, Merck, Citicorp, FedEx, Home Depot, 3M, America Online, Capital One, Intel, and Microsoft enjoy remarkable returns from innovation. But ask a senior executive at any of these companies whether innovation is a valued priority. Their answers, stated with conviction, project an attitude that virtually guarantees that innovation stays top-of-mind. These executives, for the most part, have left their egos at the door, have made themselves somewhat vulnerable, and have been willing to make the conscious choice to commit themselves and their companies to innovation. Innovation is not easy. Trying to nurture a pervasive mind-set that embraces it is challenging. That's why attitude shapes or shrouds the priority that innovation takes on within a company.

To cultivate a positive, open, and energized attitude toward innovation, stimuli that will remind, motivate, and reward all employees for making it a top priority are needed. The following five ideas vary in scope and magnitude but enable employees to live innovation consciously. They influence attitudes and therefore impact priority.

Conduct a Three-Day Innovation Summit

Imagine the urgency for innovation created if the entire senior management team went off-site for three consecutive days and held an innovation summit. The purpose would be to get every top functional leader within the company to focus on developing a plan to accelerate innovation. Topics could include the development of objectives and plans for activating the seven components of the Guaranteed Innovation system.

A summit should be viewed as a way to dramatically jump-start the entire corporate culture. Obviously, as critical as the summit itself, is

Exhibit 4.1 Attitude *Is* the Key

Courtesy of Special Olympics, Inc.

communicating the decisions made at the summit to all employees. This might include a combination of one-hour, in-person, roundtable discussions; a video made by all summit participants; or a written "declaration of innovation." The essential topics to reach agreement on at the summit include:

- What is your rationale for pursuing innovation?
- What priority do you place on innovation?
- Who will lead and be accountable for innovation?
- Should you hire or select a chief innovation officer?
- What objectives, strategic roles, and screening criteria should be in your innovation plan?
- Who should be the members and leaders of your innovation platoons?
- How will you interface and provide proper mentoring and coaching to people throughout the process?
- How will you make customer insights and problem identification research a routine and constant activity across functions?
- Will you make the appropriate technology investments in core platforms to create a portfolio of new applications and potential sources for innovation?
- How will you change your compensation system to stimulate innovation? What new rewards and forms of recognition will you create?
- What will be the specific innovation role of every senior leader attending the summit?
- How will the culture of innovation be created? (Include values, norms, and communications.)

Based on the summit topics, it should be perfectly evident that the three days will be full. This shouldn't be one of those half-work and half-play retreats. Of course, innovation is so much fun that the work will probably be viewed as play. On the other hand, fostering innovation is hard work.

Initiate Innovation Training Programs

By exposing thousands of employees and managers to innovation training, you will ensure that everyone better understands how innovation works, and a common language to be used by all employees across all functions will be established. This can have a monumental effect on shaping attitudes and building up the innovation priority. People feel more confident about and capable of doing things they understand and gain skills in. Potential training programs might include the following themes:

- What are our company's objectives and goals for innovation?
- What is innovation? How does it work? How should it work?
- What are successful innovation leadership styles?
- How can I be innovative? How can I change to become more innovative?
- What innovation process do we use at our company?
- How will I be rewarded for innovation?
- Why is our company focusing so much attention and so many resources on innovation?
- How can I better develop and implement innovative solutions to problems?

Positive and enthusiastic innovation attitudes need to be adopted by all employees. Innovation is everyone's responsibility and can be accomplished by everyone. The training should help to bolster individual self-confidence and convey that all staff members can innovate.

Create New Incentives, Rewards, and Recognition

The compensation system will need to change in order to encourage risk-taking and reward innovation on an individual and team basis. But this initiative goes well beyond compensation changes.

To ignite some excitement about trying innovation, activate some new rewards and forms of recognition. Some ideas include:

- *Innovation Platoon Award.* Based on marketplace results, team effectiveness, and risk-taking, select the top five innovation teams from across the corporation and give each of the platoon members (six to twelve people per team) a check for $25,000. Those thirty to sixty employees will become ardent spokespersons for innovation.

- *Innovation Leaders' Annual Recognition Dinner.* This event should include all leaders with direct and specific responsibility for innovation. Allow informal discussions before dinner among these leaders and top executives of the company, including the CEO, COO, and chief financial officer (CFO). Plaques, trophies, and substantial checks (e.g., $2,000 to $10,000) should be given out.
- *Innovation Phantom Stock Investors Program.* Platoon members can invest in innovation phantom stock. A separate "ownership" program is established whereby a $5,000 investment by a platoon member in a specific innovation plan could yield a $100,000 to $300,000 return if the innovations created and launched by the platoon achieve or exceed market-based performance goals.

The point is to come up with significant awards—not just a pat on the back or a wooden plaque. Significant awards usually mean peer recognition as well as money.

Write Articles and Newsletters and Deliver Speeches

Articles on innovation, proven success stories, internal innovation results, new products, new services, and processes should be communicated in multiple media. These messages should be targeted to a wide audience that includes internal employees, managers and senior management, shareholders, and customers. Upper management, platoon leaders, and experienced innovative employees could write and deliver these articles. Companies should also do far more publishing in external trade journals, magazines, and newspapers. Nothing gives innovation higher credibility to employees than senior management's external descriptions of its goals and expectations. That way, everyone knows that management's commitment to innovation isn't just lip service. Speeches, both internal and external at conferences, seminars, and so on, convey to employees that innovation is valued and management is dedicated to making it happen.

Conduct a Monthly Innovation Speakers Forum

Bring in outside authors, professors, practitioners, gurus, and thought leaders on innovation. Find a way to expose all employees to these outside perspectives on what it takes to innovate. At a minimum, a video or intranet communication should be available to everyone in the company. This also conveys the importance of innovation and energizes the dialogue.

The aforementioned attitude activators are all intended to elevate the status of innovation to new heights and bring to bear a new mindset that excites interest and gives heavy doses of enthusiasm. Making a commitment to growth through innovation calls for a can-do, we'll-make-it-happen attitude on the part of everyone. Without that proactive, permissive, and buoyant attitude in place, the naysayers will win out.

Champions

The priority for innovation will be renewed and rejuvenated if there are enough vocal and visible champions. Different kinds of champions need to serve diverse roles in the innovation priority equation. The CEO must be a brilliantly and consistently eloquent champion whose passion for innovation is genuine and credible. That's a tall order. There can never be any doubt that he or she wants everyone to adopt innovation as a new way of doing business. When the CEO is not 100 percent supportive of innovation, managers try to navigate their ideas around processes and procedures, activate a lot of informal initiatives, hide investment dollars in multiple budgets, and do clandestine research and development to protect their "personal" funding and resources. That's a lot of wasted energy and foolish mental anguish.

The CEO needs to lead innovation. However, what does "lead" mean here? The CEO as leader means he or she articulates the vision and rationale for innovation, helps to create the strategy, hires a chief innovation officer, serves on the innovation leadership team, allocates resources, communicates goals boldly, and is active in and celebrates innovation successes. "Renewal is the driving thrust of the company.

Only those with an unstinting dedication to committing to the risk and promise of those unchartable ideas will thrive," observes the former CEO of Motorola, Robert Galvin. CEOs like Jack Welch at General Electric, Jeffrey Bezos at Amazon.com, Sam Johnson at Johnson Wax, Bill Gates and Steve Balmer at Microsoft, and many others aren't afraid to state clearly and consistently their dedication to and fervor for newness, risk-taking, mold-breaking, and radical innovation.

Chief Innovation Officer
Another important type of innovation champion is a new position that should become commonplace within the next few years. Every Fortune 1000 company needs a chief innovation officer (CIO) to spearhead, mentor, and lead (along with the CEO) the innovation strategy throughout the corporation. The existence of a CIO automatically signals to the entire organization that innovation is not going to be taken lightly. It's not going to slip off the to-do list. It's here to stay; it will last for the long term.

The primary characteristic of the CIO should be his or her people-motivating, mentoring, and coaching skills. The CIO's primary job is to foster an innovation mind-set throughout the company. That won't come from an autocratic or militaristic leadership style. It requires a collegial approach with a supportive, engaging, and people-oriented manner.

This is not a two-year job. The same CIO should be encouraged to stay for a ten-year period. Compensation should be commensurate with the results from innovation that accrue to the company. This probably means that this executive's bonus will be low in the first couple of years. However, a very high upside should be put in place to reward innovation results if they positively impact the financial performance of the corporation. High-powered rewards and compensation go hand in hand with high-powered performance.

The CIO position also makes portfolio planning more effective. Resources, investments, and programs across business units, divisions, and sectors can be prioritized better, even though a wide range of different types of innovations are encouraged. Moreover, it's at this level that cross-divisional innovations will most likely be developed. Under traditional organizational forms, someone within a division usually is not rewarded for teaming up with another division to innovate. Reason: there is a "winner" and a "loser." One division gets the credit for the innovation, while the other division gets nothing. More cross-divisional innovation work avoids this inequity and capitalizes on dormant opportunities.

The major thrust of the CIO position, then, is to ensure that a culture, a process, a plan, a reward system, a training program, high-performing platoons, and metrics are in place to provide an integrated infrastructure to make innovation a core pillar supporting growth.

Taking Risks

Innovation should always result in some newness, whether in the form of new markets, services, products, processes, approaches, or policies. That means risk. But risk often makes senior managers nervous. On one level that is understandable. Make no mistake. Real innovation—the kind that creates breakthrough products, entirely new lines of business, and even start-up industries that change the way people live and work—is fraught with risk. Risk is also where innovation and growth exist. Without risk there is no innovation, and without innovation there is no genuine newness and thus no real sustainable growth. Managers are wrong to be nervous about the existence of risk. They should, in fact, be nervous if and when they haven't defined it and embraced it—because it's there, whether they see it or not.

Note the absence of the terms *line extension* and *acquisition*. Line extensions can serve very valuable new product and business strategies, but they are among the most abused marketing tactics employed today in the name of new product development. Truly new products deliver truly new benefits, but product managers wrongly tend to rely on them as remedies for risk. They tend to think that risk can be avoided with these "sure things" that involve a simple tweak to an existing, worn-out product with a claim that it's "new and improved" and then offered on discount. What could be safer?

Risk aversion leads to the same tired old line extensions that have become legendary in the packaged goods industry. After all, what risk could one more new and improved size, color, or shape create? A risk-free quick hit? Ask some of the senior managers at Procter & Gamble, the king of line extensions. Bloated inventory, alienated channel members, confused consumers—those are just a few of the consequences of overreliance on line extensions, as P&G's new innovation strategy recognizes.

Managers get a false sense of security because line extensions feel safe and easy. But in today's competitive global markets, where a customer can compare prices and features from producers all over the world at the touch of a button, most so-called "sure things" are extinct.

The same is true for acquisitions. Supporters of such tactics rely on the old saying about synergism: "One plus one equals three." Too often, the reality reflects another old saying: "Two wrongs don't make a right." Acquisitions can play an important part in a company's growth strategy, but they are not risk free and not a substitute for risk-taking and new product innovation.

The experience of McKesson, the drug distribution company based in San Francisco, is instructive about the dangers of acquisitions. In early 1999, McKesson bought HBO & Co., a medical software company, for $12 billion. It was subsequently learned that HBO & Co. had misrepresented its revenues and expenses by millions of dollars, "a candidate for financial scandal of the year" in the words of a *Barron's* August 1999 article. In a little over six months, McKesson's stock price plummeted from over $96 a share to around $30. The *Barron's* article pointed out that, despite the company's troubles and embarrassments, savvy investors viewed it as a great investment because any "risk . . . is counterbalanced by the strength of its franchise." In other words, its leadership in innovative approaches to its products, services, and markets. According to a J.P. Morgan Securities analyst, ". . . the key to McKesson regaining market share lies in investing in product development and resolving customer issues. . . ." In other words, investors had already discounted the value of the acquisition to zero, and the company's innovation in new products and services was the only thing that saved it from a total meltdown.

The moral of this story is not that line extensions and acquisitions should be avoided. Rather, there is no strategic or tactical substitute for the growth potential that innovation can offer to a company's welfare.

Working with risky projects and concepts—those that challenge the curiosity and intellect—is the reason good employees come to work. They don't come to work to practice risk aversion, at least not at the outset. They learn to avoid risk from their senior managers, who then complain that their subordinates lack imagination and initiative. But few, if any, business school graduates invest time and money in their education to devote their lives to creating new and improved replications of the same tired old products or to work on the "sauce optimization project." Product managers in many organizations are trained and motivated to engage in this kind of unimaginative line extension ("incremental innovation") because it appears to be free of risk.

For all sorts of reasons, nothing could be further from the truth. Innovation without risk is an oxymoron. Trust is a key motivator in risk-taking. Without it, people won't risk anything. Why should they? Trust is needed as the basic foundation for a risk-taking culture. Part of trust is loyalty. Loyalty from the company to the employee and vice versa. Employees who have earned their manager's trust are far more willing to take risks. They feel more secure, confident, and able to accept the consequences of making a risky decision. In short, loyalty and trust are absolutely fundamental for creating a risk-taking environment. Once this has been created, innovation's priority will float further up. As James Bryant Conant, one of the leading American educators of the twentieth century, used to say: "Behold the turtle. He only makes progress when he sticks his neck out."

In summary, attitudes, champions, and cultivation of a risk-taking culture are formidable ingredients for establishing innovation as a priority. If management is able to activate priority, the remaining six system components will be simple to execute in comparison.

Developing a Rationale for the Innovation Priority

Corporations who are successful innovators figure out why innovation should be their top priority. Developing a rock-solid rationale provides staying power. Stamina is critical; endurance is essential. There is absolutely nothing worse for innovation than to dilute the priority after a few months or so. When management stands up and shouts out the need and desire for innovation one month, and then suddenly and subtly cuts funding and removes resources the next, it's time to get out. If senior managers are coming up with excuses why the company can't focus on innovation right now, don't expect that to change a year from now. Our experience shows that if innovation gets derailed, it's usually fairly time-consuming to get it back on track. It may take two to three times as long to reignite an innovation program that has been sidetracked. The words of the old song don't apply: it's not better the second time around. Consequently, developing a strong rationale for innovation is a sort of insurance policy to help provide discipline and commitment; it offers a reason to stick to it.

Frequent explanations for setting up innovation as a core competency are to:

- Generate aggressive growth
- Create significant competitive advantage
- Enjoy time savings and cost savings
- Provide increased customer satisfaction
- Expand globally

Innovation can satisfy many strategic roles and serve different growth objectives. The first key step is to come up with a compelling and riveting reason to innovate: survive, destroy the competitor, triple stock price, quadruple earnings, capture one million more customers, and gain number one market share in a new country are examples of robust objectives.

The key to crafting the right rationale is to give it "legs" for at least three to five years. This is a must. Don't look at innovation as a one-year strategy or business approach your company is going to "test out."

It can't work in that short of a time frame. Your management team will get frustrated and begin to fret. This, of course, will enable other initiatives (that are "surefire") to creep up the priority list.

So, the bottom-line need is to develop an overall strategic rationale, clear-cut objectives, and a reason to go after innovation aggressively. Be patient, though, because it will take time for a new culture to evolve and begin to crystallize.

A strong rationale that may galvanize a company's various factions and agendas into one is: "Innovation will be used to dramatically drive up our stock price." Everyone can certainly relate to that rationale and, more important, many different constituents will directly benefit from this "cause célèbre." Ratcheting up stock price is an explanation that everyone can rally around and believe in. Linking innovation to stock price appreciation is bold but clearly an example of a benefit-laden rationale.

The main question, though, is how do you prove that innovation drives stock prices? Well, of course, you can't attribute one factor to an increased stock price. If we had figured that out, we'd buy a stock exchange seat and become traders. But you can measure, track, and carefully monitor the actual performance and returns generated from innovation. We know that a company that employs the Guaranteed Innovation system outlined in this book, views innovation as a top priority, and consistently rewards employees for successful innovations will achieve far more rapid stock price increases than competitors who don't.

Hence, if you are a middle manager who has been trying to get senior management committed to innovation, just ask them three simple questions: "Do you want your stock price to go up?" You know the response to that. Then ask, "Do you believe that successful innovation can help drive earnings?" "Sure" will most likely be the response. And finally, "Is there a direct correlation between earnings growth and stock price appreciation?" The answers to those questions are all affirmative and help to set up the premise that innovation bolsters earnings, which in turn, drives up stock price.

Let's look at some research to see how innovative companies' stocks perform relative to those of their competition. The findings are staggering.

How Innovation Drives Up Stock Prices

We'd contend, and *Fortune* rankings agree, that highly innovative companies include corporations such as Charles Schwab, Dell Computer, Southwest Airlines, Maytag, Philips, Costco, and Microsoft. Each of these innovation giants has clearly shown that true innovation pays for itself many times over.

These are corporations that are recognized for their innovativeness. They are admired by their employees, their customers are delighted by their products and services, and—oh, yes—their shareholders have been handsomely rewarded. And guess what? *Each of these highly innovative companies is the number one stock price gain leader in its industry over the last five years.*

As Exhibit 4.2 depicts, innovative companies end up with higher stock prices. It's as simple and as compelling as that. For each of the twelve industries examined, the exhibit lists the two companies that achieved the highest stock price appreciation over five years (1994–1999). The compound annual growth rate (CAGR) means that the stock price of Charles Schwab, for example, increased on average 71.5 percent each year during the past five years. The implied relationship and proposed correlation between stock price and innovation are decidedly plain.

Fact: companies that demonstrate their innovation effectiveness are rewarded robustly by shareholders and investors. People want to invest in companies that create an innovation core competency. The reason is evident. Once an innovation culture and mind-set have been created, people will feel empowered to venture out into new areas, take risks, try new things, and feel more confident to make decisions that will accelerate growth.

Exhibit 4.2 Stock Price Appreciation of Top Innovators

Industry	Company	5-Year (1994–1999) CAGR (%)
Computer hardware	Dell Computer	139.99
	Sun Microsystems	103.99
Food processing	Quaker Oats	16.37
	General Mills	4.59
Airlines	Southwest Airlines	26.55
	American Airlines	20.27
Home electronics	Sony	38.38
	Philips	35.67
Appliances and tools	General Electric	43.42
	Maytag	26.19
Automotive	Toyota	18.38
	Ford	13.84
Commercial banks	US Bancorp	16.58
	Wachovia	16.09
Household products	Colgate-Palmolive	32.62
	Estee Lauder	30.41
Investment services	Charles Schwab	71.50
	Morgan Stanley	53.16
Electric utilities	Consolidated Edison	6.03
	Duke Energy	5.63
Specialty retail	Costco Wholesale	47.94
	Wal-Mart	45.43
Computer software	Microsoft	72.51
	Oracle	66.65

CAGR = compound annual growth rate. Stock numbers provided by Dow Jones Interactive; CAGR percentages calculated by Kuczmarski & Associates.

Aggressive expansion will result. Look at the growth trajectory of Microsoft and Dell in computers, Charles Schwab in financial services, or Maytag and General Electric in major appliances. Each of these industries is totally different, ranging from high-growth, high-margin to low-growth, low-margin. The industry the company is in should in no way limit the degree of innovation potential. Your competitors matter, but what matters most is whether your management team intrinsically and fervently believes that the company can become the innovation leader or not.

It is amazing to observe how the top innovators have ended up with the highest compound annual growth rate in stock price appreciation. Even more shocking are the ten-year CAGR stock price trends. The list of companies virtually stays the same with the exception of a few corporations like Wal-Mart, which is clearly an innovator, and Estee Lauder, which wasn't publicly traded five years ago.

This ten-year trend finding may be even more significant than the correlation between innovativeness and stock price. That is, once the company becomes innovative, a momentum is created that continues to propel innovation unless there is some major shift or drastic change. A good example of this is Rubbermaid. For thirteen years, under Stan Gault's superb leadership, Rubbermaid's performance was stellar. Growing his company from $300 million to over $1.4 billion, Gault was a passionate champion of innovation. He set aggressive new product goals, met with new product teams monthly, and told the financial community that new product development was the company's number one priority and strategy. The stock soared during his reign as CEO.

But Stan "retired" and went to Goodyear. Wolfgang Schmidt came in as CEO of Rubbermaid. His focus shifted dramatically to cost-cutting, downsizing, materials management, and raw materials cost-savings; Schmidt was "leading" Rubbermaid in the opposite direction of innovation. During his three-year tenure, the stock plummeted and the company eventually was acquired by Newell. The point is that innovation won't stay on automatic pilot without proper guidance, leadership, and a steady hand of commitment at the wheel. On the other hand, once innovators learn how to fly, they usually don't forget how to teach others. They continue to build momentum and stay on course.

Exhibit 4.3 shows a review of ten years of closing stock price data (year-end) for the top four to six performers in twelve industries. The companies were sorted first by ten-year and then by five-year CAGR to achieve relative rankings within each industry. The leading innovators and stock price appreciators are ranked from high to low based on their ten-year CAGRs. Most rankings remained constant from five to ten years. Exhibits 4.4a through 4.4j present summaries of some of the new product activity, innovation history, and key points of differentiation for some of the top innovation companies.

Exhibit 4.3 Five- and Ten-Year Stock Price Appreciation of Top Innovators

Relative Ranking	Company	10-Year CAGR (%)	5-Year CAGR (%)
	Computer Hardware		
1	Dell Computer (DELL)	95.51	139.99
2	Sun Microsystems (SUNW)	53.33	103.50
3	Compaq (CPQ)	26.13	27.90
4	Hewlett-Packard (HWP)	25.42	35.43
5	IBM Corporation (IBM)	16.45	42.48
	Food Processing		
1	Quaker Oats (OAT)	8.56	16.37
2	Kellogg's (K)	6.19	1.18
3	General Mills (GIS)	7.06	4.59
4	Ralcorp Holdings (RAH)	N/A	−2.17
	Airlines		
1	Southwest Airlines (LUV)	26.16	26.55
2	United Airlines (UAL)	6.12	28.84
3	American Airlines (AMR)	8.73	20.27
4	British Airways (BAB)	5.52	2.60
5	Delta Airlines (DAL)	3.85	14.56
	Home Electronics		
1	Philips (PHG)	18.37	35.67
2	Sony (SNE)	17.87	38.38
3	NEC (NIPNY)	6.41	16.41
4	Hitachi (HIT)	4.88	10.39
5	Zenith (ZETHQ)	−42.91	−66.80
	Appliances and Tools		
1	General Electric (GE)	25.38	43.42
2	Black & Decker (BDK)	10.36	17.08
3	Maytag (MYG)	9.43	26.19
4	Whirlpool (WHR)	7.02	5.30
	Automotive		
1	Toyota Motor Corp. (TOYOY)	12.83	18.38
2	Ford Motor Company (F)	9.34	13.84
3	Volkswagen (VLKAY)	N/A	14.61
4	General Motors (GM)	5.58	11.53
5	DaimlerChrysler (DCX)	N/A	9.91
	Commercial Banks		
1	US Bancorp (USB)	15.62	16.58
2	Wachovia (WB)	12.77	16.09
3	National City Corp. (NCC)	9.25	12.86
4	Westpac Banking (WBK)	4.74	15.12

Exhibit 4.3 (continued)

Relative Ranking	Company	10-Year CAGR (%)	5-Year CAGR (%)
	Household Products		
1	Colgate-Palmolive (CL)	23.40	32.62
2	Estee Lauder (EL)	N/A	30.41
3	Avon Products (AVP)	13.60	17.18
4	Alberto-Culver (ACV)	8.75	13.63
5	Amway (AJL)	N/A	−16.58
	Investment Services		
1	Charles Schwab (SCH)	55.83	71.50
2	Morgan Stanley (MS)	N/A	53.16
3	Merrill Lynch (MER)	28.93	36.05
4	Paine Webber (PWJ)	22.74	31.16
5	Bear Stearns (BSC)	20.26	28.82
	Electric Utilities		
1	Duke Energy (DUK)	5.97	5.63
2	Utilicorp (UCU)	2.86	1.93
3	Consolidated Edison (ED)	1.71	6.03
4	Cinergy Group (CIN)	1.32	0.37
5	PG&E (PCG)	−0.70	−3.40
	Specialty Retail		
1	Wal-Mart Stores (WMT)	28.55	45.43
2	Costco Wholesale (COST)	N/A	47.94
3	Consolidated Stores (CNS)	20.66	6.39
4	Kmart Corporation (KM)	−5.38	−4.99
5	Venator Group (Z)	−14.08	−14.14
	Computer Software		
1	Microsoft (MSFT)	58.01	72.51
2	Oracle (ORCL)	47.41	66.65
3	Computer Associates (CA)	34.16	37.22
4	PeopleSoft (PSFT)	N/A	35.20
5	Hyperion (HYSW)	N/A	26.98
6	Enterprise (ENSW)	N/A	3.32

CAGR = compound annual growth rate.
Sources: Ten- and five-year stock price appreciation by Standard Industrial Classification code was calculated using Standard & Poor's Compustat statistical database. Stock price appreciation for individual companies was calculated using Dow Jones Interactive, Market Data.

Exhibit 4.4a Innovator Profile: Charles Schwab Corporation

Industry   Investment services
Subentities eSchwab (on-line trading)
               OneSource (mutual funds)
               AdvisorSource (customer referrals to independents)

Stock Price Appreciation over Time

Relative Ranking	Company	5-Year CAGR (%)
1	Charles Schwab (SCH)	71.50
2	Morgan Stanley (MS)	53.16
3	Merrill Lynch (MER)	36.05
4	Paine Webber (PWJ)	31.16
5	Bear Stearns (BSC)	28.82
	SIC Comparison (6211)	13.36
	S&P 500 Comparison	21.76

New Products/Innovation History

1989: TeleBroker introduced a 24-hour touch-tone trading service
1991: Acquired OTC market maker Mayer & Schweitzer
1992: Continued diversification, focusing on independent financial advisers
1993: Overseas expansion
1995: Acquired Share-Link (now Charles Schwab Europe)
      First launched website for investing
1996: Focus on building retirement services—new unit created for 401(k) and investment
      services
      Started building alliances with information providers like S&P, First Call, and
      Quote.com
1997: Alliance formed with securities underwriters (J.P. Morgan & Co., Hambrecht & Quist,
      and Credit Suisse First Boston) to give customers access to IPOs
1998: Reorganization to reflect new business lines acquired
1999: Joint venture formed in Japan; Charles Schwab Canada formed
      Desktop trading system (Velocity) launched for higher net worth individuals
      Moving swiftly toward "full-service" investing, with information flow as focus

Key Differentiating Factors

- Senior leadership is committed to identifying new markets and uncovering latent customer needs.
- Consumer-driven product and service development is customer value focus.
- There are multiple customer access points (E-mail, phone, Internet, branch).
- They have a full spectrum of service offerings (target research, trades, account handling, portfolio analysis, tracking, and reporting).
- There is extensive employee training focused on how to provide guidance and education to customers.

Source: Dow Jones Interactive

Exhibit 4.4b Innovator Profile: Sony Corporation

Industry	Home electronics
Subentities	Sony Electronics, Inc.
	Sony Music Entertainment
	Sony Pictures Entertainment
	Sony Development and Sony Plaza
	Sony Online Entertainment
	Sony Trans Com
	Materials Research Corporation
	Etak, Inc.
	Sony Computer Entertainment America
	989 Studios

Stock Price Appreciation over Time

Relative Ranking	Company	5-Year CAGR (%)
1	Philips (PHG)	35.67
2	Sony (SNE)	38.38
3	NEC (NIPNY)	16.41
4	Hitachi (HIT)	10.39
5	Zenith (ZETHQ)	−66.80
	SIC Comparison (3651)	14.42
	S&P 500 Comparison	21.76

New Products/Innovation History

General: Codeveloper of the CD and DVD
Developer of the Sony Playstation
Inventor of Trinitron color television
Inventor of the 3.5-inch micro floppy disk system
Inventor of Walkman personal stereo

1988: Mavica, electronic, still-image camera introduced
1990: HDTV Trinitron television introduced
1992: MiniDisc (MD) system invented
1993: Digital Betacam, component, digital VCR launched
1999: Flat TV introduced, five ambient colors
Formed an alliance with CDNOW as part of its music business

Key Differentiating Factors

- Sony positions itself as a leading entertainment company and has been forming alliances to maintain this position.
- Sony is working with Cablevision to develop next-generation digital services to parts of the country.
- Sony is working with Microsoft to create the convergence of personal computers, digital television, and consumer AV platforms.
- Sony has a new business development group that commercializes new technologies, creates new opportunities in entertainment, and develops aspects of E-business.

Source: Dow Jones Interactive

Exhibit 4.4c Innovator Profile: Koninklijke Philips Electronics

Industry Home electronics
Subdivisions Consumer products
Components and semiconductors
Information technology
Lighting
Professional products

Stock Price Appreciation over Time

Relative Ranking	Company	5-Year CAGR (%)
1	Philips (PHG)	35.67
2	Sony (SNE)	38.38
3	NEC (NIPNY)	16.41
4	Hitachi (HIT)	10.39
5	Zenith (ZETHQ)	−66.80
	SIC Comparison (3651)	14.42
	S&P 500 Comparison	21.76

New Products/Innovation History

1970s: Large research and development activity and new product development, resulting in the Laser Vision optical disc, the compact disc, and optical telecommunications systems
Acquired Magnavox and Signetics
1980s: Acquired GTE Sylvania
Acquired Westinghouse
1983: Launched the compact disc
1990s: Restructured, returning to core activities
"Let's make things better" tagline
1998: Large consumer research program and rebranding effort
1999: New flat TV introduced
Recordable CD
DVD player
Mobile computing products

Key Differentiating Factors

• Philips has undergone significant change in the last five years, becoming more market driven and customer focused. The restructuring and refocusing on core activities have positioned the company well for growth. Several new product introductions have bolstered growth as well.
• The company has strong research and development investment and deep technology capability.

Source: Dow Jones Interactive

Exhibit 4.4d Innovator Profile: Maytag Corporation

Industry Appliances and tools
Brands Maytag (premium)
JenAir (premium)
Magic Chef (midprice)
Performa (midprice)
Hoover

Stock Price Appreciation over Time

Relative Ranking	Company	5-Year CAGR (%)
1	General Electric (GE)	43.42
2	Black & Decker (BDK)	17.08
3	Maytag (MYG)	26.19
4	Whirlpool (WHR)	5.30
	SIC Comparison (3632)	N/A
	S&P 500 Comparison	21.76

New Products/Innovation History

1991: Consolidated European operations and formed an alliance with Bosch-Siemens
1993: New CEO Leonard Hadley reorganized, selling Hoover Australia and closing down European operations
1995: Purchased G.S. Blodgett (commercial ovens) and ECC International's vending machines
1997: Launched the Neptune washer (revolutionary top loading)
1998: Signed an agreement with Sears to begin selling Maytag
1999: Acquired Jade Range, premium cooking products and refrigeration units
New CEO Lloyd Ward (formerly COO)
Launched the Maytag Gemini range (revolutionary two-oven design)
Realigned business units to facilitate innovation strategy (September)

Key Differentiating Factors

• Lloyd Ward, CEO Maytag (10/4/99): "An innovation company depends on a steady stream of ideas and waves of innovation that create shareholder value. Cash-flow return on investment will help us measure and evaluate which ideas, products and businesses are creating value for shareowners, and which are not. It's one more tool that will enable us to become smarter, faster and better at innovation as the driver of profitable growth."
• Lloyd Ward, CEO Maytag (10/4/99): "Innovation is key to how we have created share-owner value. Now, we are taking that strategy to every business, every product line, and every brand."
• Greg Jordan, Chief Technology Officer, Maytag (9/20/99): "Our alliance with RISD is one more building block in our innovation network and our commitment to delivering continuous discovery, invention, and rapid deployment of innovation. We believe RISD can increase our capabilities in industrial design and providing total system-oriented solutions to meet consumer and commercial customer needs."

Sources: Hoover's, Market Guide, www.maytag.com

Exhibit 4.4e Innovator Profile: Sun Microsystems

Industry Computer hardware

Stock Price Appreciation over Time

Relative Ranking	Company	5-Year CAGR (%)
1	Dell Computer (DELL)	139.99
2	Sun Microsystems (SUNW)	103.50
3	Compaq (CPQ)	27.90
4	Hewlett-Packard (HWP)	35.43
5	IBM Corporation (IBM)	42.48
	SIC Comparison (3571)	8.93
	S&P 500 Comparison	21.76

New Products/Innovation History

1986: Went public
1987: Signed an agreement with AT&T to develop enhanced UNIX system
1988: Introduced the SPARC processor and licensed it
      Lotus and WordPerfect appeal increased
1993: Expanded technology to sell computer chips
1995: New push to network and Internet computing
1996: Java builds as industry standard for programming
      Purchased Cray Research and Integrated Micro Products
1998: Purchased i-planet, Net Dynamics, and other Internet communications software
      firms
      Won Internet advantages against Microsoft and formed alliance with America Online
1999: Sony and Philips agreed to use Sun's technology in making networked computer
      devices
      Agreed to buy program developer Forte Software

Key Differentiating Factors

- Sun is the largest company to build computers with its own design, chips, and operating system.
- Java (programming) is the strongest threat to Microsoft's operating system monopoly, thus they are in constant battle.
- Since 1996, solid partnerships have helped Sun grow its Internet software and E-commerce share.
- Sun is continuing to expand technologies into digital cameras and other consumer devices.

Sources: Hoover's, Market Guide, *PC Magazine*

Exhibit 4.4f Innovator Profile: Dell Computer Corporation

Industry Computer hardware

Stock Price Appreciation over Time

Relative Ranking	Company	5-Year CAGR (%)
1	Dell Computer (DELL)	139.99
2	Sun Microsystems (SUNW)	103.50
3	Compaq (CPQ)	27.90
4	Hewlett-Packard (HWP)	35.43
5	IBM Corporation (IBM)	42.48
	SIC Comparison (3571)	8.93
	S&P 500 Comparison	21.76

New Products/Innovation History

1988: Went public and started to sell to government agencies
1990: 64% drop in profits, largely due to design and production of proprietary hardware
1991: Entered retail arena by agreeing to have CompUSA/Staples sell its PCs at mail-order prices
1992: Xerox sold Dell in Latin America
1993: Opened subsidiaries in Japan and Austria
1994: Refocused to mail-order and retooled its notebook computers
       Introduced a line of servers
1995: Pentium notebook introduced
1996: Increased operations in the Pacific Rim
1997: Entered workstation market
1998: Plant opened in China, plans made for Brazil
1999: Introduction of $999 PC
       Dell Latitude notebook praised as thinnest and lightest

Key Differentiating Factors

- Dell is the best-performing stock in the past decade measured against other companies in the S&P 500 index.
- Dell has built-to-order boxes, which lower inventory and costs. This lower inventory has allowed the company to offer the latest technologies.
- Dell's website claims up to $18 million in computer sales daily and is expected to be processing half of Dell's transactions by the year 2000 (dellnet.com).

Sources: Hoover's, Market Guide, *PC Magazine*

Exhibit 4.4g Innovator Profile: Southwest Airlines

Industry Airlines

Stock Price Appreciation over Time

Relative Ranking	Company	5-Year CAGR (%)
1	Southwest Airlines (LUV)	26.55
2	United Airlines (UAL)	28.84
3	American Airlines (AMR)	20.27
4	British Airways (BAB)	2.60
5	Delta Airlines (DAL)	14.56
	SIC Comparison (4211)	18.75
	S&P 500 Comparison	21.76

New Products/Innovation History

1986: Introduced Fun Fares, an advance-purchase discount

1987: Frequent flyer program Rapid Rewards introduced, based on the number of flights
(not miles, the industry benchmark)

1992: Herb Kelleher, CEO, starred in advertising campaigns
Became the official airline of Seaworld and painted a plane as a whale

1993: Expanded to East Coast service

1994: Ticketless system launched
New computer reservation system for automated passenger booking

1996: Expansion to more markets
Partnered with Icelandair for Cleveland passenger through travel

1997: Extended Icelandair agreement to other destinations

1998: First transcontinental flight

1999: Continued eastward expansion of routes

Key Differentiating Factors

- Southwest uses smaller airports to avoid congestion; offers single-class, open seating and no meals.
- It uses only one type of plane, the Boeing 737, to cut down on maintenance and training.
- Customer service and humor is emphasized.
- Employees own 13% of the company.
- Southwest uses a ticketless, proprietary reservation system.
- The company is 85% unionized, yet has never had a strike.

Sources: Hoover's, Market Guide

Exhibit 4.4h Innovator Profile: Ford Motor Company

Industry Automotive
Subentities Ford Automotive
Ford Motor Credit
The Hertz Corporation (81%)
Kwik-Fit Holdings (UK)
APCO (car warranties)
Visteon Automotive Systems (parts)

Stock Price Appreciation over Time

Relative Ranking	Company	5-Year CAGR (%)
1	Ford Motor Company (F)	13.84
2	Volkswagen (VLKAY)	14.61
3	DaimlerChrysler (DCX)	9.91
4	Toyota Motor Corp. (TOYOY)	18.38
5	General Motors (GM)	11.53
	SIC Comparison (3711)	21.06
	S&P 500 Comparison	21.76

New Products/Innovation History
1988: Introduction of the Ford Taurus and Sable (captured 21.7% market share)
1989: Purchased the Associates (financial services) and Jaguar
1990: Sold Ford Aerospace to Loral
1994: Acquired Hertz
1996: Acquired Budget (sold in 1997)
1997: Increased stake in Mazda
Sold heavy-duty truck unit to Daimler-Benz
Spun off 19% of Hertz
Entered the Chinese vehicle market
1998: Sold off its direct stake in Kia Motors
Jacques Nasser, longtime Ford veteran, became president/CEO
1999: Purchased Volvo's car-making operations
Acquired Kwik-Fit Holdings (UK) to boost after-market presence
Acquired APCO (extended service contracts)
Started purchasing junkyards to move into used auto parts
Agreed to buy Mazda's credit division
Planned to spin off auto parts division (Visteon) to employees
Formed joint venture with Microsoft to provide on-line services to customers
Launched the Ford Focus, a new car aimed at Generation Xers

Key Differentiating Factors
• Ford is diversifying products and services to gain more share of wallet with customers.
• Consumer-based research is leading to the development of campaigns targeted to specific segments (e.g., the new Ford Focus targeted at Generation X and Echo Boomer markets). The company is using the Internet and a national TV campaign to reach these segments.

Sources: Hoover's, Market Guide, www.ford.com

Exhibit 4.4i Innovator Profile: DaimlerChrysler

Industry	Automotive
Subentities	Mercedes-Benz
	Smart
	Chrysler
	Plymouth
	Jeep
	Dodge

Stock Price Appreciation over Time

Relative Ranking	Company	5-Year CAGR (%)
1	Ford Motor Company (F)	13.84
2	Volkswagen (VLKAY)	14.61
3	DaimlerChrysler (DCX)	9.91
4	Toyota Motor Corp. (TOYOY)	18.38
5	General Motors (GM)	11.53
	SIC Comparison (3711)	21.06
	S&P 500 Comparison	21.76

New Products/Innovation History
1995: Mercedes launched new E-Class (series 210), with more than 30 technical innovations

Chrysler's hybrid-electric car won the Discover award for technological innovation
1996: Mercedes presented the new SLK

Mercedes-Benz won the brand competition of the International Touring Car Competition, achieving 86 wins from 1986 to 1996

Chrysler introduced the Plymouth Prowler, the world's first mass-produced hot rod
1997: Mercedes introduced the M-class, all-activity vehicle

Mercedes introduced the first city bus with an emission-free fuel cell engine

Chrysler introduced the Durango, Concorde, and Intrepid (hybrid propulsion) lines
1998: Chrysler merged with Daimler-Benz as "equals"
1999: Introduced the Vaneo, a new vehicle concept van (October)

Management board restructured to complete the global integration program

Key Differentiating Factors
- In 1999, the company reorganized into three brand-focused divisions (Mercedes/Smart, Chrysler/Plymouth/Dodge/Jeep, and commercial vehicles). It is looking at integrating opportunities and building cross-divisional products.
- The company is seeking a competitive edge, and vehicle technology is becoming more important to North American operations. As such, it is consolidating its supplier programs and implementing a global procurement strategy.

Sources: Hoover's, Market Guide, www.daimlerchrysler.com

Exhibit 4.4j Innovator Profile: Microsoft

Industry Computer software

Stock Price Appreciation over Time

Relative Ranking	Company	5-Year CAGR (%)
1	Microsoft (MSFT)	72.51
2	Oracle (ORCL)	66.65
3	Computer Associates (CA)	37.22
4	PeopleSoft (PSFT)	35.20
5	Hyperion (HYSW)	26.98
6	Enterprise (ENSW)	3.32
	SIC Comparison (7372)	14.06
	S&P 500 Comparison	21.76

New Products/Innovation History
1986: Went public
1990: Launched Windows 3.0
1990s: Antitrust lawsuits started
1995: Launched Windows 95 worldwide
Began buying start-up companies and their technologies, investing in their development and then selling their resulting products
MSN, a proprietary on-line network, launched
1996: Licensed Java Web programming language from Sun
Introduced Internet Explorer
Launched expedia.com, an on-line travel service
1997: Set up a UK research laboratory
1998: Launched Windows 98
Justice Department filed antitrust charges against MS
Streamlined MSN.com
1999: Reorganized the company along customer groups instead of product lines
Agreed to invest $5 billion for a minority stake in AT&T
Agreed to buy Visio (drawing and diagramming software specialist)

Key Differentiating Factors
- Visionary leaders are fully committed to innovation.
- The company has a mind-set and an attitude that encourage risk-taking and aggressive investment in technology and innovation.
- Microsoft's approach to buying technologies rather than developing them in-house appears to have helped propel it to the forefront of the industry.

Sources: Hoover's, Market Guide, *PC Magazine*

The Ultimate Synergy: Stock Price Drives Priority, Priority Drives Stock Price

One more interesting point supporting the case that innovation affects stock price is a recent Kuczmarski & Associates Best Practices Study (1999) conducted with over two hundred companies. "The 'best' innovation companies have higher stock prices than their competitors more frequently than the 'rest'," is a key conclusion. Over three-quarters (76.2%) of the "best" companies described their stock prices as appreciating significantly more than those of their top three competitors; in contrast, just over one-third (34%) of the "rest" make the same statement. The best innovators outperform their competitors relative to stock price appreciation.

Another interesting insight from this study is that 78 percent of the best companies recognize the contribution of innovation to their stock prices—far more than the rest (only 26.4%). This finding is very revealing regarding priority. Companies that recognize, acknowledge, and truly believe that innovation can drive their stock prices are more apt to devote resources to it and make it a top priority. This is the reason this chapter emphasizes that companies with consistent innovation achieve higher stock prices than competitors who don't innovate well. If management buys into the argument that innovation influences stock price, reaching the priority level that an innovative culture needs will be much easier. Thus, recognizing that stock price is positively affected by innovation will reinforce its stature as a high-priority initiative. Likewise, once innovation has been clearly set as a top priority, the cumulative results from innovation efforts that build up over time will help drive up stock price.

The Main Ingredient

Innovation, in effect, needs to come close to being an obsession. If it's really going to take hold, everyone needs to think, breathe, and act innovation. Companies like Intel and Motorola, for example, invest heavily in research and development, and aggressively pursue strategies for developing new business lines and entering totally new segments and categories. Both manage innovation by investing in many different types of ventures to hedge their bets and create a port-folio of varying risk-return innovations.

Corporations that achieve priority for innovation usually invest heavily to gain insights from their customers on a continuous basis. This is so critical, in fact, that it's one of the GI system's components—problem orientation. Systematically uncovering customer and non-customer needs and wants signals that innovation has become a business discipline and core competency. 3M, for example, keeps extensive information on consumer complaints, suggestions, and pref-erences. This sets the framework for continuous innovation.

Enron is another example of a company whose stock price has mir-rored its successful practice of innovation. It transformed the utili-ties industry by creating new products, new services, new markets, and new pricing structures. By transporting gas to customers from inex-pensive locations, trading natural gas futures, and offering "total energy solutions" to customers, Enron has radically changed this sleepy and heretofore noninnovative industry.

In 1999, Hewlett-Packard got a new CEO and a new slogan: invent. Both help to reinforce the significance and importance of innovation to this company. Its instruments division, for example, makes sure it gets customer insights on a continuous basis. Scanning units, teams of technical and marketing people who visit current and former cus-tomers to gain input on their perceptions of needed improvements as well as other needs, concerns, and issues, have been set up.

The discipline of regularly gathering consumer insights has a lot to offer the care and feeding of priority. It helps to protect innova-tion from the cultural resistance to new ideas that entrenches itself over time. It helps to dissipate comments like: "We tried that before, and it didn't work," "We can't make that profitable," "Customers won't really be willing to pay a premium for that," and "Senior man-agement will never go along with that." Customer research cuts through the negative internal clutter and accelerates a team directly to the market truth. This can be a huge benefit for keeping the pri-ority for innovation well supported.

Priority means tracking the results of innovation over time. By knowing the results from investments made through innovation, managers' desire to fund innovation will be reinforced further. Success, when calibrated, provides innovation with precedence over other strategies and growth programs.

"It's clear that companies that innovate effectively all across the enterprise grow sustainably and create value faster. Equity markets, in turn, accord those companies a premium," states Ron Jonash from Arthur D. Little, Inc. Wall Street analysts agree that innovation is a key driver of market valuation. Priority and stock price do go hand in hand.

The Power of Innovation

When you consider the incredible resource base of Fortune 1000 companies, the United States has the power to produce a cataclysmic and volcanic innovation reaction. According to a February 2000 *Economist* article, the Price Waterhouse Coopers 1999 study on innovation said: "Innovation will be the dominant value proposition for the next century." One of the driving forces that will keep the urgent need and desire for innovation buoyant will be its ability to raise stock price and reward shareholders and management. Trevor Davis in PWC's London office summarized: "There was a close relationship between innovation and financial performance. We found that those companies that were generating more than 80 percent turnover from new products and services at least doubled their market capitalization over a five-year period." This is certainly another profound testament to the power of innovation on stock price.

The Fortune 1000 companies have access to more than 27 million employees, as depicted in Exhibit 4.5. The key challenge is for the nation to harness this incredible talent pool of people and unleash their psyches to be innovative. Imagine if, on Monday morning, 27 million people were converted into innovators who thought differently, felt secure, explored new ways to grow, and took risks. It truly would revolutionize and transform the world. The same could

Exhibit 4.5 Fortune 1000 Revenues and Employees (Year Ending 1998)

Companies	Annual Revenues	No. of Employees
Fortune 1 to 500	$5,740 trillion	21,852,671
Fortune 501 to 1000	$671 billion	5,614,965
Total	$6,411 trillion	27,467,636

happen if even 50 percent of those employees adopted an innovative and risk-taking mind-set and attitude.

Consequently, this country has a huge potential opportunity to better use the valuable resources of its corporate network. If it does, and the people and financial resources are converted into innovation leaders, it will be the global economic leader for years to come.

But corporate leaders need to give some thoughtful discussion and analysis to the long-term role they want innovation to play. Remember, priority will set the stage for innovation to happen. It all starts with the creation of the right culture that enables everyone to ACT. Through the combined energy of champions and innovation teams, as well as the right attitude and risk-taking environment, innovation will take off. However, there are six more components that need to be in place for the GI system. The hardest component to establish, priority, will serve as a catalyst to activate the other components.

CHAPTER 5

POLICY

Policy is one of those words that seems like an abstraction that you can pay lip service to and then ignore. In fact, nothing could be further from the truth. Continuous innovation starts with a proactive plan for achieving innovation goals. This plan is driven by an *innovation policy* that expresses the goals, expectations, and success criteria for innovation, as well as the proper alignment of resources that should characterize every innovation initiative in the company. Like priority, it contributes significantly to innovation success or failure in a company. A clearly articulated policy enables more effective planning.

Innovation efforts can easily get offtrack—or never get started on the right track. Invariably, one of the contributing factors is policy related. The following are common sources of trouble:

- *Lack of understanding of past performance in innovation.* Some companies develop and launch innovations without understanding past performance—either their own or their competitors'—in areas in which they are attempting to innovate. Although innovative companies should live in the present with an eye to the future, knowledge of past performance helps focus the efforts of innovation platoons as they move forward. Every so often, one reads about a company that, in its enthusiasm for innovation, forecasts selling a million units of a product that has a user universe of only three hundred thousand individuals—or projects 18 percent growth when it has never grown more than 6 percent in a year. How can such a thing happen? Odds are, no one looked at the history of the product category or the market. The lack of predefined goals and targets, usually stemming from not understanding past performance, provides insufficient and inadequate planning inputs and virtually ensures failure.

- *Lack of breakthrough innovation.* As previously mentioned, some companies focus all their innovation efforts on low-risk, minor improvements in the mistaken belief that they are avoiding risk. Nothing that is truly new and different gets developed. One of two things invariably happens: either the company strangles on its own line extensions, or the company loses its customers and ultimately its business to competitors who take risks and innovate. Typical symptoms are incentives and career paths that don't encourage risk-taking, short planning horizons, and leadership styles that do not accept (let alone reward) failures.

- *Lack of strategic alignment.* Platoons often work on innovation projects that are not linked to the company's strategy and goals. These projects often sound like good ideas, but they don't match the company's objectives, which probably haven't been defined or articulated clearly. Eventually these projects get killed or die a slow death. Team members become frustrated and feel their time has been wasted.

- *Lack of focus.* Underallocation and fragmentation of resources are two symptoms reflecting the same problem: lack of focus. Many companies set aggressive goals for innovation but dedicate only a handful of people to the effort. This simply won't work. Real innovation can produce blockbuster results precisely because it isn't easy, and it isn't free. It takes time, talent, hard work, and resources.

At the other extreme, some companies devote too much attention to too many initiatives. They virtually refuse to kill projects. They delay difficult decisions and allow projects to meander on too long. As a result, the company's resources are stretched too thin across too many projects, and no project receives the attention it needs. Managers and team members become frustrated when nothing is seen through to completion. The root cause is the inability to set priorities and to say no to certain projects. Successful innovators focus on a limited number of high-priority initiatives.

- *No predefined criteria for success.* In an attempt to be entrepreneurial, some companies do not consistently define and apply screening hurdles to innovation projects. "Bring me your ideas, and I'll know a successful one when I see it" is the phrase heard from all too many senior managers. In actuality, this attitude has a demoralizing impact on innovation platoons. Without predefined goals and targets, teams get insufficient guidance. How do you hit an undefined, moving target? Go/no-go decisions are perceived to be (and often are) based on the unpredictable gut feeling of a few senior managers.

Innovation Policy Components

Having an innovation policy in place can encourage a more disciplined, structured approach to innovation and help prevent many of these common pitfalls. An innovation policy provides an overall description of the role that innovation will play in satisfying the growth goals of the company. It establishes the criteria for setting strategies, priorities, and agendas. It provides the framework for a disciplined, structured approach to innovation.

Specifically, a policy contains the following five components:

- *Vision.* The scope and boundaries for innovation
- *Growth gap.* Financial expectations for innovation revenues and profits, typically over a five-year period
- *Strategic roles.* The strategic objectives that innovation should serve in supporting the business strategy
- *Screening criteria.* Filters that help determine which ideas are most attractive to pursue in order to yield success
- *Resource strategy.* An outline of the resource requirements—financial, human, and the like—necessary to support the desired innovation goals and initiatives

An effective innovation policy integrates these components into a consistent call to action. For example, if the innovation growth goals are aggressive, then the vision and strategic roles must support a higher-risk portfolio, and the screening criteria must establish aggressive hurdles to be overcome.

Innovation Vision

An *innovation vision* is a concise, future-oriented statement that defines the markets in which a company will compete and where it will focus innovations within those markets. The purpose of crafting the innovation vision is to create a high-level road map to guide the initiatives a corporation will seek to implement over the next three to five years. Although the vision itself may not change significantly during that time, it should be revisited often to ensure that it properly captures the essence of the corporation's self-identity with respect to innovation.

While the focus of the vision is on the future, its roots are in the past. An audit of a company's past innovation performance and an analysis of innovation strengths and weaknesses provide required direction and input for the identification of target markets and specific innovation roles. Specifically, data from an innovation audit can help shape the three components of an innovation vision:

1. *A definition of the market where the company competes or wants to compete* (e.g., the scope or boundaries that define which markets or market segments should be targeted for innovation and which are out of the company's scope). The more aggressive a company's growth goals, the more broadly it may need to define its market scope.

2. *The company's desired position in its target markets.* How does the company define its leadership role in the market? Does it want to be the most profitable? Does it want to be the dominant player in certain niches?

3. *A definition of the range of benefits to be provided to customers*
(e.g., the benefits the company will focus on delivering to customers). Will the company focus on reducing delivery time or
customer wait time, improving personalized service, applying
technology to improve ease of use for customers, providing wider
customer access? Corporations need some broad guidelines for
the types of benefits they should focus on delivering through
innovations.

The Innovation Audit

Entire books have been written about how to conduct marketing
audits and analyses, but it isn't possible to go into that level of detail
here. Exhibit 5.1 provides the key questions to ask during an innovation audit. This checklist can serve as an outline in structuring data
collection efforts and interviews with innovation participants. The two
major components of an innovation audit are past innovation performance interviews and a strengths-and-weaknesses assessment.

Past Innovation Performance Interviews

Understanding past innovation performance starts with gathering
company new product performance records. These records should
include overall revenues, profits, and budgets, as well as individual
project costs, forecasts, revenues, and profits. Once this background
data is collected, interviews and analysis can begin.

An objective team should conduct interviews with key upper management and innovation participants. The objective is to get their views
of the primary factors influencing innovation success, as well as their
perceptions of internal strengths and weaknesses compared to those of
the competition. It is important to interview or survey all innovation
managers until a clear picture of the company's situation emerges. An
example of a questionnaire for a strengths-and-weaknesses assessment
is presented later in this chapter.

With this overview of innovation performance at the company
level, the team can then turn to collecting past innovation project data,

Exhibit 5.1 Diagnostic Audit Checklist

The following questions can serve as a miniaudit—as a backdrop against which key topics can be focused on. The answers to these questions should provide a snapshot of some of the challenges facing your company in the new product arena and indicate how badly the company needs a full audit.

- What have been the major internal factors influencing your company's new product performance during the past three to five years?
- What new products have competitors introduced within the past five years? How have their new products performed in comparison to yours? Why?
- Which current functional strengths have had the greatest and most frequent impact on successfully commercialized new products? What specific shortfalls should you correct in the following areas?
  —Sales and marketing
  —Manufacturing
  —Research and development
  —Engineering
  —Finance
  —Market research
- What strategic roles have new products satisfied for your company, and how has performance contributed to the company's financial objectives?
- On what types of new products has your company focused (e.g., totally new-to-the-world, new lines to the company, line extensions and adaptations, new additions to existing lines, cost reductions)?
- What screening criteria are used to evaluate new products that have been under development? Under what circumstances have the criteria changed?
- How effective are the communication and coordination between the sales/marketing, manufacturing, and engineering functions? How does your current process address the need for multidisciplinary integration in the development process?
- What formal and informal communication mechanisms foster team interaction in the development process?
- How does your current organizational structure enhance the management of the new product process?
- What are your company's major weaknesses?
- How can the current process, approval procedures, and development time be streamlined to decrease the gestation time of new products?
- Who does your company hold accountable for new products, and who measures the performance of new product managers? To whom in the organization should the new product effort report?
- What types of compensation incentives or reward systems does your company use to support its objectives, structure, and process?
- What role has top management played in the new product program?

In answering these questions, your company will begin to understand some of the reasons for its new product performance. The answers, moreover, will indicate the types of objectives and roles that new products will play in meeting the overall growth objectives of the company. Now you are ready to take a deeper look at your past products and seek out key lessons learned to carry forward into tomorrow's new product program.

Source: Thomas D. Kuczmarski, *Managing New Products: Using the MAP System to Accelerate Growth*, 3d ed.

which provide specific additional support for broader, company-level observations. The team should start by interviewing product or project managers, current and past, to get their insights and perceptions about projects they were involved in. If the company uses multifunctional innovation teams, it is important to interview at least two team members to account for any biased perceptions.

Strengths-and-Weaknesses Assessment

Identifying a company's internal strengths and weaknesses relevant to innovation is a question of interpretation and judgment. It is highly subjective, qualitative, and difficult. The farther away a company moves from its existing strengths, the greater the degree of risk. That is not to say that the company should not take risks by going outside of its identified pool of strengths, but even new-to-the-world innovations can draw on internal strengths. These might be in the forms of technology applications or brand name equity that will bring perceived value to an offering; a proprietary manufacturing process that can be used in making an offering; or management expertise or familiarity with a given category that can be applied in developing new products or services.

The best way to conduct an assessment is on a division-by-division basis. Of course, strengths and weaknesses vary from company to company, but they tend to fall into four common groups: costs and manufacturing, technology, demand and marketing, and sales and distribution (Exhibit 5.2). Whatever the chosen categories, the team should identify a set of key competitive attributes. Then a simple three-point rating is applied to each attribute. A score of 1 signifies a significant competitive disadvantage in a market category; 2 signifies relative equality; and 3 indicates a very strong competitive advantage.

After completing this assessment, a company will have a picture of how it stacks up against the competition in terms of major innovation building blocks. These insights can then provide the needed direction for an innovation vision statement. Although the structure and format of an innovation vision are different from company to company, understanding the key elements of an effective vision can best be achieved through examining a couple of real-life examples.

Exhibit 5.2 Strengths-and-Weaknesses Assessment for a Market Category, Comparison to Top Competitor

	Company Strengths Compared to Top Competitor (Score 1–3)
Cost and Manufacturing Factors	
1. Low-cost producer: role that unit cost plays in the profitability of the product line. Low-cost producer scores 10; high-cost producer scores 1.	_____
2. Patented processes: degree to which patented processes provide a genuine competitive advantage that cannot be easily duplicated or is costly to replicate.	_____
3. Automated equipment: importance of robotics and automated machinery in achieving cost economies. Compare burden or overhead costs of competitor's cost structure.	_____
4. Low material cost: portion of raw materials in cost stream. Determine whether competitor has low-cost materials advantage.	_____
5. Low-cost labor: portion of labor costs in cost stream. Identify whether competitor has low labor costs.	_____
6. Unique source of supply: determine relative substitution capabilities of raw materials and competitive strongholds with suppliers.	_____
7. Productivity programs: compare competitor's formalized activities and programs in cost reduction and productivity enhancements.	_____
Subtotal	_____
Technology Factors	
8. Product patents: patented products score 10; products without patents score 1 if patented product exists, if not, score 5.	_____
9. Design patents: score 10 if design patents exist and are a key advantage in the manufacturing process; score 5 if they exist but are not important; score 1 if they do not exist.	_____
10. CAD/CAM systems: assess competitor's use of CAD/CAM and degree of importance of design adaptability and efficiency.	_____
11. Research & development spending: competitor spending most in R&D scores 10; the least scores 1. Weighting determined by the effect R&D has had on new products developed previously within this category.	_____
Subtotal	_____
Demand-Related and Marketing Factors	
12. Product differentiation: the degree of perceived uniqueness of a proposed product line that can be developed relative to existing offerings.	_____
13. Price advantage: lowest price in market scores 10; highest price scores 1.	_____
14. Packaging advantage: the contribution of packaging in stimulating purchase—unique design or protective qualities.	_____

15. Advertising expenditures and exposures: importance of advertising in motivating purchase intent, total advertising dollars spent, and reach and frequency achieved by competitor.   _____

16. Advertising creative: level of aided and unaided recall by consumer and degree to which any one competitor's creative has built awareness of the category.   _____

17. Distribution network: role that channel management and multichannel distribution play in product-offering success.   _____

18. Promotion impact: the importance of consumer promotions and trade discounts in moving product off the shelf. Compare competitor's spending levels for each.   _____

19. Public relations: extent to which publicity influences consumer trial-and-repeat purchase of the product.   _____

20. Focused market niche: how each competitor positions its product within the category. Who has the most memorable and useful positioning?   _____

21. Brand name recognition: degree to which brand name is the major factor influencing purchase. Competitor with highest brand name awareness and perceived price/value benefit scores 10.   _____

22. Loyal consumer base: competitor with strong consumer franchise scores 10.   _____

23. Management expertise: tangible and recognizable experience by managers in the category who provide a competitive advantage.   _____

24. Market research: already completed market research that will offer insights into a category (especially good if research is too costly for competition to conduct).   _____

Subtotal   _____

Sales and Distribution Factors

25. Sales coverage breadth: geographic penetration and sales force coverage, importance of broad sales coverage in selling product.   _____

26. Channel and distribution-cost advantage: low-cost distributor scores 10; high-cost distributor scores 1.   _____

27. Selling costs: cost per sales call and selling costs per revenue dollar generated relative to competitor.   _____

28. Market/buyer clout: degree to which other product line offerings or trade relationships give competitor an edge with buyers in the category.   _____

29. Delivery turnaround time: extent to which quick delivery is important to buyers in the category.   _____

30. Strategic distribution centers: geographic coverage of distribution centers strategically positioned to offer lower shipping costs and better delivery times.   _____

Subtotal   _____

Total   _____

Source: Thomas D. Kuczmarski, *Managing New Products: Using the MAP System to Accelerate Growth*, 3d ed.

Innovation Vision: Examples

The innovation vision should provide a general scope for both internally and externally focused innovations. For example, the portion of the statement that describes the range of benefits that will be provided to the company's customers can refer to both internal and external customers.

What does an innovation vision statement look like? Consider the following examples from the high-tech industry:

> We strive to lead in the creation, development, and manufacture of the industry's most advanced information technologies, including computer systems, software, networking systems, storage devices, and microelectronics. We translate these advanced technologies into value for our customers through our professional solutions and services businesses worldwide.

> Our mission is to connect more people and organizations to information in more innovative, simple, and reliable ways than any other networking company in the world. Our vision of pervasive networking is a world where connections are simpler, more powerful, more affordable, more global, and more available to all.

Notice that the first statement is more technology focused, and the second is more market focused. There is no right or wrong way to define an innovation vision, but it should be noted that effective visions must be customer focused. The first example is from IBM. The company's vision clearly describes its intent to focus on innovation in the information technology, computer system, software, network, storage device, and microelectronics markets. Its focus on customer value and innovation breakthroughs has helped IBM become a global technology leader in a variety of product and service markets.

The second example is from 3Com Corporation. 3Com's vision, similar to IBM's, specifies where and how the company seeks to compete. Its focus on connectivity and customer-oriented innovation has fueled its reputation as one of the most innovative, customer-oriented corporations of the digital age. 3Com's innovation vision has helped influence both internal and external perceptions of the company and its innovation programs.

Innovation Growth Gap

The *innovation growth gap* defines the financial goals to be achieved through innovation. Specifically, it describes what has to be accomplished for a company to realize the ambitions described in its vision. The difference between current revenues and expected future revenues highlights the gap to be filled through some combination of current businesses, innovation, and acquisitions. The future revenues illustrate the anticipated growth that will be expected from the company's innovation efforts. Exhibit 5.3 shows an example of an innovation growth gap.

Without an innovation growth gap, success cannot be measured. Resource requirements cannot be determined. A long-range business plan usually contains some optimistic "hockey-stick" graphs and charts. These often-lofty goals are a starting point to get the process under way. However, developing *realistic* innovation financial targets is critical. Targets that are too low tend to drag down people's potential; targets that are too high create frustration and anxiety and cause people to lose their sense of commitment. While revenue and profit goals may be a stretch and deliberately challenging, they should be attainable. If not, this alone will be debilitating for innovation participants, drive down morale, and weaken the innovation foundation.

With the historical perspective of the innovation audit, additional questions that should be addressed to help assess the validity of the innovation growth gap are:

- Which internal and external factors will likely impact this growth rate during the next five years?
- How is competition changing?
- What has been the historical rate of innovation?
- Will customer demand continue to grow at historical levels?
- What is the projected growth rate of the total market category over the next five years?

These questions provide benchmarks against which to measure a company's innovation growth projections. If a category is forecasted to grow at 8 percent a year, and a company is projecting a 25 percent annual growth rate in that category, management may have unrealistic expectations. However, if the company is planning to take a price reduction, substantially increase its advertising budget, expand its distribution base, or the like, then a 25 percent growth rate for the company may be feasible.

A five-year innovation growth gap can be developed by building up the revenue projections estimated from each growth mode. Determine for your own company what percentage of future growth is expected to come from each source. Then, percentages or absolute revenue dollar projections can be applied to each growth mode. This framework will begin to calibrate the relative degree of importance of innovation to alternative growth routes. Exhibit 5.3 shows a company's $134 million growth gap for innovation and other sources of growth. Nearly 13 percent of the company's revenues in five years is expected to come from internally developed innovations.

One of the useful things that can come from growth gap analysis is the identification of a range of financial and nonfinancial issues that help set the direction for innovation platoons and programs. For

Exhibit 5.3 Defining the Innovation Growth Gap

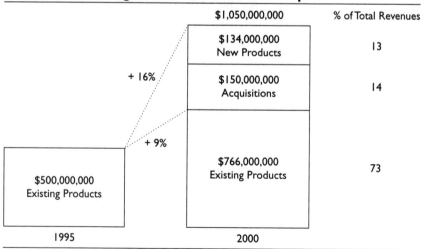

example, the implications for the company in Exhibit 5.3 include the following:

- The innovation and acquisitions expectations are roughly evenly balanced. The company wants to add $150 million from acquisitions and $134 million from innovation.
- The mix of line extensions and additions versus new-to-the-company innovations is also relatively balanced.

Separate innovation platoons may be needed for the new-to-the-company innovations, whereas line extensions might be managed by current product managers. If the balance is skewed to line extensions and minor improvements, the innovation effort might be best carried out by existing business marketing managers.

Management must recognize that revenues from innovation will not begin flowing in for at least one to two years. (Development time is often overlooked in setting innovation targets.) Thus, the $134 million in sales from innovation should be expected to materialize within a three- to four-year period. This may be an overly optimistic goal. The company wants to more than double its size within five years. With 27 percent of total revenues coming from innovation and acquisitions, a high degree of focused attention and dedicated resources will be required to achieve these goals. The assumption should be that innovation platoons are already or will soon be in place.

The financial growth gap helps to break down and better define innovation targets. It provides a reality check on innovation objectives, as well as a framework for financial and human resource requirements. For example, a telecommunications supplier established a five-year goal of $300 million in incremental revenues from innovation. However, in the previous five years, only three new offerings that achieved greater than $30 million in annual revenue had been launched in this company's entire industry. Assuming a success rate of 60 percent and a balanced portfolio, this company would need to seriously vamp up its innovation development activities: approximately thirty-four new offerings over the next five years (including fourteen expected failures)! To do so, it would have to dramatically increase the resources dedicated to innovation to achieve such aggressive goals—more people, more capital spending, larger research and development and information technology budgets, more market research and test marketing, and more advertising and promotion. And, most important, more management time and attention.

Creating an innovation growth gap requires focused attention and unbiased, unfiltered self-examination. Key inputs into the growth gap are perspectives from senior managers, the company's historical innovation performance, historical innovation performance of competitors, and company financial and strategic plans. The ultimate benefit from assimilating these inputs is an agreed-upon target and expectations for innovation efforts. This creates a common understanding among employees about the effect that the corporation intends innovation to have, and it also serves as a tool for measuring annual progress. The growth gap itself must fit in with the overall philosophy described in the innovation vision as well as with the other elements of the innovation policy. For example, companies with more aggressive growth gaps may need to define their innovation vision more broadly than they currently do and establish strategic roles that encourage greater risk-taking.

Innovation Strategic Roles

A strategic role is a clear, concise label used to categorize innovation developments. Its title should intuitively convey the purpose of the innovation ideas that will be used to fulfill that role (e.g., high growth, defense). *Innovation strategic roles* provide a framework for linking new innovation with a company's strategy and goals. Often an organization's strategic plan does not provide enough guidance on the types of innovations to be developed. As a result, innovation platoons are often left guessing rather than having concrete answers to strategic questions such as:

• What objectives is the company trying to support with innovation?

- What types of innovations would fit the company's strategy, and what types would be out of its scope?
- To what degree should the innovation portfolio help the company explore totally new areas as opposed to concentrating on core competencies?
- What level of risk is the company willing to accept with its innovation portfolio?
- How expansive should the innovation portfolio be?

Strategic roles provide a framework to ensure that the innovations developed will support the business strategy. In particular, they define how innovations can help solidify and grow the current business, as well as propel the company into new areas. The key requirement is that all strategic roles must support a business objective.

Innovation strategic roles can be classified as either requisite or expansive. *Requisite roles* describe functions that innovation can satisfy in defending, enhancing, or increasing the competitiveness of existing business, within existing areas, for existing customers, and for solving existing problems. *Expansive roles* help direct a company to develop innovative offerings for going outside the confines of the current business into new areas, offering new benefits, applying new technologies, and/or targeting new segments.

Strategic roles help define and guide the desired portfolio mix of corporate innovations. By keeping these roles in mind, a corporation is better able to carry out its innovation vision and fulfill the financial growth gap. Losing sight of its strategic roles can lead a corporation to expend energy on innovation projects that may be great ideas but that don't support its desired innovation end state.

The innovation vision and growth gap help identify the proper mix of requisite and expansive roles for the corporation's pipeline of innovations. The quantity and nature of each variety of these roles should be congruent with the corporation's stance toward innovation and risk. Offerings that satisfy requisite roles (e.g., cost reductions, repositionings, improvements, and productivity enhancement) are typically less risky. Innovations that satisfy expansive roles (e.g., new platforms, new-to-the-company ideas, and new-to-the-world innovations) are typically more risky.

Each innovation can potentially fill many different roles. In addition, strategic roles can vary greatly from one company to the next. The key is that no one role is better than another because the appropriateness of each is dependent on a company's individual business strategy. However, successful companies understand the power of innovation for building competitive advantage and often have strategic roles that reflect this.

Innovation Screening Criteria

Screening criteria are objective measures for evaluating the relative attractiveness of innovation opportunities. If risk or resources were not relevant considerations, screening criteria would not be necessary. Of course, defining and managing risk in the face of limited resources is the basis of all innovation, and screens provide a common basis by which to evaluate projects throughout the corporation. Attached to each screening criterion are specific hurdles that a specific innovative need, idea, concept, or prototype must "pass" in order to move on to the next stage of development. Each potential innovation is compared against each screen and rated to assess its desirability based on that aspect. Specific screening questions vary with the type of product and industry, but several screening categories are applicable to virtually all businesses. These same screening categories can be applied at different points in the innovation process to evaluate and prioritize opportunities. As a starter list, the following seven broad screening categories should be considered:

- *Strategic fit.* The extent to which needs, ideas, or concepts fit in with or satisfy the innovation vision and strategic roles
- *Market attractiveness.* The overall size, growth rate, and competitiveness of the markets or segments being explored
- *Customer need.* The overall intensity of a need or appeal of an idea or concept

- *Sustainability*. The time over which needs, ideas, or concepts will likely be appealing and unique in the customer markets or segments being explored
- *Uniqueness*. The extent to which an idea or concept is new and different relative to current offerings in the market
- *Feasibility*. The degree to which an idea or concept leverages existing capabilities versus required new capabilities
- *Financial attractiveness*. The overall size and return potential of an idea or concept, including the likely impact on existing business

The reasons for developing and applying innovation screening criteria are as follows:

1. **To focus investments.** Screening criteria help eliminate ideas that do not appear to meet corporate objectives. As a concept moves through the development process, the investment goes up. Screening criteria help an organization choose those opportunities that offer the highest utilization of scarce resources.
2. **To more rapidly complete high-potential projects.** By focusing innovation development efforts on projects with the highest potential, companies can put more dedicated resources against them to ensure timely completion.
3. **To provide objective goals.** Screening criteria provide objective measures that innovation can shoot for, mitigating the "gut feel" or champion-driven screening approach used by many companies. In one case, two CEOs from the same city—one representing a utility company and the other a telecommunications company—struck an agreement to develop and test-market a new energy management system. This system would enable homeowners to monitor their energy usage by appliance and by time of day and then modify their usage behavior to save money. The initiative provided positive public relations value for both companies and also helped satisfy a regulatory requirement for one of them. Customers, however, were not very interested. The benefits were not compelling enough to warrant using the product. Screening criteria established in advance would have set a hierarchy of standards to meet. The innovation platoon could have weighed the public relations attractiveness

against the financial problems, and senior management could have made an informed choice with respect to the product. Unfortunately, objective measures were replaced with subjective, management-driven measures. The platoon felt powerless to kill the project even after determining it would not achieve reasonable financial hurdles. Both companies ultimately suffered financial losses, and eventually the test marketing was discontinued.

To receive the greatest benefit from developing and applying screening criteria, several key principles should be followed:

- *Screening criteria should be agreed to in advance.* This reduces the likelihood of surprises and midcourse changes. Nothing is more frustrating for innovation platoon members than to think they have met the corporate hurdles only to find out the hurdles have changed.
- *Screening results should be presented to a cross-functional management team.* All appropriate functional areas of the company should be involved in critically evaluating ideas and offering opinions as the ideas move through the process. By making sure that the important issues get raised and addressed early in the process, the overall time to market can be reduced.
- *Screening is not a one-time event.* It should be performed at several points throughout the development process, always prior to committing to the next level of investment in a project. Screening builds momentum for and provides education about an innovation to the broader organization throughout the process. If momentum is there and education occurs, fewer roadblocks crop up late in the process that might kill a good idea.
- *The same categories of screens should be maintained throughout the process.* Although the specific questions and hurdles may change, the categories of screening criteria should remain the same to ensure consistency.
- *As a project moves through the process, the hurdles associated with each screening category should become more rigorous and the measures more quantifiable.* Rigor should increase because the cost of failure goes up dramatically as ideas move into later stages of development.

- *Screening hurdles should vary by type of innovation.* Offerings with higher risk (e.g., new-to-the-world, new-to-the-company) may be allowed more development time but must meet higher financial return hurdles. Similarly, innovations with lower risk (e.g., line extensions, product improvements) may have lower financial requirements to get approved for launch.

Innovation Resource Strategy

After completing the strategic elements of the innovation policy, it is time to align the people and financial resources required to successfully carry out the plan. This is where the rubber meets the road. Taking into account the innovation opportunities with the highest potential payoff and comparing them with the company's key internal strengths, innovation projects can be prioritized. From there, the opportunities with the overall highest priority should receive first crack at company resources.

For example, on putting together an aggressive innovation policy that called for the launch of more than thirty innovations over five years, a midsized energy company calculated that it needed to allocate twenty-one full-time employees, with a significant number of new hires, to innovation-related positions. Furthermore, the company realized it needed to allocate close to $1 million to cover payroll and associated expenses for this group for the next five years.

After calculating the human resource requirements, the next step was to estimate the financial resources required to support the innovation effort. As it turned out, filling the aggressive growth gap was going to require the company to invest close to $300 million in acquisitions. In addition, an estimated $150 million would be required to stimulate the existing business lines to achieve the required growth rates, while another $30 million was needed to support innovation initiatives that its new dedicated staff would be developing.

It becomes quite clear that innovation is often expensive. However, the extra effort a company puts into "priming the innovation pump" early on can help keep the flow of innovations running efficiently and effectively in the future. The short-term sacrifice made by dedicating the company's top-flight resources to innovation will be greatly over-shadowed by the tremendous long-term benefits that disciplined innovation can bring. And most important, everyone involved has an idea of what is required. Shooting from the hip isn't part of the equation. Everyone has a clearly defined target and commitment.

The Policy Framework

The innovation policy is the framework for stimulating innovation within a corporation. To get results, it must be backed by several organizational practices. The adoption of these practices supports the innovation process and ensures that the proper corporate environment exists for facilitating innovation. The innovation policy is the vital link that corporations need to translate company goals into innovation realities. By taking on the disciplined approach to innovation that the policy encourages, corporations will be much more likely to develop an enduring, regenerating pipeline of innovations instead of an occasional flash-in-the pan breakthrough. In the next chapter, we take a look at how a corporation can best fulfill its innovation policy by creating an ideal human dynamic for facilitating innovation among its dedicated personnel.

INNOVATION PLATOONS

There's no way around it: innovation takes time. A corporation— especially a large one—simply cannot become a successful innovator overnight. But it can get results, one step at a time. And teams are where results happen. But there are teams, and then there are teams. The term *teams* has been overused and trivialized to the point of being almost meaningless. Companies are establishing teams to do everything from creating the strategic plan to orchestrating the annual Christmas party!

We have participated on scores of corporate innovation teams, some more successful than others, but the most effective innovation teams had at least one thing in common: they were established and operated differently from other teams in the company and bore little resemblance to past groups. Effective innovation teams' actions, behavior, culture, and results are dramatically different. They tap into the power of the logarithmic function, and their impact is lasting—both for the company and the individuals. Time and again, the feedback from team members who have participated on effective innovation teams is that the experience was the best of their entire career. The difference is the spirit of the platoon.

Innovation Platoons Versus Traditional Teams

The term *platoon* is a much better descriptor than *team* of what companies need to create to manage their innovation initiatives. War veterans will tell you that wars are fought and won at the platoon level.

Small groups of soldiers band together, fight together, and live or die together. They understand the big picture—their overall mission—and how they support this mission. But each platoon must work together on a local (detail) level to accomplish the goal of the mission.

Operating under an established charter, the ultimate allegiance of platoon members is to their mission and to one another. This is the core difference between a platoon and a team. A platoon is a little community that creates its own identity, values, and operating norms. Each person brings different skills to form an interdependent unit. Although each individual is critical to successfully accomplishing the goal, no one person—not even the leader—can make it happen alone. And everyone in the platoon knows deep down that this is true. At best, members are cross-trained so they can substitute for one another if a platoon member is promoted or has to leave.

Most companies think their innovation teams are, in fact, platoons. In most cases, they aren't. Effective innovation platoons have two profoundly distinct characteristics:

1. *They exhibit an unwavering commitment to their mission.* When people truly believe they are doing something important and worthwhile, their efforts go beyond those they typically exert for "work." More than money, what motivates people's hearts and souls is a commitment to a greater purpose, a noble mission.

2. *They exhibit an unwavering commitment to one another.* Platoons throw away the "what's in it for me" individualism that pollutes the minds of most employees today. Platoon members spend time nurturing the individual. They intentionally take time to know one another, serve one another, and celebrate individual and team efforts.

In his first letter to the Corinthians, the apostle Paul laid out a picture of what platoons look like, using the human body as an analogy:

> *The body is a unit, though it is made up of many parts; and though all its parts are many, they form one body. . . . But God has combined the members of the body and has given greater honor to the parts that lacked it, so that there should be no division in the body, but that its parts should have equal concern for each other. If one part suffers, every part suffers with it; if one part is honored, every part rejoices with it.*
>
> 1 Corinthians 12:12, 24–26

Although effective innovation platoons depend on the unique characteristics of each individual, they are not an elusive "state of mind" that can only be achieved when the right chemistry is present or the stars are in alignment. Tangible actions can increase the likelihood of a platoon's success. Specifically, innovation platoons require very careful attention when they are set up and ongoing support while they operate. In addition, when a particular mission is over, the company can "seed" the organization with platoon members to disseminate the spirit of innovation throughout the organization. Exhibit 6.1 illustrates and summarizes the following three stages of innovation platoons:

- *Starting.* Setting up platoons for success
- *Sustaining.* Helping platoons thrive and survive as they progress
- *Seeding.* Strategically leveraging platoon member experiences to further broaden innovation competency

Exhibit 6.1 Three Stages of Innovation Platoons

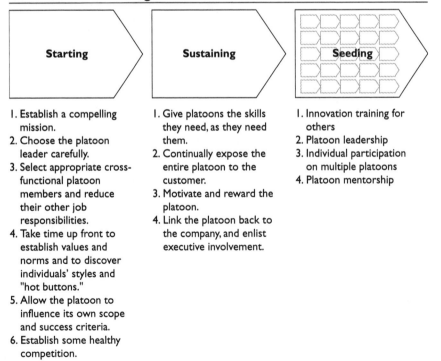

Starting	Sustaining	Seeding
1. Establish a compelling mission.	1. Give platoons the skills they need, as they need them.	1. Innovation training for others
2. Choose the platoon leader carefully.	2. Continually expose the entire platoon to the customer.	2. Platoon leadership
3. Select appropriate cross-functional platoon members and reduce their other job responsibilities.	3. Motivate and reward the platoon.	3. Individual participation on multiple platoons
4. Take time up front to establish values and norms and to discover individuals' styles and "hot buttons."	4. Link the platoon back to the company, and enlist executive involvement.	4. Platoon mentorship
5. Allow the platoon to influence its own scope and success criteria.		
6. Establish some healthy competition.		

Stage I: Starting Platoons

In too many instances, innovation platoons are set up to fail. Any number of things can doom a platoon before it ever gets off the ground. Perhaps the wrong leader or team members are selected. Maybe the mission statement is muddy or dull. Or perhaps, after the platoon receives its new orders, members are still expected to carry out all of the duties of their "real" jobs. Compounding this challenge is the all-too-human one: the need to deliver early successes for a "newfangled," high-profile initiative. After all, the first few innovation platoons will model different behaviors and operate under different norms; thus, they are expected to produce benefits to justify the changes. Therefore, the successes of the first few innovation platoons are particularly critical.

The good news is that innovation platoons can be set up to succeed. While this alone won't ensure success of the project, an effective foundation is a prerequisite. It is exceedingly difficult to go back after the fact and try to remedy or restart a poorly chartered platoon. In working with a wide variety of innovation platoons, we have identified six key ingredients for starting up a successful platoon:

- Establish a compelling mission.
- Choose the platoon leader carefully.
- Select appropriate cross-functional platoon members and reduce their other job responsibilities.
- Take time up front to establish values and norms and to discover individuals' styles and "hot buttons."
- Allow the platoon to influence its own scope and success criteria.
- Establish some healthy competition.

Companies that adhere to these six principles create a fertile environment in which platoons have every opportunity to flourish.

Establish a Compelling Mission

On the battlefield, a platoon's mission is ultimately worth dying for. Although corporate platoons might not require quite this same level of commitment, they need a worthy cause to bring out the best efforts of each individual. Platoon members must know that their particular mission is of the utmost importance for the success of the division, business unit, or company. The great news about innovation is that without it a company eventually dies. So, creating a compelling mission around the need for and importance of innovation isn't unusually difficult.

People are eager to be part of an effort that is worthy of their best. Not because they are being paid to do it. Not because they have received a promotion that entitles them to do it. Not because it will ensure their job for another year. And not because it is a requirement to climb to the next rung on the corporate ladder. These motivations are short-lived and unworthy of people's best work. Rather, people long to be part of something significant, something meaningful, something lasting, something bigger than themselves. Give them a real reason to participate in an innovation platoon.

Not long ago, we participated on an innovation platoon where the vice president of sales and marketing offered a few "motivational words" at the kickoff meeting: "There are no innovations left in this business. The last major innovation was in 1955, and for the rest of our lives, products in this market will continue to look the way that they do today." What a way to get people excited about their mission! Fortunately, the CEO was very excited about and supportive of the team, but this executive naysayer continued to try to find the dark cloud for every silver lining the platoon created. Ironically, the team identified and developed a new product innovation that became the company's most successful—and profitable—new product introduction in a generation.

The key to an effective mission statement is that it should be clear, concise, aggressive yet achievable, and aligned with company strategy. It should evoke emotion, either because of its own significance or because of what it promises to do for customers. One innovation platoon charged with creating new food products in a certain category created the following mission: "To make healthful eating more convenient and enjoyable." Their simple mission was to transform people's thoughts and behaviors toward healthy eating, at least in the product category they were exploring—no small task. This mission provided focus to keep them on track and passion to keep them energized.

Choose the Platoon Leader Carefully

The platoon leader makes or breaks the team. End of story. We find that successful innovation platoons *always* have an effective leader. And platoons find it exceedingly difficult to overcome the impact of a poor leader, even if each of the members is individually strong. The platoon leader must be selected with great thought and care.

One recent example from an information technology services company illustrates how a good or poor choice is difficult to distinguish. At first, the individual chosen looked strong. He had good marketing expertise and a solid track record in prior jobs. In addition, senior management wanted to provide him with a challenging opportunity to enhance his professional development. He looked like a good choice for platoon leader. However, platoon members quickly realized that he was very politically motivated, always looking at how executives perceived him. He thought of himself first, second, and third. The platoon and its members were a distant priority compared to his own self-interests and personal/professional agenda. We were not surprised to see this platoon falter almost immediately, while another platoon established at the same time was thriving. Different platoon members tried to rise to the occasion and overcome the leader's deficiency in caring for the team, but with limited impact. Fortunately, partway through the assignment, this platoon leader decided to leave the company for a new opportunity. Another member of the platoon was selected to take over leadership, and the team flourished almost immediately. The new leader quickly galvanized and energized the team, creating magnetic relationships with his team members. Their efforts ultimately resulted in a portfolio of successful innovations launched in the market.

Too often companies believe that tenure and technical expertise are the most important characteristics to evaluate in selecting a platoon leader. Our experience has shown that emphasizing these two elements does *not* serve a company well. Beyond a certain amount of experience needed to understand the company culture and gain some exposure to executives, tenure in and of itself is not required. Some of the most effective platoon leaders we have worked with were considered relative newcomers to the company or held fairly junior positions. In addition, a leader's gaps in technical expertise can be overcome by surrounding him or her with appropriate platoon members and providing appropriate outside resources.

What platoons really need is leaders who possess the following characteristics:

- *They are highly "others focused."* More than the goal itself, effective platoon leaders are focused on people—specifically, people other than themselves: customers, platoon members, platoon members' bosses, company executives, and other company employees. They have a customer orientation that is reflected in a passion for understanding customers and uncovering their needs. Medical professionals often work in teams, but the Mayo Clinic provides an example of the unusual extent this customer focus can reach. Dr. Lynn Hartmann, a medical oncologist at the clinic, describes how Mayo teams function: ". . . each team is driven by the medical problems involved in a case and by the patient's preferences. Sometimes that means a team must be expanded—or taken apart and reassembled."

- *Platoon members are focused outward and upward within the company.* They presell ideas with executives. They involve a broad range of cross-functional managers early to build internal momentum and obtain buy-in. They keep others in the company informed as to the project's status and progress. Finally, effective platoon leaders show intense concern for each platoon member. For each person, they ask:

  —"What are this member's unique needs and work style?"
  —"What roles will motivate him or her?"
  —"What personal development opportunities is he or she looking for?"
  —"How can I increase his or her exposure to senior management?"
  —"What can I do to make this an outstanding experience for him or her?"
  —"How can I recognize his or her contributions?"

—"How can I enhance his or her career?"

—"How can I reduce conflict with his or her boss?"

- *They are outstanding communicators, both within and outside of the platoon.* Innovation platoons tend to make people uncomfortable. They may investigate areas where others have not looked or rethink strategies that were previously dismissed. Regardless, they tend to be surrounded with a lot of questions, concerns, and politics. Effective platoon leaders keep the environment open, both inside and outside of the team. Inside the team, they work to create an environment where people feel free to share opinions and work through conflict. They clarify the mission and goals, people's roles, and the short-term plan. Outside the team, they work hard to knock down political and organizational barriers so the platoon can do its job unhampered by other people's baggage. An effective platoon leader tries to reduce the mystery and jealousy that can build up in a larger organization and to prepare it for what will come from the platoon's efforts.

- *They are comfortable sailing into uncharted waters.* Innovation platoons tend not to have a detailed map that clearly identifies exactly where they are going and how they will get there. Although companies may have an innovation process, such a process serves more as a tool to provide general guidance rather than step-by-step directions to be followed. In mountain climbing, you proceed up the mountain in stages, moving the base camp up the mountain as you go. If you take a wrong turn or run into difficult weather, you need go back only to the previous base camp rather than all the way down the mountain. Similarly, each stage of an innovation process provides a new foundation for the platoon, moving it farther ahead. So, if members take a wrong turn, they have to go back only a few steps in the process, not all the way back to the beginning. Still, within each stage of the process, the platoon will encounter a great deal of uncertainty in terms of customers, competition, and internal capabilities. Therefore, an effective platoon leader must be comfortable leading in an environment fraught with uncertainty, yet be able to instill confidence and trust in platoon members that they are moving in the right direction to accomplish the mission. Quite a difficult balance! If a potential platoon leader needs everything buttoned down before the journey begins, he or she is probably not the right person for the job.

Of course, these attributes are not the only ones to look for in an effective platoon leader. For example, great project management and planning skills and meeting facilitation skills are a plus. But such skills can be taught or supplemented without too much difficulty. The key is to be very selective in choosing the platoon leader and pay particular attention to the three attributes described here.

Select Appropriate Cross-Functional Platoon Members and Reduce Their Other Job Responsibilities

Innovation is part of everyone's job, or so people are told in many companies. The problem is that these same people are given no time for innovation, especially people in functions that are not traditionally associated with it, such as sales, finance, information technology, customer service, and manufacturing. In a post reengineering environment where many people's job responsibilities have already been stretched to the breaking point, what time is left for innovation? A large insurance company identified approximately one hundred "high-potential" employees, gave them a "development opportunity" to participate on specific innovation initiatives, and assigned them to teams. The first question was: "Are they expected to participate in this innovation initiative on top of their current responsibilities, or will some of their current responsibilities be off-loaded to free up time?" The answer was predictable: Innovation was thrown in the "other duties as assigned" category.

If innovation is truly a top priority, then innovation platoons should receive additional resources from various functions in the company. This may mean taking resources away from other priorities, putting certain initiatives on hold, or canceling them altogether. Across industries, this does not appear to be the case. Kuczmarski & Associates' recent Best Practices Study indicates that only 2.4 percent of companies describe their resource allocation for innovation as highly effective. On the contrary, an energy company we recently worked with was suffering from short-term financial pressure because the extremely mild winter reduced people's usage of natural gas. But the company viewed innovation as so critical to its future that other initiatives were cut or put on hold so that an innovation platoon could move forward. This company backed up its goal to be more innovative with the resources to accomplish its goal.

Reducing platoon members' other commitments starts with the leader. If at all possible, platoon leaders should dedicate a majority of their time—100 percent, if at all possible—to leading the platoon. Depending on their role, other team members should dedicate at least 20 percent to 25 percent to the innovation platoon. The goal should be to have representation from each function that is necessary for the innovation platoon's success, with the core platoon comprising no more than ten to twelve members (Exhibit 6.2).

Expect many objections to this approach. Perhaps the biggest objection will come from the sales organization, where shifting part of an individual's time away from sales activities will have a negative short-term impact on the company's revenues and on that person's sales commissions. Another frequent objection is that some functional areas "aren't needed" until later in the process. For example,

Exhibit 6.2 Core Innovation Platoon

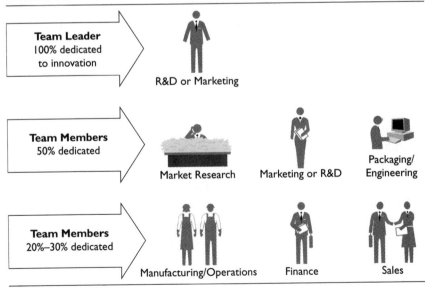

representatives from packaging design, manufacturing, advertising, customer service, or sales may not be deemed necessary at the beginning. In reality, participating from start to finish as part of the platoon builds a critical foundation of customer understanding, enhances communication and teamwork, provides multiple functional perspectives and expertise, and reduces time to market—all of which increase the likelihood of success. Be careful not to give in to organizational pressures to strip away time and talent from the platoon.

A typical innovation platoon is supplemented by a hub-and-spoke system, with subteams being formed outside of the core platoon as needed (Exhibit 6.3). In this way, the core platoon can remain reasonably small and still draw resources from and make changes in the overall organization. Subteams form and disband to accomplish specific tasks as the innovation platoon proceeds.

Exhibit 6.3 Platoon Hub-and-Spoke System

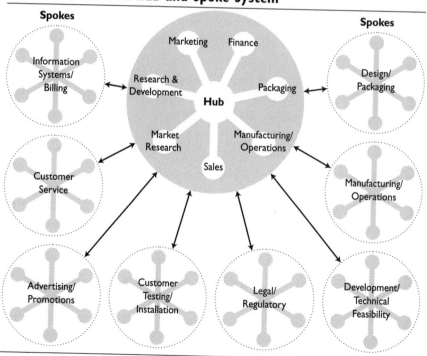

Take Time Up Front to Establish Values and Norms and to Discover Individuals' Styles and "Hot Buttons"

All too often, innovation platoons get the perception that time spent building their "teamness" is a waste. We have observed that the opposite is true. Platoons enhance their effectiveness by taking time at the beginning and throughout their existence to develop a strong culture. In war, spending time in the same foxhole facilitates getting to know your platoonmates on a deeply personal level. Innovation platoons need to build in activities that foster a deeper understanding of and appreciation for each individual.

Some specific activities can help stimulate the start-up process:

- *Prekickoff interviews by the platoon leader with each individual.* When a platoon leader takes the time up front to understand each individual's strengths and weaknesses, and then shapes a role that reflects this understanding, platoon members start off feeling valued and energized. In interviewing one platoon member, a platoon leader uncovered that the woman wanted opportunities for greater executive exposure, including presenting to senior management where appropriate. Unfortunately, she was extremely reserved and lacked experience in making executive presentations. The leader took time prior to each presentation to design a specific role for this team member and rehearse with her. The results were phenomenal. The platoon member received the exposure she wanted and represented the platoon extremely well during each executive interaction. She maintained a high level of performance throughout the project, and ultimately her career took off.

- *A multiday off-site kickoff meeting with structured activities that facilitate understanding.* Platoons feel pressure to get on with their mission. An extended kickoff can help them take adequate time up front to start the process of creating and nurturing their culture. Certainly much of the kickoff time will be spent planning and preparing for their mission. But time spent conducting an exercise around the Myers-Briggs personality profile, or having pairs of individuals break out and discuss their unique styles and needs, can help platoon members begin to understand and appreciate their differences. Meals allow downtime to begin uncovering the interests and priorities of each platoon member.

- *Development of platoon values and operating norms during the kick-off.* A platoon needs to agree on what it believes and how it will operate. It may choose to operate quite differently from the historical company culture. To start defining its own culture, a platoon can design its own values and norms. *Shared values* are beliefs or principles that are jointly held by all platoon members. *Norms* are the specific behaviors that support these values. For example, one value might be to respect platoon members' outside family commitments. A norm that supports this value might be starting and stopping meetings on time. Platoons can get as creative as they desire in crafting the kind of culture they want, right down to the rewards and penalties for keeping or breaking the agreed-upon values and norms. The key is to spend precious time designing the platoon's desired culture in advance rather than letting it flow out of the company's current culture—much of which may not currently support innovation.

Once the values and norms are established, the platoon's effectiveness should be measured regularly. Effective platoons take time to discuss how they are performing, what is working well, and what could be improved. A consumer products company we encountered distributes a team effectiveness survey every few months to all active innovation teams. It tracks team performance over time and can compare teams against "the best" to identify and head off potential problems.

Allow the Platoon to Influence Its Own Scope and Success Criteria

Although executives will want to define the high-level mission, platoons need room to influence this charter. Dictated goals can shut down platoons, leaving them feeling they are doomed to fail before they ever begin. Often executives fear a platoon will stray from the mission or define too small a goal. In reality, platoons typically come up with a better direction and perhaps even more aggressive goals if they are allowed to influence them. Some back-and-forth negotiation may be necessary, but platoons and executives should be able to mutually agree on a charter.

Prior to any significant innovation initiative, the first stage of the process should be devoted to establishing an innovation policy (as outlined in Chapter 5). This brief step enables the platoon to take the time to get different internal perspectives on the mission, begin to understand the relevant external market and trends, and uncover whatever research already exists on the topic. Once informed, the platoon is better able to establish its own charter in terms of:

- The scope of the innovation efforts (e.g., markets, customer segments, types of innovations, technologies considered)
- Success criteria (specific goals the platoon plans to achieve, and how the platoon will measure its success)

Allowing the platoon to define its own scope and success criteria represents a structured way of creating a contract between the platoon and the company. It also helps ensure alignment of the platoon's scope, goals, and resources. Once this contract is in place, the platoon can operate without the need for day-to-day involvement from the executive team.

Establish Some Healthy Competition

One final ingredient for starting up an effective innovation platoon is creating some form of healthy competition. Platoons operate at their best when presented with a challenge, and competition can help create the right environment. The most obvious form of competition is external, where a company selects a particular competitor and challenges the team to steal market share, get to market with new products sooner, be the first to penetrate specific customer segments, and the like. Competition, however, does not have to mean winners and losers—it can be strictly internal. For example, one consumer products company initiated two platoons at the same time with charters to innovate in two different market categories. Both platoons were expected to deliver a portfolio of innovations that would generate substantial revenues and profits. While the platoons did not consider one another the enemy, this healthy internal competition sparked each to rise to the challenge in an effort to outperform the other.

Stage II: Sustaining Platoons

In war, a platoon experiences difficulties, retreats from certain battles, requires updated instructions from headquarters, needs additional supplies and reinforcements, and celebrates small victories along the way. Similarly, innovation platoons encounter hardships as well as victories as their initiatives progress. In trying to sustain high levels of performance, executives and platoon leaders should pay particular attention to four areas: resources, customer focus, a reward system, and organization-wide involvement. The ways to address these areas are:

- Give platoons the skills they need, as they need them.
- Continually expose the entire platoon to the customer.
- Motivate and reward the platoon.
- Link the platoon back to the company, and enlist executive involvement.

Give Platoons the Skills They Need, as They Need Them

Innovation often requires platoon members to work outside of their traditional areas of expertise and develop new skills. Some of the particular skills needed might include:

- Conducting market research through customer interviews and focus groups
- Performing data analysis to uncover customer problems, insights, and trends
- Systematically screening ideas from a large list to find those with the greatest potential
- Writing, testing, and evaluating new concepts

- Writing a business case for high-potential concepts
- Assessing alternative partners needed for developing or delivering a particular innovation
- Packaging and delivering an executive presentation

Except for areas that require a high level of technical expertise, many of the necessary skills can be taught, practiced, and improved over time. One innovation platoon devoted two hours of its weekly team meetings to training. The platoon leader worked hard to identify in advance the types of skills needed and either used an expert from within the platoon—such as the market researcher who taught customer research techniques—or an outside expert—such as the president of a local construction association who talked about building codes.

An environment in which all platoon members are proficient in certain core skills encourages cooperation, provides flexibility to substitute for one another, and creates greater equality of contributions. Each platoon member then wears a generalist hat for these core skills, as well as a specialist hat representing his or her unique area of expertise. Because of this need for ongoing skill development, we recommend involving a representative from human resources from the start—either as part of the team or as an executive committee member.

Continually Expose the Entire Platoon to the Customer

During the innovation process, platoon members must undergo an "intuition transplant." Most of them come to the initiative with little understanding of the customer or, worse yet, misperceptions of customers' needs. The problem is a platoon member's natural inclination to use his or her own needs, attitudes, experiences, observations, and behaviors as a proxy for those of the customer. Unfortunately, these rarely provide an accurate understanding of the needs, attitudes, and behaviors of target customers. Professional managers typically are not the target customer for most innovations. As a result, none of the platoon members initially understands the customer at a level required for successful innovation. Like many transplants, an intuition transplant takes time to take hold, although intensive "deep dives" into the lives of customers can shorten the transplant time frame. Bruce Claxton, an industrial designer who participated in one of the Motorola multidisciplinary teams that designed the Talkabout—the first Motorola product to ever sell a million units in a year—described the need for an intense level of customer understanding: "Now we have to develop inquiring minds, an almost anthropological interest in the world, and learn a lot about linking human behavior to new products . . . To be innovative a company must take mental excursions into the lives of their customers and observe patterns of behavior related to its products" (*Philadelphia Inquirer*, April 10, 1999).

On a positive note, the procedure is fairly simple: continuous exposure to target customers through interviews, observations, group discussions, customer diaries, and the like. Over time platoon members replace their old intuitions with those of the customer and can begin to anticipate and even predict where customers are headed as well as how they might respond to various innovations.

Not long ago, we helped a company develop new household cleaning products. It didn't take our platoon long to realize we knew very little about the topic. In one particular in-home interview, we watched a woman put Turtle Wax on her bathtub. Dumbfounded, we asked the logical question: "Why?" It turns out, cleaning the tub was such a difficult and distasteful job, she was willing to go to great efforts— even taking a risk that family members might slip on the freshly waxed surface—to reduce mold, mildew, and soap scum. All to ease the cleaning burden. We visited several other consumers who had invented equally unique home remedies for similar purposes. So, people were willing to take extra time and effort up front to reduce their job later. This insight led to the development of a daily bath and shower cleaner, sprayed on after each shower or bath, that keeps dirt and soap scum from sticking to bathroom surfaces. Daily bath and shower cleaners, including Clean Shower and ShowerShine by Scrubbing Bubbles, have revolutionized the bathroom-cleaning category, reinvigorating growth in a previously stagnant market.

Ultimately, the platoon is substantially more effective and efficient if all members undergo an intuition transplant. Communication improves. Decision making speeds up. Everything moves more quickly because all members are operating out of a deep, acute understanding of the customer. The platoon creates shared experiences—customer war stories—that revolve around actual customers with actual behaviors and actual needs. The conversations start to make a noticeable shift. Platoon members spend more time talking about what customers need rather than what management thinks, what the company wants, what their current capabilities can or cannot do, and what past efforts have been tried and have failed.

Motivate and Reward the Platoon

If companies desire different results, then surely the reward and recognition systems require change. However, few companies do much in the way of specifically rewarding innovation at any level—executives, business unit managers, or innovation platoons. Our recent study on best practices in innovation revealed that fewer than 25 percent of companies have created reward and recognition systems specifically to encourage and support innovation. The purpose here is not to go in-depth on any particular method but to highlight how innovation platoons should be motivated through monetary and nonmonetary rewards, and some of the alternatives to consider (Exhibit 6.4).

Monetary Rewards

Monetary rewards fall into four primary categories: equity based, performance sharing, milestone based, and career path.

- *Equity-based methods.* These methods include stock or options in a company that are spun out or phantom stock created for a particular product, service, or business. For phantom stock, valuation becomes a key issue. Usually, a proxy revenue or EBIT (earnings before interest and taxes) multiple can be established using benchmarks from a relevant set of publicly traded companies. With either method, employees benefit if their stock appreciates due to the performance of their innovation. The number of shares or options dis-

Exhibit 6.4 Platoon Rewards and Recognition

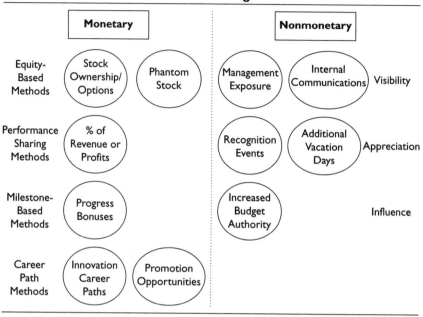

tributed to each platoon member might vary based on their level of involvement.

- ***Performance sharing methods.*** With these approaches, a predefined percentage of future revenues, gross profits, or pretax profits is distributed to platoon members. The performance measure may start out as a percentage of revenues for a period of time, then shift to a percentage of profits in order to change the focus during later stages of the innovation's life cycle. Performance sharing methods tend to be easier to implement than equity-based methods because they are easier to measure. Also, most companies have a similar bonus system already in place for some functions or levels of management.

The Mayo Clinic's incentive system is an unusual example of performance sharing. Conventional incentive systems in medical practices can create perverse outcomes because doctors, ostensibly collaborating on a case, are actually competing for financial gain, either directly in terms of credit (and payment) for a case or in terms of referrals (and future cases). Mayo physicians receive a set income, so the pernicious effects of competition are eliminated. They are willing (and encouraged) to ask for advice from a colleague in another area of expertise. Even more important and unusual is that doctors feel comfortable contacting each other on an informal basis (a "curbside consult") because the focus is solely on the outcome for the patient. This practice encourages freewheeling debates among medical staff and a constructive questioning of advice from outside consultants.

- *Milestone-based methods.* These methods pay for progress and good judgment. Bonuses (either money or company stock) are paid when a platoon completes critical stages in the process or recommends "killing" a concept. With these methods, platoons must meet certain measurable hurdles before moving on to the next stage in the process. One caution with milestone-based methods: unless platoons are rewarded for using good business judgment—even if that judgment means killing a project—the bonuses may encourage them to push poor ideas forward for too long.

- *Career path methods.* These methods provide a means of valuing time spent on innovation platoons by propelling individuals' careers. For many platoon members, time spent on an innovation initiative may actually inhibit their career progress. They return to their functional area and find their bosses do not value the time spent on innovation because it took them away from other responsibilities. Separate career paths established for employees who desire a career in innovation, as well as enhanced career benefits and promotion opportunities for employees who participate part-time on an innovation platoon, is a great way to reward and motivate platoon members.

Nonmonetary Rewards

Nonmonetary rewards are less expensive ways of recognizing and celebrating accomplishments. Such rewards can and should be handed out after crunch times, after interim milestones are met, and after specific results are known. A few examples include:

- Increased management exposure
- Recognition events and awards banquets
- Recognition in internal newsletters
- Additional vacation days
- Increased authority

Key reward and recognition issues include who is allowed to participate in the program (anyone who ever touched the innovation versus only the core team) and the extent to which rewards are more team based rather than individual based. It is important to avoid overemphasizing individual rewards, as this can be detrimental to the health of the platoon.

Link the Platoon Back to the Company, and Enlist Executive Involvement

Finally, successful innovation platoons do not hibernate from the rest of the organization. Although platoon members benefit from frequent contact with and proximity to one another, isolation from the larger organization is detrimental. Platoons can end up isolated—disconnected from the very people they need in order to be successful. If communication back to the organization is limited, a veil of secrecy may surround a platoon, resulting in resentment building up among other employees and managers. Except in those instances where a platoon will be spun off as a separate operating entity, isolation tends to harm its future impact.

Successful innovation platoons continuously communicate with and look for ways to involve the rest of the organization in their initiative. They invite nonmembers to:

- Attend customer research activities
- Participate in brainstorming sessions
- Provide expert input when needed
- Help screen ideas

- Sit in on team meetings
- Attend status updates

In particular, platoons that actively engage the executive team in their process are able to build that team's information base, trust level, and buy-in—which can help overcome risk aversion. We particularly enjoy holding a separate executive brainstorming session during the appropriate stage of the process. Such a session informs executives about customer needs, enables them to participate in shaping the ultimate solutions, and provides an opportunity for them to "take a dip" in the team's culture so they can experience different norms and behaviors.

We recently worked with an innovation platoon that conducted a brainstorming session with its executive team. Platoon members provided the executives with background customer research and gave a homework assignment to bring one idea to the session. Near the beginning of the session we had each executive read his or her idea. When we reached the CEO, he wanted to show everyone that he was prepared. He offered an idea, which included a very detailed description of a potential new concept, a picture of what the product might look like, and even a potential product name and advertising slogan. That was enough to raise the bar and engage each executive's competitive spirit. The ideas flowed, the executives enjoyed the session, and best of all, they engaged in the process. By constantly checking in with the executive team, inviting them to participate in customer research, and reviewing status updates with them, the platoon acquired buy-in and built momentum along the way.

Stage III: Seeding the Organization

The last stage in creating effective innovation platoons is *seeding*, leveraging past platoons for maximum impact on the company's culture and overall innovation competency. By strategically seeding past innovation platoon members in new initiatives, their organizational impact is enlarged.

In many cases, innovation platoon members either go back to their previous jobs and roles or get promoted to new positions. An innovation platoon is merely a one-time assignment or career stepping-stone. Yet, if leveraged in the right way, past platoon leaders and members can serve as innovation evangelists who ultimately develop a much broader base of innovation disciples. Rather than being viewed as an initiative du jour, innovation can be systematically infused in a company through this seeding process.

Unfortunately, in most companies, innovation is not a career path. As a result, time spent on an innovation platoon may be viewed as negative, or neutral at best, to one's career growth. To support the seeding process for future innovation platoons, company reward systems and career paths must encourage such participation.

Leaders interested in seeding their organizations with innovation evangelists can do so in four ways:

- *Innovation training for others.* Previous innovation platoon members can conduct innovation training sessions for new platoons, conduct management training sessions, and lead innovation discussions at new-hire orientation sessions.
- *Platoon leadership.* Previous platoon members can be offered the opportunity to lead a future platoon, thereby challenging them to develop new skill sets.
- *Individual participation on multiple platoons.* Some members may immediately serve on a newly formed platoon. In addition, platoons often come to a point where they need to divide up and focus on separate initiatives. Past members may be leveraged across multiple initiatives, thereby providing new platoons with experienced guides.
- *Platoon mentorship.* For those who can't immediately participate on new platoons, their expertise can still have an impact. One effective way to make this happen is to establish mentor relationships. New platoons receive informal coaching from those who have already been through the process.

One company we worked with was particularly effective at the seeding process. The company kicked off two pilot innovation platoons in two different business units, with ten cross-functional members on each platoon. After demonstrating success with these two pilots, the company decided to start a new innovation platoon every few months for a different business unit, charging each platoon to create a portfolio of innovations for a specific product category. As a platoon neared the end of an initiative, the company seeded a few of its members in the next available innovation platoon. Furthermore, some of the innovation platoons would identify multiple opportunities and then split into separate platoons, bringing in new people to each of the new groups. They engaged past platoon leaders as coaches, trainers, and spokespersons for future platoons. Within a short time, the initial twenty platoon members had directly influenced hundreds of other employees.

The main point is that a few successful innovation platoons will not, in and of themselves, create the kind of lasting, significant change that most companies desire. They will create interest and demonstrate that innovation is possible, thereby overcoming some of the skeptics. But they will not create new behaviors outside of their particular platoons. The seeding process brings about a deeper, longer-lasting innovation competency within the entire company.

Platoons—The Heart and Soul of Innovation

Research shows that companies are, in increasing numbers, adopting cross-functional teams for innovation. A 1999 Kuczmarski & Associates study of innovation best practices reveals that nearly 50 percent of companies use cross-functional teams for their innovation initiatives. Few of these teams, however, resemble true innovation platoons. As described in this chapter, innovation platoons require a different mindset, leadership style, resource commitment, management involvement, and "care and feeding." The good news is that all of these elements are within a company's control. When they are activated, they provide fertile ground where innovation platoons can create lasting growth for the company and for the individuals involved.

Platoons are where innovation takes place. They represent the front line in any effort to infuse innovation. Without them, effective innovation processes, strategies, organizational structures, and research approaches will fall short. With them, companies can model new behaviors, encourage appropriate risk-taking, and generate tangible results.

CHAPTER

PROCESS

Successfully managing innovation requires designing a well-defined, disciplined innovation process that is consistently understood and used by all of a company's managers. As might be expected, different companies in different industries use different approaches to innovation, but there are common elements of effective processes that can serve as guiding principles for all companies. These elements and principles are the focus of this chapter.

The *process* is the essential set of tools that platoon members use to give form and substance to the company's innovation priority and the initiatives stated in its policy. The purpose of an innovation process is to:

- Provide a structured approach for systematically and continuously generating innovations
- Enable formal decision and go/no-go approval points to guide innovation decisions and prioritization
- Efficiently track the number of innovations in each stage of development to ensure that an organization is on target to meet its stated financial and strategic goals

Without a clear, well-communicated, consistently applied process in place, innovation teams are likely to fail in their efforts to identify and develop successful new offerings. Product development in companies without a disciplined process tends to be slower and less efficient and produces lower success rates overall than innovation in organizations with such a process. Sadly, however, the findings of

141

most innovation studies to date reveal that many companies' processes are nonexistent or seriously deficient.

The Benefits of an Innovation Process

Despite the clear link to innovation success, many companies still resist spending time designing and executing a staged development process as a road map for innovation. Some managers believe that development processes take too long to execute, stifle creativity, and/or reduce the likelihood of identifying breakthrough innovations by screening out too many good ideas. As hypercompetition, globalization, the Internet, and other megatrends create new challenges and opportunities for companies, many managers are facing new pressures to reduce innovation development cycles and at the same time increase success rates, fueling discussion about the practicality of formal development processes even more.

While these concerns are understandable, most of them are not based in fact. Developing and using a staged development system or similar process to move innovation projects from needs and ideas to concepts and launches actually has far more benefits than costs. Among the many benefits of innovation processes are that they help managers achieve the two seemingly conflicting goals most often faced: reduced innovation cycle time and higher success rates. Other key benefits of an effective innovation process include:

- *Improved up-front direction setting.* As stated earlier, innovation often succeeds or fails largely at the outset, before anything has "happened."
- *Strong customer orientation.* Effective processes provide this critical element.
- *Improved coordination and communication across functions.* These are essential to reducing or eliminating customer insight "translation errors" that contribute to failures.
- *More effective prioritization of needs, ideas, and concepts.* All things are possible, just not at the same time. Setting priorities makes it possible to focus on the best opportunities.

- *Higher quality of execution.* The structure and discipline of a good process enhance the quality of the product, which increases the likelihood for success.

These outputs can lead an innovation platoon down the most fruitful roads for breakthrough innovation. Conversely, a weak strategy can lead to inefficient research focus, poor decision making, wasted time and energy, and strategically irrelevant findings and ideas.

Evidence supporting the benefits of innovation processes is strong. The 1999 Kuczmarski & Associates study of winning innovation practices among over two hundred companies across industries revealed that nearly three-quarters of the most successfully innovative corporations (73.6%) have a formal new product development process in place versus just over half (55.7%) of the less successful ones. Not surprisingly, the "best" companies also have significantly lower cycle times and higher new product and service hit rates. In fact, nearly a quarter (23.5%) of the best new product and service companies described their speed to market as extremely effective versus only 1.2% of the "rest." A well-designed innovation process can make or break a project's desired outcome.

Overview of Staged Innovation Processes

One particularly effective general process for moving innovations from needs to launches is called a staged innovation process, or stage-gate system. Popularized by Robert Cooper in his book, *Winning at New Products*, the term *stage-gate system* is used to describe an innovation process with a predetermined set of stages, each with well-defined, cross-functional, and concurrent activities. Each of the stages in the system is followed by an approval point, or gate, which serves as a go/no-go decision point prior to the beginning of a new stage. Filtering tools called screening or success criteria—which are developed as part of the innovation policy—are used at each approval point to help make the prioritization of innovations more efficient and less subjective.

Stages

A staged development process breaks the entire innovation development cycle into distinct stages in which all of the members of the innovation platoon participate. Each stage is designed to gather information and valuable customer insights that help to reduce development uncertainty and help the team better identify high-potential opportunities to investigate. The information collected by the team at each stage is evaluated by the innovation steering committee or senior management at regular approval point meetings. A "best of class" staged innovation process is shown in Exhibit 7.1. The key stages in the Guaranteed Innovation (GI) system process are:

1. *Problem identification.* Refers to the exploration of customer needs and wants
2. *Ideation.* Comprises problem-focused idea generation
3. *Conceptualization.* Includes concept development, shaping, and business analysis, which describes the potential revenue and overall attractiveness of innovation concepts
4. *Development.* Includes the actual design and development of an innovation prototype
5. *Testing.* Includes prototype testing and/or marketplace trials to verify and validate the specifications and overall value perception of the proposed innovation
6. *Launch.* Revolves around commercialization of the innovation, including the initiation of full production, marketing, and selling

Exhibit 7.1 The Guaranteed Innovation System Process

Stage 1	Stage 2	Stage 3	Stage 4	Stage 5	Stage 6
Problem Identification	Ideation	Conceptualization	Development	Testing	Launch

In the GI system, the development of innovation policy precedes problem identification and ideation. This essential step is described in Chapter 5. The policy defines the role of innovation and describes how innovations relate or contribute to the overall goals of the business. It also sets up clear expectations and goals for the types of innovations being sought and defines the boundaries for them. In other words, it sets the direction for process. However, because the innovation policy is more "global" in nature and less tactical than the other process stages, it is not included in the system diagram.

A second stage not included in the GI system process is the post-launch checkup stage. The objective of this stage, which occurs after commercialization, is to monitor and analyze the performance of innovations relative to original forecasts six and twelve months after launch, and annually thereafter. This step, often overlooked, can provide valuable insights that can be used to identify opportunities and avoid mistakes in the future.

All members of a cross-functional innovation platoon participate in each stage of the innovation development process. There are not steps that are the responsibility of one function and others that are the responsibility of a different function. Rather, each of the team members is involved in each stage to maximize customer understanding and innovation results and minimize development errors. The involvement of cross-functional resources in the early stages of innovation development is a major departure from traditional norms in most companies.

Approval Points

Each stage ends with an approval or go/no-go point. Decisions are made about the opportunities being explored using predefined screening criteria. The seven different categories of screening criteria described in Chapter 5 are used at each approval point in the GI system process to evaluate and prioritize innovation opportunities. Exhibit 7.2 describes the five major approval points in the innovation process and the key screening criteria categories used at each approval point.

Exhibit 7.2 Guaranteed Innovation System Process Approval Points

1. *Problem Approval.* This gate follows the problem identification stage and focuses on the evaluation of customer problems and opportunities.

    Key problem approval screening categories include strategic fit, market attractiveness, customer need, and sustainability.

2. *Idea Approval.* This gate follows the ideation stage and focuses on the evaluation of innovation ideas.

    Key idea screening categories include strategic fit, customer need, sustainability, and uniqueness.

3. *Concept Approval.* This gate follows the conceptualization stage and focuses on the evaluation of innovation concepts.

    Key concept approval screening categories include customer need, sustainability, uniqueness, feasibility, and financial attractiveness.

4. *Prototype Approval.* This gate follows the development stage and focuses on the evaluation of innovation prototypes.

    Key prototype screening categories include customer need, feasibility, and financial attractiveness.

5. *Prelaunch Approval.* This gate follows the testing stage and focuses on the evaluation of final user tests and business cases.

    Key prelaunch screening categories include customer need, feasibility, and financial attractiveness.

Screening criteria are used at each approval point to evaluate the information collected, prioritize opportunities, and help determine which innovations will continue to be explored and which will be put on hold or killed. Furthermore, at each approval point, the screens become more detailed and specific. As the amount of information about each opportunity increases, the rigor of the screens used to judge them increases as well. At the problem and idea approval gates, for example, screens are simple and highly qualitative. Later in the process, screens become more rigorous and quantitative. Examples of specific screens used at each approval point are described later in this chapter.

Although different categories of screens are emphasized to different degrees at each of the major approval points of the GI system process, screens from each of the seven screening categories are applied at some level at each gate. As shown in Exhibit 7.3, there is typically a heavier emphasis on the strategic fit, customer need, and sustainability screens at the problem and idea approval points because

Exhibit 7.3 Emphasis of Screening Categories at Process Approval Points

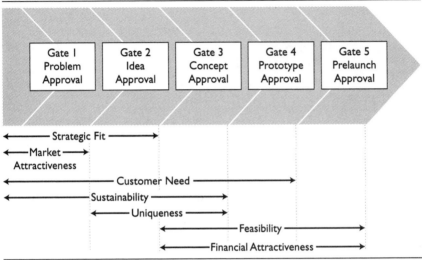

the merit of new markets, needs, and ideas is being judged with limited information. At the concept, prototype, and prelaunch approval points, emphasis shifts to the feasibility and financial attractiveness screening categories. The screens at these gates are usually more finance oriented because there are well-defined concepts and more detailed information to evaluate.

Staged Innovation Processes and Innovation Risk

Not surprisingly, even the best innovation processes and screening criteria do not guarantee desired results all the time. In fact, even the most successful companies only reach their goals about two-thirds of the time. Despite this disheartening statistic, strong evidence supports the notion that a systematic, well-defined, and commonly understood innovation development process is a required ingredient for successful innovation in large corporations. In fact, among best-of-class innovation companies, an effective process is quickly becoming a given, not a differentiator, for successful results. Fortunately for organizations without an optimized process in place, best practice techniques and proven methodologies are available to provide teams with assistance and guidance.

Stage 1: Problem Identification

The first stage of the GI system process is called the problem identification stage because it is the place where customer problems and opportunities are first identified and explored. The innovation platoon selects research categories and targets customers to study, using the goals and roles outlined in the innovation policy as guidelines. Then, in each of the selected research categories, iterative rounds of research with customers and select noncustomer experts are conducted to identify and understand customers' key frustrations, problems, needs, and wants in a given product or service category. The needs and wants focus can be broad (e.g., category product or service usage processes or routines) or narrow (e.g., product and service feature, benefit, or service dissatisfactions).

The most effective research techniques for surfacing and exploring customer problems are qualitative: focus groups, in-depth interviews (IDIs), observational interviews, projective interviews, and lead user groups. More detail on these qualitative research tools, along with the advantages and disadvantages of each, is provided in Chapter 8. Ultimately, customer problems and opportunities identified in this stage provide a foundation for focused idea generation in the next stage.

The Problem Approval Gate

In most instances, a large number of intense problems surface at the problem identification stage, so the primary use of screening criteria is to evaluate and prioritize problem and opportunity categories for idea generation. As mentioned previously, screening criteria at this gate are usually very simple:

SCREENING CRITERIA CHECKLIST

Strategic Fit
➤ Is the problem or opportunity consistent with the innovation vision, roles, and goals outlined in the innovation policy? (Y/N)

Market Attractiveness
➤ Is the overall size and growth rate of the market(s) in which the problem or opportunity exists sufficiently large? (Y/N)

Customer Need
➤ How intense is the problem or opportunity to customers? (Score 1 [lowest] to 5 [highest])

Sustainability
➤ Is the problem or opportunity sufficiently stable? (Y/N)

Uniqueness
➤ Is the problem or opportunity currently unmet? (Y/N)

Feasibility
➤ Can the problem or opportunity potentially be addressed? (Y/N)

Financial Attractiveness
➤ How profitable would solving this problem likely be if a solution was offered to customers? (Score 1 to 5)

Case Study: Building Products Manufacturer

An innovation platoon in the building products industry began stage 1 by discussing the broad research categories it wished to explore. In its innovation policy, the platoon had outlined aggressive innovation growth goals—a 40 percent compound annual growth rate (CAGR) over five years—and decided to focus on satisfying expansive innovation roles with new-to-the-world and new-to-the-company concepts. Given these objectives, it was clear that the platoon needed to establish a broad category definition and select research categories inside and outside of the company's traditional target markets. In the end, eight research categories were selected and a research plan was created that included research with homeowners, builders, architects, and building industry experts. The research plan extended for ten weeks and included thirty-six focus groups, twenty-seven in-home observations, and three lead user groups in nine cities across the United States.

Three iterative waves of research were conducted in stage 1. Each wave comprised three cities and included twelve focus groups, nine in-home observations, and one lead user group. In wave 1, the platoon began by exploring broad life and business problems and opportunities with homeowners, builders, and architects. The focus was on generating a large list of potential customer needs and issues to further explore in wave 2. At the end of the first wave, twenty problems were identified across the eight research categories.

In the second wave, the twenty problems were explored in great detail. The platoon focused on understanding which problems were the most intense and why. At the end of that wave, twelve high-potential problem areas remained. These problems were summarized and converted into concise problem statements and taken into wave 3 for confirmation and prioritization by customers and select nonconsumers.

After the third wave, the problem statements were evaluated using the problem approval screens, and six high-potential problem and opportunity statements were recommended for stage 2. Key insights for each of the recommended problems were created and distributed to the innovation steering committee and later to the platoon's idea generation session participants as stimuli prior to brainstorming.

Problem Identification Stage Pitfalls

The problem identification stage is arguably the most important stage of the entire GI system process because it establishes a foundation for the development of breakthrough innovations by identifying creative, customer-based problems and opportunities. One of the most common mistakes companies make during front-end product development is to skip the problem identification stage and move right into idea generation. The right approach to creating successful innovations is to begin with customer problem research. This ensures that idea generation is aimed at creating solutions that resolve, address, or improve highly intense, customer-identified problems, hassles, complaints, or unmet needs.

This problem-solving approach to idea generation results in higher-potential new product and service ideas and, ultimately, higher innovation success rates. Developing a customer problem orientation mind-set is a standard practice in highly successful and innovative companies, and it is one of the seven components of the GI system. Specific strategies and techniques for identifying breakthrough customer problems and needs is the focus of Chapter 8.

Stage 2: Ideation

The second stage of the innovation process is called the ideation stage. The main objective of the ideation stage is to generate dozens, sometimes hundreds, of innovation ideas, each of which addresses one or more identified customer needs or opportunities. Idea generation sessions are conducted with various constituencies, including employees, management, suppliers, and customers to solicit creative innovation ideas. An *idea* in this stage is defined as a one- or two-sentence description of an innovation that details what the product or service is, how it works, and the primary benefits it offers customers. Once all of the idea generation sessions are completed, ideas are consolidated and "scrubbed." That is, duplicates are removed, and partial ideas are completed or discarded prior to screening.

Idea screening usually occurs in three steps. In the first step, "must-pass" screens are applied to all of the ideas to eliminate those that do not meet the required criteria. Next, "should-pass" criteria are applied to the remaining ideas. High-level feasibility screens also may be applied but only for the purposes of ensuring that a well-rounded mix of short- and long-term ideas are being explored, not for the purpose of eliminating potential ideas. Only ideas that are judged to be technically impossible (i.e., ideas that defy the laws of chemistry or physics) should be eliminated with feasibility screens at this stage.

A simple weighted-average scorecard method can be used to evaluate results of the should-pass criteria screening and determine which ideas are the strongest. Finally, the screened ideas are examined by the platoon and the top ones are recommended. Following the idea approval gate, the ideas move to the conceptualization stage.

The Idea Approval Gate

Ideas identified in the ideation stage are evaluated and prioritized using the three-step approach already described. Screens in the strategic fit and customer need categories are commonly must-pass criteria, whereas screens in the other categories are more often should-pass criteria.

SCREENING CRITERIA CHECKLIST

Score each question from 1 (lowest) to 5 (highest):

Strategic Fit
➤ To what extent is the idea consistent with the innovation vision, roles, and goals outlined in the innovation policy?

Market Attractiveness
➤ How large is the potential market(s) in which the idea exists?
➤ How attractive are the growth prospects in the potential market(s) in which the idea exists?

Customer Need
➤ To what extent does the idea address an intense customer need?

Sustainability
➤ How stable is the problem or opportunity driving the idea?
➤ How protectable is the idea?

Uniqueness
➤ To what extent is the idea different from other solutions?

> **Feasibility**
> ➤ How technically feasible is the idea?
> ➤ How easily can the idea be manufactured or delivered?
>
> **Financial Attractiveness**
> ➤ How profitable is the idea likely to be if offered to customers?

Case Study: Building Products Manufacturer

Using the six problem areas identified in stage 1 as the foundation for brainstorming, the innovation platoon conducted eight separate idea generation sessions in stage 2. Sessions were conducted with managers from a variety of functions, including marketing, research and development, and customer service, as well as with the company's advertising agency, customers, builders, architects, and the platoon itself. Sessions lasted three hours each and generally identified 100 to 150 ideas each.

Through the eight idea generation sessions, over six hundred ideas and idea fragments surfaced. Once duplicate ideas and idea fragments were removed, the platoon was left with about 250 unique, complete ideas. Each of the remaining ideas was then evaluated by each platoon member using screens in the must-pass categories—strategic fit and customer need. This initial round of screening reduced the list of ideas to about one hundred high-potential ideas.

These ideas were then evaluated using the should-pass screens and prioritized using a simple weighted scorecard method. Approximately twenty-five ideas were eliminated in this second round of screening (they were judged by the team to be technically impossible), and the last seventy-five ideas were taken into a final round of screening prior to the idea approval gate.

In the final screening, the platoon members choose twenty-five ideas from the seventy-five that had passed all of the idea screening criteria. These ideas were recommended for movement to stage 3, and the other ideas were catalogued by the platoon for use at a later time. The twenty-five recommended ideas were examined by the innovation steering committee at the stage 2 gate. Following the gate meeting, twenty-four of the ideas were moved forward into the conceptualization stage.

Ideation Stage Pitfalls

Companies often make a couple of mistakes during the ideation stage. The first is that they don't provide idea generation session participants with adequate problem stimuli in advance of the sessions and, as a result, brainstorming is not focused directly on identified customer problems and opportunities. This leads to ideas with low consumer need or without a valued, unique point of difference. One- to two-page problem area summaries should be prepared by the innovation platoon and distributed to idea generation participants at least two days before the session to maximize the absorption of customer needs and insights.

Arguably, the biggest mistake that companies make in the ideation stage is to eliminate too many ideas too early during screening. Often, the platoon throws out ideas that are radically new or technically challenging before any significant effort is made to identify ways to execute the idea or modify it to make it more feasible. Radical ideas are often the source of breakthrough innovations, and platoons should make every effort to see that the best of these ideas are kept in the process through the ideation and conceptualization stages.

To ensure that too many innovative ideas aren't screened out, platoons should view the technical feasibility screens in this stage as prioritization (i.e., should-pass) screens, not go/no-go (i.e., must-pass) screens. The only ideas that should be eliminated with technical screens in the ideation stage are those that the team agrees are technically impossible. All other ideas should be considered for movement into stage 3.

Stage 3: Conceptualization

In the third stage of the innovation process, high-potential ideas are turned into concept statements, shaped and tested with customers, and evaluated financially through business analyses. Concept statements are usually one to two pages in length and briefly describe the problem the product or service is attempting to solve, its intended use, key features and benefits, and unique points of differentiation.

The concept statements are shaped and prioritized in iterative rounds of qualitative research with customers and select other decision makers and influencers. As in the problem identification stage, qualitative techniques including focus groups and in-depth interviews are used most often to shape concept statements. Low-need concept statements are screened out after each round of research and high-potential concepts are moved to the business analysis phase.

Business analysis involves the formulation of market size and cost estimates that can be used to estimate the potential revenue and profit potential and the overall attractiveness of an innovation concept. Generally, analyses include rough, three-year financial pro formas on concepts that estimate the future financial performance and the impact of the innovations on existing businesses. High-potential concepts that meet the required financial hurdles are moved into the development stage.

The Concept Approval Gate

At the concept approval gate, screening criteria and a high-level business analysis are used to evaluate the attractiveness of innovation concepts to determine which will move forward into the development stage and which will be put on hold or dropped. Although many of the screens at this gate are similar to those used at the idea approval gate, there is a much greater emphasis on feasibility and financial attractiveness screens at the concept approval gate. This is because concept approval is the final gate prior to the development stage and the last point at which a project can be put on hold or killed prior to making significant investments of capital or people. Because a large spending commitment must be made for most of the concepts that pass through this gate, the financial screens and business analysis are an important part of the evaluation. Results from screening and business analyses are reviewed, and concept recommendations are developed.

SCREENING CRITERIA CHECKLIST

Strategic Fit

➤ To what extent is the concept consistent with the innovation vision, roles, and goals outlined in the innovation policy? Score 1 [lowest] to 5 [highest]

➤ Does the concept satisfy one or more strategic roles? If so, which ones? (Y/N)

➤ Does the concept fit with one or more of the established brands in the category? If so, which ones? (Y/N)

Market Attractiveness

➤ How large is the potential market(s) in which the concept exists? ($)

➤ What are the expected growth rates in the potential market(s) in which the concept exists? (%)

Customer Need

➤ To what extent does the concept address an intense customer need? (Score 1 to 5)

Sustainability

➤ How stable is the problem or opportunity driving the concept? (Score 1 to 5)

➤ How protectable is the concept? (Score 1 to 5)

Uniqueness

➤ To what extent is the concept different from other solutions? (Score 1 to 5)

Feasibility

➤ How technically feasible is the concept? (Score 1 to 5)

➤ How easily can the concept be manufactured or delivered? (Score 1 to 5)

➤ What is the expected development timeline for the concept? (years)

➤ What are the expected development costs for the concept? ($)

➤ What is the environmental impact of the concept? (Score 1 to 5)

> ➤ What is the legal impact of the concept? (Score 1 to 5)
> ➤ What is the regulatory impact of the concept? (Score 1 to 5)
>
> **Financial Attractiveness**
> ➤ What is the expected revenue of the concept? ($)
> ➤ What is the expected margin of the concept? (%)
> ➤ What is the expected new product value/return on investment of the concept? ($)
> ➤ What is the expected payback period of the concept? (years)

Case Study: Building Products Manufacturer

The innovation platoon began the conceptualization stage by converting the twenty-four ideas that passed the idea approval gate from one-sentence ideas into one- to two-page concept statements. Each concept statement included a name, a brief problem setup, a description of the concept and how it would work, and a reassurance statement that tried to address any fears or concerns that customers might have.

Concepts were then shaped by customers in iterative rounds of research similar to the approach used in the problem identification stage. Three waves of research were conducted in stage 3, and each wave again comprised three cities and included nine focus groups and twelve in-depth interviews. In wave 1, the platoon gathered broad concept feedback, including confirmation of the primary benefit and key likes and dislikes. The objective of this wave was to identify major concept suggestions and improvements, as well as screen out weak concepts. At the end of the wave, eighteen concepts were moved to wave 2 and six were dropped.

In the second wave, the eighteen concepts were shaped in greater detail. The platoon asked customers specific questions about the appeal of the concepts and ways to make them stronger. At the end of the wave, twelve high-potential concepts remained. The innovation platoon took these concepts into a final wave of research for final confirmation and prioritization by customers.

After wave 3, the twelve concepts were evaluated by the platoon using the concept approval screens and high-level business analysis.

Based on the results of the screening and business analysis, five high-potential concepts were recommended for prototype development. Lists of key insights and issues for each of the recommended concepts were created and distributed to the innovation steering committee prior to the concept approval gate meeting. At the review, all five of the recommended concepts were accepted and moved into stage 4.

Conceptualization Stage Pitfalls

In most cases, during the conceptualization stage, a concept can be effectively communicated to customers through a one- to two-page written concept description, which gives its idea form, substance, and shape. The description also may include a rough rendering or chart to help customers visualize how the product or service might look and be used or delivered. This allows valuable information to be collected about the concept at relatively low expense.

However, when highly innovative new-to-the-world or new-to-the-company concepts are being shaped, a rough, nonworking prototype, called a *protocept*, may be created as a supplement to the concept statement. By giving customers a 3-D mock-up to react to, protocepts can provide additional clarity so customers can more accurately evaluate a breakthrough product or service idea.

Additionally, the most innovative corporations generally conduct two or three rounds of qualitative concept shaping research with customers before fielding any quantitative tests. Optimizing concepts qualitatively—prior to spending the time and resources required to field a larger quantitative study—can give innovation platoons valuable insights about why customers like or don't like specific concepts or concept features, allowing major modifications to be made to the concepts prior to the concept approval gate.

Stage 4: Development

The fourth stage of the GI system process is called the development stage. In this stage, concepts that pass the gate 3 concept screen are turned into full-scale, working prototypes and detailed market test and launch plans, and production or service delivery plans are developed. Additionally, a more detailed business case is completed and final technical, environmental, legal, and regulatory issues are addressed. The time required to complete this stage varies significantly based on the specific product or service industry and the types of innovations being pursued. Line extensions in low-capital, low-technology markets can sometimes be developed in a couple of months, whereas development of new-to-the-world innovations in high-technology industries can take five years or more.

As high-potential concepts are converted into final mock-ups or prototypes, cost of materials and manufacturing or service delivery costs can be calculated precisely. The process is usually iterative and involves creating rapid prototypes, working models, initial prototypes, and final prototypes. Small customer acceptance tests may be conducted after each major iteration to ensure that the innovation concept still meets customer needs and expectations. The ultimate objective of this step is to complete one or more prototypes in final form for testing and validation in the next stage of the process.

Concurrent to the development of final prototypes is the creation of detailed market plans, market launch plans, and production or service delivery plans, using the market size estimates developed during the business analysis in stage 3 and the precise cost calculations developed by technical personnel during the prototyping process. The updated information is used to prepare a final business case. While the financial analysis is being completed, any remaining environmental, legal, or regulatory issues also should be resolved.

The Prototype Approval Gate

Prototype approval is the fourth major gate in the innovation development process. At this gate, small-scale customer tests and updated financial analyses of high-potential prototypes are evaluated to determine which projects will move forward into the testing stage and which will be put on hold or dropped. Additionally, the test plans, market plans, and operations or service delivery plans for each of the prototypes are reviewed for feasibility and effectiveness.

Not surprisingly, the criteria used to judge prototypes are the same as the screens used to evaluate concepts in stage 3. Again, they place a heavy emphasis on financial attractiveness screens based on the new, more accurate financial data collected during this stage. The revised business cases created during stage 4 are judged against company financial hurdles for innovations and, from these evaluations, final recommendations are developed.

Case Study: Building Products Manufacturer

The technical members of the innovation platoon began the development stage by attempting to develop working prototypes for each of the five recommended concepts. At the same time, the marketing, market research, sales, and finance team members focused on preparing the launch and production plans, as well as documenting the outstanding legal and regulatory issues that needed to be addressed.

After approximately six weeks, the technical team had successfully developed three of the five prototypes. Significant technical issues delayed the development of prototypes for the other two concepts. While work continued on the two more challenging concepts, cost estimates and production plan estimates for the remaining three concepts suggested that two of the three ideas would be profitable and meet the required financial hurdles of the company.

As a result, detailed launch plans were completed for the two potentially profitable concepts, and recommendations were made to move the two concepts to the testing stage (while work continued on the two technically challenging projects). The recommendations were quickly approved by the innovation steering committee at the prototype approval gate meeting.

Development Stage Pitfalls

Not surprisingly, the emphasis in this stage is on technical work, specifically the development of final innovation prototypes. However, just as the technical innovation platoon members need to be involved in the front end of the development process, nontechnical members need to stay involved in the back end of the process. Many companies make the mistake of moving nontechnical team members on to other assignments in the development stage, leaving the customer prototype testing and the development of detailed test plans and market launch plans to new marketing managers working in the base business. This is a potentially costly mistake.

The marketing and technical activities should be very closely coordinated in this stage. Marketing and market research platoon members, who are intimately familiar with the concepts and customer insights, should manage the customer feedback research on the prototypes during the technical development process. As prototypes evolve, they should be taken almost immediately to customers for assessment and feedback. Similarly, team members have a distinct advantage in developing the test and launch plans given their intimate knowledge of the specific market and technical issues that need to be addressed.

Finally, as described previously, companies should view the conceptualization stage as a final opportunity to kill concepts that cannot be manufactured or delivered profitably after thorough in-house development and testing. Innovation platoons are often afraid to kill projects at this stage because of the significant time and resources that have been applied against them to date. However, in reality, terminating projects in development prior to investing additional capital and resources in large-scale testing and ramp-up is financially prudent. Platoons should be commended, even rewarded, when they discover and recommend that a project be killed during this stage. Failure is a regular part of successful innovation programs, and the development stage screens are designed to identify potential failures sooner rather than later.

Stage 5: Testing

The fifth stage of the innovation process is called the testing and validation stage. In this stage, prototypes that pass the gate 4 screen are judged in product performance and customer acceptance tests in a last attempt to validate the innovation and its economics. In addition to in-house and market tests, final financial analysis is conducted that incorporates any additional assumptions or new calculations generated during stage 5. The time required to complete this stage is usually about one month.

In-house product tests are conducted on high-potential prototypes to validate quality or performance under controlled environmental conditions. Results are compared to customer-driven product or service performance specifications to identify potential quality gaps. At the same time, field trials or market tests are conducted to assess and debug the product or service under real or near-real market conditions, as well as to more precisely gauge market and customer interest in the new offering. Lastly, revised market plans, market launch plans, and production or service delivery plans are developed using new assumptions and information collected during stage 5 and the business case developed during stage 4.

The Prelaunch Approval Gate

Prelaunch approval is the fifth and final formal gate in the GI system innovation development process. As a result, this is the last point at which an innovation project can be killed before a full-scale launch is initiated. The major focus at this gate is on the evaluation of the revised financial analysis, market plans, market launch plans, and production or service delivery plans. Criteria for passing the gate are generally a combination of financial attractiveness screens and subjective, judgment-based assessment of the appropriateness and completeness of the launch and operations start-up plans.

Of the high-potential prototypes evaluated at this gate, generally all of the projects are approved for launch in stage 5. However, depending on how many projects an organization wishes to launch simultaneously, the projects may be prioritized and/or scheduled to determine which will be introduced first, second, third, and so on. Furthermore, depending on which projects are approved, additional equipment or people may need to be purchased or added and manufacturing lines may need to be adjusted in preparation for the new product or service innovations.

Case Study: Building Products Manufacturer

The innovation platoon recommended conducting in-house and market tests on one of the two recommended projects. The project for which testing would be skipped was viewed as an innovative line extension that the company felt comfortable moving forward immediately. The other project was more radical and needed to be tested to better understand actual performance and market acceptance. While final testing details for the radical concept were being finalized, a breakthrough was made on one of the two technically challenging prototypes from the previous stage. Financial analysis quickly confirmed that this project would be profitable too, so plans were made to test it along with the previously approved radical project.

In-house performance tests revealed that both prototypes met or exceeded the efficacy and performance standards set by customers and reflected in the screening criteria. Additionally, while one concept was clearly more appealing in market tests than the other, both concepts also exceeded the customer appeal and financial performance hurdles, so the recommendation was made to move all three concepts (two new-to-the world and one line extension) into stage 6.

Testing Stage Pitfalls

This stage, while extremely important, is often shortchanged or omitted entirely by companies trying to save time and get to market more quickly with their innovation. Although speed is unarguably an important ingredient in successful development, speeding a failure to market is extremely costly—particularly given all the time and resources that have likely been invested in an innovation in this stage of the process. Occasionally, performance glitches or quality issues are discovered in innovations during in-house product tests or test markets that were not visible or apparent in artificial conditions prior to the testing stage.

Despite their potential advantages, many companies feel that test markets aren't really worth all the time and trouble they can cause. Executives argue that in-house tests and test markets are expensive and time-consuming. Additionally, a regional or national test market often gives an organization's competitors a glimpse of future innovations and allows them to start working on copying new products or services more quickly.

There is no single right or wrong answer to the question of whether to conduct product tests and test markets, but research in the field of innovation suggests that undergoing activities in the testing and validation stage improves innovation success rates and profitability in nearly all cases where speed and the competitive situation are not overwhelmingly crucial factors in the ultimate success or failure of the project. If two organizations are racing to introduce a similar product or the risk of launching a nonoptimized product into the marketplace is low, it may be quite logical—even smart—to skip many or all of the activities in this stage. But organizations need to make a more conscious decision regarding this step, bearing in mind the risks of omission—namely, the increased chances of a failed launch.

Stage 6: Launch

The last stage of the innovation process is the launch stage. In this stage, final prototypes that pass the gate 5 screen are introduced to the sales force and, shortly thereafter, to the trade and customers. The primary goals of this stage are to initiate awareness of the new product or service innovation, as well as to stimulate trial among customers in the designated target segments. The time required to complete this stage varies depending on the scale of the launch. Generally, the launch stage varies from a month or two for small-scale launches to a year or more for national or international launches.

As its name implies, this step focuses on the implementation of the marketing launch plan and production or service delivery plan. Timing, coordination, and a well-planned execution are the cornerstones of a successful launch. Additionally, if the sales force has not been adequately educated and trained regarding the specific features and benefits of the new product or service and the key points of differentiation, this should also be a focus at this stage.

Case Study: Building Products Manufacturer

After nearly fourteen months of hard work, two of the three concepts—one new-to-the-world concept and the line extension—were launched nationally two months into stage 6. The final concept, which initially was launched regionally, was launched nationally six months later.

To date, two years since the launch of the last innovation, the three concepts have all been successful in the marketplace, generating nearly $250 million in cumulative revenues and $30 million in profits for the building products company. The final prototype for the last stage 4 concept has not yet been completed, but technical resources are still working to identify feasible alternatives in an effort to identify a future technology platform for the company.

Launch Stage Pitfalls

Once the test results for a new innovation have met all of the hurdles and the decision is made to go forward, many companies feel as though they are "home free" and that the process is over. Unfortunately, this carelessness leads to a lack of coordination between the functions and mismanaged activities that can result in suboptimized or failed introductions. According to the 1999 Kuczmarski & Associates survey, poor execution in the launch stage accounts for nearly half of all new product and service failures. What a shame it is for an organization to make it this far in the process only to let a sloppy launch ruin what might otherwise be a highly successful and profitable new offering.

In addition to carefully coordinating the launch of a new product or service, companies should also focus on educating and properly motivating the sales force to garner their commitment to selling the new innovation to the marketplace. Companies often neglect this important step and fail to keep in mind that sales representatives must be persuaded to sell just as customers must be persuaded to buy.

Postlaunch Review

Once the innovation process has been completed and one or more new offerings have been introduced to the marketplace, it may seem that all of the work is done. However, the most successful organizations continue to review new introductions at regular intervals—six, twelve, eighteen, and twenty-four months—following commercialization to ensure that they are on track and to identify course corrections that can be made to current offerings or new products to maximize innovation effectiveness and results now and in the future.

Responsibility for this step is usually put in the hands of a category or brand team charged with managing the current business because the innovation platoon is most often dissolved after stage 6. At each postlaunch review, the innovation's performance should be measured against original revenue, profit, and timing forecasts to assess performance. Additionally, key lessons learned—both positive and negative—should be documented to ensure that future innovation platoons leverage the things that went well and avoid the things that didn't work during the innovation process.

PART III

FUELING
THE
SYSTEM

PROBLEM ORIENTATION

Throughout this book, we've stated how important it is to have all seven Ps of the Guaranteed Innovation (GI) system in place, so it is a little difficult to say now that one is more important than the others. Nevertheless, knowing your customer—that means knowing his or her likes and dislikes, needs and wants, and problems—is so basic that without it you don't have a business. Nearly everyone agrees with that, and they buy and read at least some of the hundreds of books and articles devoted to the importance of "knowing your customer," "listening to your customer," "relating to your customer one-on-one," and so forth. Yet, according to Kuczmarski & Associates' 1999 Winning New Products & Services Best Practices Study, nearly 90 percent of companies not only begin their new product process with internal idea generation rather than customer needs and wants research, they never engage in any serious customer problem research before a new product is launched.

Talking *about* your customer is very different from talking *to* your customer. Ironically, idea generation is the worst place to begin innovation development efforts. Companies that fail to conduct effective customer problem research prior to idea generation do not develop as many highly innovative, differentiated new ideas and concepts as those that do such research well. Innovations created without customer problems at their source tend to fail for several reasons; they:

- Miss key customer opportunities and trends
- Address low-intensity needs

- Fail to provide a tight problem-solution fit
- Fail to provide a unique, differentiated positioning

The Three Ds and the Problem Orientation Approach

Conducting customer problem research is only the first step. It needs the direction and focus reflected in the "three Ds": dedication, design, and depth (Exhibit 8.1).

- *Dedication* refers to the time and resources a company dedicates to customer problem research activities. When a company relies too heavily on its own perceptions of customer needs (instead of spending time with customers), there often is a significant gap between what it thinks customers desire and what customers actually value. Many new product failures, including the busts of Apple's and AT&T's personal digital assistants (PDAs), resulted

Exhibit 8.1 The Three Ds of Problem Orientation

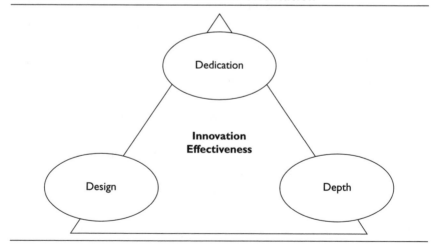

from companies trying to guess what customers wanted instead of spending the time and resources to ask them directly.

- *Design* is the way in which the research is scoped and focused. Typically, design problems occur when companies conduct narrow, targeted research focused on dissatisfactions with current products and services instead of exploratory research designed to understand customers' broader life issues. Current products or services may be outside the scope of those bigger problems. Most targeted research provides only limited insights into customer needs and doesn't help companies understand the true source of the needs or the trade-offs that customers make between satisfying different needs or issues.

- *Depth* refers to the number of interactions with customers and the specificity of information collected on individual problems and needs. Companies increase their chances of launching innovation failures when they do not interact with consumers in enough depth to fully understand the nature and importance of their problems and needs. Companies that go beyond the basic levels of customer insight identify more sophisticated and subtle customer needs that form the basis for new innovations that are highly unique and valued.

Improving innovation effectiveness and managing the three Ds require more than just checking in with customers occasionally. They require a dedicated, systematic new approach to customer problem orientation and research. By adhering to key principles of problem orientation, which is discussed in detail in this chapter, companies can beat the odds by generating a more consistent stream of truly new innovations.

The heart of the GI system approach is its heavy emphasis on identifying and addressing breakthrough customer needs and wants. Although a great deal has been written recently about the importance of having a strong customer orientation throughout the product development process, less has been written about specific methods for identifying breakthrough customer problems and needs consistently—

the problems and needs that form the basis for innovative new-to-the-world (NTW) and new-to-the-company (NTC) ideas and concepts.

Characteristics of Breakthrough Needs

A breakthrough customer problem is a frustration or desire that represents a significant functional, psychological, emotional, or financial strain or tension—or a lack of something wanted—for an identified set of customers. Such problems generally have five common characteristics:

- *Highly intense.* When customers describe or react to these needs, they project extremely strong feelings, emotions, or tensions, using expressions like "I really hate it when . . ." or "I can't stand it that . . ." or "I would really love it if. . . ." These needs really matter to customers and it shows, even in relatively low-involvement product and service categories. For example, OXO International designed its line of highly successful kitchen utensils with soft, wide handles to solve a very difficult basic life problem for elderly people with arthritis: trying to cook. Introduced in 1990, the line now has a 15 percent share of the kitchen utensils market.
- *Unique.* These aren't "me-too" frustrations that everyone in the industry understands and is already working on. These are the problems that are generally very difficult to find and comprehend, the "needles in the haystack" of a specific product or service category. Nokia raised the innovation bar to new heights in the cellular telephone market by identifying and fulfilling unique needs related to customers' desire to personalize their high-tech equipment. The company's new lines of cellular phones enable customers to change the look and operation of their phones with customizable menus and individual face plates to match the style and décor of the customer's other accessories.
- *Not easily articulated or verbalized.* Although customers are generally good at describing what they don't like, they often can't

express, formulate, or brainstorm ideas and concepts to solve their greatest needs with any clarity or effectiveness. Again, this contributes to making certain problems and innovations difficult to identify and explore. High-technology breakthroughs like the home information terminal (HIT) and networked appliances—PC-like devices for the home that display vital household information, including daily schedules, health records, and grocery inventories—are innovative solutions to breakthrough needs.

- *Textured.* These needs aren't just surface-level problems. They often are caused by or related to a very precise or specific element of a product, service, process, or experience. For example, when one of our clients—a major food manufacturer—was exploring problems with its customers, it learned that the surface-level "A.M. rush" problem that many people describe having each day as they hurry out the door in the morning was actually being driven by a more subtle emotional need. Specifically, research revealed that most people believe their day begins the moment they leave their house in the morning, not when they arrive at work. As a result, people often rush out of the house in a fury only to stand in line for coffee for twenty minutes before getting to their offices.

- *Costly.* These needs usually impact the lives or behaviors of customers in a significant way. They usually have major time or cost implications, and solutions to them represent a tangible value to customers. This value can be financial or nonfinancial (e.g., risk or time reduction). Palm Computing's Palm Pilot electronic organizer is a perfect example of an innovative solution to a costly customer need. The time people spend creating, updating, and accessing calendars and Rolodex files can be significant. The Palm Pilot provides fast, easy access to electronic versions of these and other essential business tools. The results are time savings and convenience, which are extremely valuable to a large segment of the business population.

Not surprisingly, breakthrough customer problems are a critically important ingredient in the GI framework and, along with sound technology platform research, provide the fuel for a consistent stream of breakthrough new product and service ideas.

Categories of Customer Needs

There are several categories of customer needs, as shown in Exhibit 8.2. Each need category can produce highly intense, breakthrough problems that may lead to breakthrough innovations. However, each category also represents a unique marketing challenge and requires a different set of market research tools to understand and exploit. While all of the need categories may not be represented in a particular product category or market, they should all be understood and monitored because new needs emerge over time. The five categories of customer needs are:

- Explicit
- Observable

Exhibit 8.2 Categories of Customer Need

Explicit Needs

↓

Observable Needs

↓

Tacit Needs

↓

Latent Needs

↓

Emerging Needs

Source: Adapted from Elizabeth Sanders, "Converging Perspectives: Product Development Research for the 1990s," *Design Management Journal.*

- Tacit
- Latent
- Emerging

For the purpose of illustration, brief definitions and examples of customer needs in each of the five need categories will be described for customers in the glass cleaner market. The glass cleaner market is mature and has low customer involvement (demonstrating that needs can be found anywhere), it's easy to relate to (most people have cleaned glass), and it has rich examples of different types of customer needs.

The first category of breakthrough needs is explicit needs. Explicit needs are those that are easily recognized and articulated by customers in focus groups, in-depth interviews (IDIs), and surveys. These are generally the easiest needs to identify and understand. Often referred to by companies as the "low-hanging fruit," these needs most often form the basis for solid line extensions and incremental product improvements. While explicit needs are not frequently the source of breakthrough innovations, at the same time, companies shouldn't ignore them because they can be quite simple (and profitable) to solve in many cases.

In the glass cleaner market, product dripping—the frustration that customers experience when a liquid glass cleaner runs down the glass onto the window frame before it can be wiped up—is an explicit need. Glass cleaner customers cite this as one of their first frustrations regarding things they don't like about current glass cleaner products. S.C. Johnson, the manufacturer of Windex, recently addressed this explicit need with a successful line extension called Windex No-Drip.

The second category of needs is observable needs. Observable needs can be discovered by watching customers use or interact with the product or service, most often while being interviewed (an in-depth observational interview). In many cases, customers cannot or do not think to articulate these observable needs or wants in traditional market research settings (focus groups, IDIs, surveys, etc.), so they can lead to intense, highly unique insights.

An observable customer problem in the glass cleaner market is that customers often have difficulty finding and removing all of the dirt and streaks from a window the first time. Some people will even use two products to clean a window—an all-purpose cleaner to remove the dirt and then a glass cleaner to shine the glass and remove the streaks. This process is time-consuming and inconvenient. While a consumer may not clean windows or glass often enough to recall this as a problem in a focus group, a series of observational interviews probably would reveal it.

A third category of needs is tacit needs. Tacit needs are those that customers recognize they have but have difficulty or don't think about expressing or describing to researchers. When these problems are introduced in traditional research settings, customers can identify with them and expand on the insights described to them. Making an initial identification of tacit needs can be challenging though, and usually involves the use of a mix of qualitative research tools, including focus groups, IDIs, and observational research.

A tacit need in the glass cleaner market is cleaning outside windows. Most people really dislike the process of climbing up on a ladder; using a bucket, sponge, and squeegee to clean the windows; and still seeing streaks when they are finished. As a result, most consumers choose not to clean the outside windows on their homes. They just accept the fact that the windows will be dirty and learn to live with it. Only after they are asked about it will consumers say they would really like to be able to clean these windows more easily and often. It's just not something they think to talk about naturally. S.C. Johnson also recently discovered and addressed this need with the introduction of Windex Outdoor, which attaches to a garden hose and sprays the product onto outdoor windows, eliminating the need for ladders, buckets, sponges, and so on.

A fourth needs category is latent needs. Latent needs are those that customers don't even recognize they have, even when the problem or frustration is introduced to them in a research setting. These needs are extremely difficult to identify and usually must be unearthed using a variety of different research techniques. The specific process for finding latent needs is described later in this chapter.

In the glass cleaner market, cleaning windows manually is a latent need. Consumers just assume and accept that they will always need to clean windows by hand. Even though cleaning windows consumes a significant amount of time and energy, the act of cleaning is so ingrained in people's household cleaning routines that suggesting that it shouldn't need to be done at all sounds unbelievable to most consumers. On the other hand, if technology were developed that allowed windows to become self-cleaning, the resulting product would most likely revolutionize the category and be very successful. However, given that the product would solve a latent need, consumers might not recognize it or believe the benefits of a self-cleaning window until they saw or tried it.

The last category of needs is emerging needs. Emerging needs are needs customers don't have currently but likely may have in the future. Unlike latent needs, which customers might recognize if a product or service that addresses them is introduced, products that address a future need will most likely not be immediately accepted by mainstream customers. Of all the customer need categories, emerging needs are the hardest to identify and address with new products and services. Usually, special groups of progressive, creative customers called *lead users* must be the focus of research efforts designed to identify emerging needs. Additionally, secondary environmental trends research may provide clues to what future needs may develop in a specific product or service category. Unlike in the other needs categories, mainstream customers will most often not be very helpful in providing insights about emerging needs.

Emerging needs in the glass cleaner market are not easy to describe. One could hypothesize that next-generation glass cleaners will do more than simply clean windows and keep them cleaner longer. Maybe customers in the twenty-first century will look for glass cleaning products that clean and protect glass surfaces from damage. Maybe they will harness the power of the sun to keep the window streak-free longer. Maybe they will reduce glare and furniture fading. Maybe they will better insulate the home from the heat of the summer sun and the cold of winter. Lead users and other sources of consumer trend information probably hold the key to these answers.

Guaranteed Innovation System
Problem Orientation Success Factors

Dozens, maybe hundreds, of factors contribute to the identification and understanding of breakthrough customer problems and needs. After working with scores of clients across dozens of industries, we have identified five critical success factors:

- Link customer problem research to innovation strategy goals
- Use a mix of qualitative and quantitative research tools
- Start by exploring broad customer problems and issues
- Conduct iterative waves of problem research
- Use platoon members across functions to conduct problem research

The remainder of this chapter discusses each of these success factors: how they are defined, why they are important, and how you can implement them.

Link Customer Problem Research
to Innovation Strategy Goals

The first step in creating a problem orientation is to create a link between customer problem research and the elements of the innovation policy, which reflects overall corporate business strategy (see Chapter 5). Specifically, the innovation growth gap, vision, and strategic roles should form a blueprint or road map that helps guide the selection of specific research categories and the scope of topics to be explored with customers, as well as the types of innovations desired. Failure to create this link can result in the identification of customer needs, ideas, and concepts that aren't consistent with the strategic direction of the company or aren't technically or financially feasible.

Innovation platoons should establish the link between problem research and the innovation policy by first examining the financial growth gap, which is the overall financial goal for innovation. The size of the growth gap, and specifically the portion of the gap that is expected to be filled by internally developed innovations, plays a major role in determining the number and size of opportunities that must be identified through customer research. For a company with an extremely large growth gap, the number of research categories will probably be greater than if the growth gap is small. An examination of past innovation performance, at both the company and industry levels, can help the platoon members better gauge the specific number of categories that should be examined.

The vision and strategic roles, two other major outputs of the innovation policy, serve a similar function to the growth gap. Namely, they can be used to help the innovation platoon define the specific discussion topics and need categories that should be explored during the customer problem stage, as well as the areas that should be emphasized less or avoided altogether.

For example, in our work with a major building products manufacturer, our innovation platoon was charged with filling a growth gap that called for aggressive growth through internally developed innovations. Specifically, a $400 million division was challenged to double in size over a five-year period. This large gap, combined with an extremely broad innovation vision and roles, suggested a need to focus NTW and NTC innovations both inside and outside of the division's current markets. The first step of our initiative focused on identifying high-potential new markets that were consistent with the innovation vision and large enough to accommodate the incremental growth that the division sought. By linking our opportunity assessment and research objectives closely with the innovation policy outputs, we were able to quickly identify three strategically relevant new markets that were large enough to warrant problem exploration. The NTC and NTW innovations in these markets eventually allowed the division to exceed its growth goals.

In this way, the innovation growth gap, vision, and strategic roles serve to direct the customer problem research scope and design. It is important to point out here that the innovation policy elements should be specific enough to provide platoons with helpful direction but broad enough to allow them the freedom to explore new markets and offerings required to meet the stated growth goals. If an innovation policy or vision appears to be too narrow or confining, a platoon should raise this concern to the innovation champions prior to the initiation of research so that additional discussions and/or revisions can be considered.

Establish a Broad Category Vision

As already described, in order for aggressive growth goals to be achievable, it is important to have a broad innovation and category vision. An expansive vision sets the stage for truly creative exploration with customers. Without this breadth, companies will most likely develop more line extensions or product restages. These typically offer only incremental growth to the existing business. An expansive category definition increases the likelihood that customer problem research will yield exponential growth opportunities, enabling companies to catapult into new categories and develop innovative new offerings with breakthrough benefits.

To realize its aggressive growth goals several years ago, the Glade division of S.C. Johnson reexamined its category vision. Glade's original vision was to be the leading manufacturer of odor-masking products, including instant and continuous air fresheners, in and away from home. Glade maintained a large share of the mature market and was searching for new ways to grow the business. To open up new possibilities for breakthrough innovation, Glade broadened its vision to be the leading manufacturer of air treatment products (e.g., odor masking and neutralization, air filtration, etc.) both in and away from home. This more expansive view of the category has helped Glade continue its pattern of impressive growth. For example, in 1999, Glade launched an innovative new line of aromatherapy products that is creating an entirely new market for the company.

When attempting to define an expansive category definition, an innovation platoon should start with the existing business and innovation visions, as well as previous research studies and trend analyses, as key inputs. The platoon should then brainstorm and ask questions to determine, from the given internal and external inputs, what research categories might be attractive. Questions may include:

- What primary and secondary benefits do our products and services offer customers?
- For what reasons are customers buying our products over competitive offerings?
- How might the strengths of our current products and services be leveraged in new categories and markets?
- How might we extend our current technology platforms in new categories and markets?

Use a Mix of Qualitative and Quantitative Research Tools

Although some suggestions for selecting research tools will be offered here, it should be noted that there is no single best research design. Each research tool has certain advantages and disadvantages, and successful companies use a variety of tools in combination to achieve breakthrough results. In most cases, trade-offs must be made between time and cost constraints and the quality and depth of information collected.

Identifying and Understanding Customer Problems: Exploratory Qualitative Research

Based on our experiences with clients over the past two decades, we believe the best place to start customer problem identification is with exploratory qualitative research. Some criticism has been levied against qualitative research because of its traditionally small sample sizes, but it is the best way to identify and understand the in-depth problems, feelings, and motivations of customers. Rather than providing reading reports filled with tables of data containing numerical rankings of needs, qualitative research gives innovation platoons and other participants the opportunity to identify, observe, and record customers' specific thoughts on various research categories and topics in their own language. It allows platoon members to determine the factors that are driving key needs and the reasons they are important to customers.

Additionally, qualitative research can significantly improve the efficiency of quantitative research. It can surface detailed hypotheses and issues that can later be evaluated and measured more precisely to determine specific need rankings and product and service attribute levels, establish market potential estimates, and determine marketing support requirements.

Conversely, quantitative techniques are not particularly effective as a means of identifying and understanding broad customer needs. They help to rank and prioritize the "whats" but do very little to help understand the "whys" underlying consumer perceptions and attitudes. Quantitative techniques don't explore the specific elements that contribute to positive and negative product and service experiences and drive customers to make trade-offs among competitive offerings. For that reason, relying on quantitative methods at this stage of product development can actually hinder an organization's ability to deliver breakthrough new products consistently.

The most common qualitative tools include focus groups, IDIs, observational interviews, projective tests, and lead user groups. Exhibit 8.3 describes each of the primary qualitative tools and the primary advantages and disadvantages of each.

Each of these qualitative tools can effectively uncover different types of customer needs more or less effectively in different situations. In some situations, quickly establishing a large list of highly intense needs using focus groups is the best approach. In other situations, an in-depth understanding of broad needs is the goal, and IDIs are the best technique. In still other cases, companies are focused on identifying tacit and latent needs, and observational or lead user techniques are the most effective tools to use. Most often, innovation platoons experience a variety of these types of situations at different points in time, so a mix of research techniques is generally the best answer.

Using a mix of tools also helps companies identify discrepancies or fallacies in their understanding of customers. A vacuum cleaner manufacturer that had traditionally only used focus groups to

Exhibit 8.3 Qualitative Problem Research Tools: Advantages and Disadvantages

Research Tool	Description	Advantages	Disadvantages
Focus groups	Group discussion with 8–12 people on a specific set of topics designed to quickly identify and clarify broad needs and wants and why they are important	• Interaction among respondents • Quick execution • Cost-effective	• Possible inconsistencies between participants and target • Possible misrepresentation of facts by participants • Moderator bias
In-depth interviews (IDIs)	One-on-one interviews designed to elicit in-depth perspectives on customer motivations and attitudes	• Elimination of group pressure • Opportunity for in-depth probing	• Time-consuming • Expensive • No group dynamics
Observational interviews	Interviews involving the recording of customer behavior and the characteristics of usage of a product or service	• Ability to observe what customers actually do • Less moderator bias • Possibility of tacit or latent needs surfacing	• No observation of motivations, attitudes, and beliefs possible • Difficult-to-interpret findings • Time-consuming • Expensive
Projective tests	Group discussion or exercises designed to understand customers' deep emotional attitudes and feelings	• Ability to tap customers' subconscious attitudes and feelings • Penetration of customers' natural defense mechanisms	• Difficult-to-interpret findings • Time-consuming • Expensive
Lead user groups	Group discussion with customers from the "leading edges" of a company's target market designed to explore future needs and wants and emerging trends	• Ability to understand emerging needs of customers • Ability to create hypotheses to test with target customers	• Difficulty in finding lead users • Time-consuming • Expensive

identify customer problems got very different results when observational research was used. The relative severity of problems that customers had described in focus groups was ranked differently. For example, customers had described stair cleaning in focus groups as a major problem. However, through observation and IDIs, it turned out that most customers had developed simple techniques for stair cleaning, eliminating the need for an expensive, complex solution.

Focus Groups   A focus group consists of eight to twelve participants who are led by a moderator in an in-depth discussion on a specific set of topics. One of the goals of focus groups in customer problem research is to quickly understand the most significant explicit needs and wants customers are experiencing in a given product or service category and why the needs are intense or bothersome. Another goal is to explore, in depth, customer problem hypotheses that have surfaced through other avenues. Normally, direct questions are avoided to encourage open discussion and to give participants an opportunity to lead the discussion into areas where they have interest, passion, or emotional involvement.

Focus groups, like all other forms of research, have distinct advantages and disadvantages. On the positive side, the interaction among respondents that occurs during focus groups can stimulate a great breadth of ideas and thinking, some of which may never surface through one-on-one interviews or surveys. Another advantage of focus groups is that they can usually be executed more quickly and cost-effectively than many other research techniques. This makes them a particularly useful way to quickly identify and begin to understand high-potential customer needs and wants that warrant further discussion and exploration.

On the negative side, given their small sample size, focus groups may produce insights that are not representative of target customers in a given product or service category or market. As a result, several groups, rather than just one or two, should always be conducted on each topic being studied to reduce the risk that the insights obtained represent only a small fraction of customers.

Successful innovators like Apple, Sony, and Microsoft use focus groups to surface ideas for new technologies. Sony performs extensive focus group research in the early stages of the innovation process to quickly identify problems and needs that can form the basis for breakthrough offerings. In many cases, the early direction Sony receives from customers allows the company to get user-centered products and technologies to the market quickly, often forcing Sony's competitors to launch me-too imitation products.

In-Depth Interviews In-depth interviews are generally one-on-one interviews that probe and elicit detailed perspectives on specific topics to uncover customer motivations and attitudes. An important goal of IDIs in customer problem research is to understand explicit needs in depth, including the underlying aspects of and reasons for an intense customer problem. Such interviews are also an extremely valuable tool to identify or better understand needs that are more difficult to unearth (observable, tacit, and latent needs).

The advantages of IDIs relative to focus groups include the fact that group pressure is eliminated in the one-on-one setting, allowing respondents to talk more freely and openly about specific personal frustrations and their origins. Additionally, the greater time devoted to each respondent allows the innovation platoon to get into greater depth on each topic and move beyond a surface-level understanding of the problems and needs being explored. Furthermore, IDIs, in some cases, become the only alternative in situations where a company is interested in getting perspectives from industry competitors who would otherwise be placed in the same room.

The disadvantage of IDIs compared to focus groups is that they are much more time-consuming and expensive, especially when viewed from a per-interview perspective. Additionally, IDIs do not usually allow for the same breadth of information collection as focus groups. The respondents do not have the advantage of hearing comments from others and building on thoughts and insights from the group.

An innovation platoon from a major chemical products manufacturer in Japan used IDIs to discuss personal issues related to home cleaning with Japanese housewives. The interviews were conducted at customers' homes and the small, intimate setting allowed the team to achieve an in-depth understanding of specific frustrations that customers experienced when they cleaned their bathrooms. Many of the insights that the platoon garnered would never have surfaced in larger focus groups.

Observational Interviews Observational interviews record customer behavior and characteristics of usage or interaction with a product or service with little or no verbal communication on the part of the researchers. Such interviews are useful to identify observable customer problems and needs, as well as to develop hypotheses about other types of needs that can be tested and explored verbally through other forms of qualitative and quantitative research. Observational interviews can also be an effective tool to identify breakthrough problems that are difficult or impossible for customers to articulate in traditional market research activities—focus groups, IDIs, surveys, and so on. However, the needed information must be observable, repetitive, or predictable, and of a short duration for observational interviews to be useful, cost-effective, and time-efficient.

The primary advantage of observational interviews in customer problem research is that platoon members see what people actually do, instead of what they say they do. Unfortunately, there is a significant difference between the two in many cases. In addition, the potential of researchers to bias respondents into identifying certain problems or describing certain needs as being more intense than they truly are is reduced or eliminated in observational interviews. Lastly, as discussed previously, many tacit or latent needs that likely wouldn't surface in a focus group or survey can sometimes be identified through observation. These difficult-to-articulate needs can form the basis for breakthrough innovations.

The primary disadvantage of observational interviews is that only behavior and physical characteristics can be observed. There is no way to observe motivation, attitudes, beliefs, and perceptions. Unlike more traditional question-and-answer research activities, the findings uncovered during an observational interview can be difficult to classify and interpret. For this reason, a skilled researcher is usually responsible for conducting observational interviews. Observational research, like IDIs, can be quite costly and time-consuming to implement.

Maytag uses observational research to study how customers actually use products and behave in their own environments. Cross-functional teams at Maytag go into customer homes and watch them interact with appliances. Maytag uses this research, among other things, to identify compensatory behaviors, actions that customers take to address an unmet need. By solving these subconscious problems, Maytag has been able to identify and launch several profitable innovations, including a new top-loading, vertical axis clothes washer.

Projective Tests Projective tests are methods of understanding customers' deep emotional attitudes and feelings about products, services, processes, and the like. The most common forms of projective tests include word association and fill-in-the-blank exercises, photo sorts, drawings, and third-person techniques. The main objective of each of these techniques in customer problem research is to identify hard-to-surface tacit and latent needs that customers are unaware of or are uncomfortable talking about. Projective tests often allow innovation platoons to gather richer, more in-depth data than standard questioning techniques. Projective tests can also be intermingled with more standard probing questions to add additional insights during an IDI.

Specific advantages of projective tests are that they penetrate customers' natural defense mechanisms (because respondents are usually talking about something or someone else) and that they provide insight and understanding about customers' inner feelings that often are missed in more traditional forms of qualitative research.

The biggest disadvantage of projective tests is that they are arguably the most subjective of all qualitative research tools to interpret. Even skilled researchers have to make some substantial interpretations of customers' true feelings, meanings, and motivations. Although this can lead to unique and valuable insights, it can also result in erroneous conclusions and recommendations. Like many of the other one-on-one techniques, projective tests can be quite expensive and time-consuming to execute.

Projective tests have helped companies like Visa identify opportunities for innovation. Several years ago, Visa asked credit card customers to draw pictures that best described their view of Visa. Through this exercise, researchers learned that the image of Visa was that of a wholesome, married female. To change this image and begin to appeal more to professional men, Visa launched a number of new offerings, including its "Everywhere You Want to Be" advertising campaign. Results of the innovation initiative were highly successful.

Lead User Research   Lead user research is a special type of workshop, focus group, or IDI in which a group of customers from the "leading edges" of a company's target are brought together to discuss their needs and wants, as well as emerging trends, in the product or service category being explored. Lead users have needs that are well ahead of those of more mainstream customers (Exhibit 8.4). In all like-

Exhibit 8.4 Innovation Adoption Curve

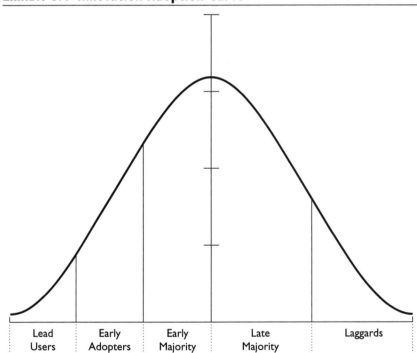

| Lead Users | Early Adopters | Early Majority | Late Majority | Laggards |

lihood, over time, more and more mainstream target customers will develop the same needs as lead users. Understanding these future needs before they become pervasive is a key to identifying breakthrough ideas and innovation technology platforms that can serve as the basis for innovative new products and services in the future.

The most significant advantage of lead user research is that it is one of the only ways to identify and begin to understand the emerging needs of customers in a specific market or industry. Emerging needs are often a great source of breakthrough new product and service ideas and concepts. More often, insights from lead users help to clarify and stimulate the creative energy of a company's research and development and internal product development resources to think up and develop new products and services that suit a company's needs and markets.

There are several disadvantages to lead user research. First of all, true lead users are hard to find. Searching them out requires extensive time and resources, and companies usually need to network extensively in their target market and other related fields and markets to find these customer "visionaries." Additionally, lead user research can be quite expensive and time-consuming to conduct. Lead user workshops typically last two to three days and often involve assembling individuals from all areas of the country or around the world. Finally, as with many of the other more nontraditional market research techniques, interpreting the results of lead user research is far from an exact science.

3M has been using lead user research for several years to identify emerging technologies that can serve as platforms for breakthrough innovation. Recently, an innovation team from 3M's medical supplies division used lead user research to identify innovative new surgical product concepts, including a new removable surgical tape that will likely become a profitable addition to 3M's product portfolio.

Confirming and Prioritizing Customer Problems: Quantitative Research

Once high-potential customer needs and wants have been identified and are well understood, quantitative research tools become extremely valuable as a means to confirm and prioritize breakthrough insights. Prior to generating ideas and concepts, quantitative techniques can provide value by confirming or measuring the frequency or intensity of customer problems or perceptions of identified opportunities. This encourages more fact-based decision making and often makes recommendations easier to sell to bottom line–driven senior managers and innovation champions.

The most commonly used quantitative research customer problem survey approaches include door-to-door or mall-intercept interviews, telephone interviews, mail surveys, direct computer surveys, and Internet surveys. Since far more has been written about traditional quantitative survey approaches in the field of marketing research than has been written about exploratory qualitative research techniques, much less time is devoted to discussing individual survey approaches and their unique advantages and disadvantages here.

The one exception to this is Internet surveys, a relatively new technique that gained tremendous popularity in the late 1990s. A unique advantage of Internet surveys is the possibility of creating, distributing, and receiving data from the questionnaire within hours of writing it. Furthermore, data are obtained in electronic form so that statistical analysis can be performed almost instantaneously. A second key advantage of Internet surveys is that they are extremely inexpensive to implement. Printing, mailing, keying, and interviewer costs are eliminated, and the incremental cost of sending additional surveys is almost negligible. Yet another benefit of these surveys is the ability to reach large numbers of people in a short time.

The biggest disadvantage of Internet surveys is that Internet users are not currently very representative of the population as a whole. A second major disadvantage is that most surveys today are unrestricted Internet samples. This allows individual users to fill out a survey more than once or misrepresent their demographic or product use characteristics to qualify as respondents. However, as Internet research becomes more popular and widely adopted, more sophisticated security and screening utilities are being developed and used, reducing the potential impact of this problem.

Start by Exploring Broad Customer Problems and Issues

The "exploratory" customer needs research conducted by many organizations tends to be a misnomer. Rather than using a wide-angle approach to explore broad, highly intense customer life issues, the research focuses on narrow topics such as product dissatisfaction and ways to optimize current offerings. Without question, this targeted research can be strategically important to organizations because it helps them identify the shortcomings of company and competitor products and services, as well as opportunities to address existing deficiencies.

However, most targeted research provides only limited insight into breakthrough customer needs. It doesn't identify the relationships between and intensities of customer problems or desired benefits and the trade-offs customers make between these problems and benefits in their purchase decisions. As a result, companies generally get a rather myopic view of the world and rarely identify anything more than low-hanging fruit and "innovationless" product and service line extensions and restages rather than products and services with exponentially new benefits (e.g., NTW products).

Broader exploratory initiatives enable companies to uncover a wide spectrum of needs that, in many cases, help to identify innovative products capable of transforming a category or market. The recommended approach for identifying breakthrough customer problems and needs is summarized in Exhibit 8.5. From this chart, you can see that the place to begin exploratory research is looking at customers' broad life problems and needs. Depending on the demographic, economic, and lifestyle characteristics of the target customer being studied, the life problems that surface will be quite different. Futurists like Faith Popcorn and others have attempted to identify major life issues of the general population in the United States. Exhibit 8.6 shows ten trends that Faith Popcorn has identified. These trends are examples of some of the types of needs that may be unearthed as part of exploratory research.

To most innovation platoon members, customers' overall life problems often seem unrelated to the product or service category they are

Exhibit 8.5 Exploring Broad Customer Problems and Issues

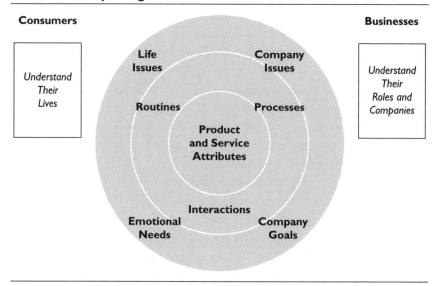

Exhibit 8.6 Faith Popcorn's Top 10 Population Trends

1. **Cashing Out:** the desire to escape the rat race and have a slower but more rewarding lifestyle

2. **Cocooning:** the desire to stay home when the outside world becomes too tough or scary

3. **Down-Aging:** the desire to act—and feel—younger than one really is

4. **Egonomics:** the desire to develop an individual style to be more distinct than others

5. **Fantasy Adventure:** the desire to get away from the monotony of everyday life by escaping emotionally

6. **99 Lives:** the challenge of juggling multiple roles and responsibilities in one's personal and professional lives

7. **S.O.S. (Save Our Society):** the desire to make society more socially aware and responsible

8. **Small Indulgences:** the desire to relieve the stress of everyday life through occasional emotional fixes

9. **Staying Alive:** the desire to live a longer, more rewarding life

10. **The Vigilante Consumer:** a person who no longer tolerates shoddy products or poor service

Source: Philip Kotler, *Kotler on Marketing: How to Create, Win, and Dominate Markets.*

working in. The fact of the matter is that most companies have an ability to significantly or partially solve one or more major customer life issues with their products and services. These solutions are what very often end up becoming breakthrough innovations. By starting with highly emotional, intense problems as the foundation for product and service ideas, companies focus on creating offerings that are truly meaningful and valuable to customers.

In our work with a major food manufacturer, the client effectively identified the broad life issues of its target customers. One of the most significant issues, the stress for working moms of not being able to spend enough time with their families, was the foundation for several innovative new products that allow moms and children to cook meals together and have more free time afterward. The products make it possible to blend work and play in a time-pressed environment.

Once the broad life issues have been identified, the next step is to examine the process steps or consumption chain activities of products and services in order to create links between customers' life issues and the product or service category. In this step, the focus of the research turns to understanding how customers acquire, use, and dispose of a product or service and identifying which steps in those processes contribute most significantly to broader life issues. The innovation platoon may even try to map the processes involved with customer interactions with a product and use the maps to identify whether the company can introduce innovations that address an intense dissatisfaction or frustration in one of the process steps. In his book *Kotler on Marketing*, Kotler describes a comprehensive list of the questions, developed by authors Ian MacMillan and Riat Gunther McGrath, that should be asked in this step. Exhibit 8.7 lists a sample set of these questions.

Finally, once the product and service consumption processes and routines have been studied, a more detailed examination of specific high-potential product or process dissatisfactions identified in the previous stage can be explored in greater detail. At this stage, the features, attributes, and processes studied can all be traced back to a highly intense, emotional customer life issue or routine. Conducting

Exhibit 8.7 Questions for Understanding Product and Service Processes and Routines

1. How do customers first identify their need for your product or service?
2. How do customers find your offering and/or competitive offerings?
3. How do customers make their final selections among competitive offerings?
4. How do customers make their orders and purchases?
5. How is your product or service delivered?
6. How is your product installed?
7. How is your product stored and/or reused?
8. What are customers actually using your product for?
9. What do customers find difficult or need help with when using your product?
10. How is your product repaired or serviced?

Source: Philip Kotler, *Kotler on Marketing: How to Create, Win, and Dominate Markets.*

this targeted research as a starting point to exploratory research can lead to the solution of problems that may address truly significant customer problems and needs.

The competition between Kellogg's and Nestlé to enter the Indian breakfast food market serves as a good example of the value of understanding broad life issues. Kellogg's, leveraging its strong brand name and image, quickly introduced cornflakes to the Indian market. Although the product was initially successful, sales have since dropped significantly. Nestlé, on the other hand, spent time talking with middle-class Indian consumers before launching a product and discovered that they were not just interested in breakfast but in a fast, convenient breakfast to accommodate their rushed morning schedules. Nestlé's offerings, instant breakfast mixes that can be prepared and consumed in five to ten minutes, have been very successful and have helped the company take the lead in the market.

Conduct Iterative Waves of Problem Research

Achieving a breadth and depth of unique customer insights and understanding can rarely be accomplished in a single wave of qualitative or quantitative research. When a series of focus groups, interviews, or surveys are conducted together over a relatively short period, the innovation platoon doesn't have the time necessary to process and absorb key findings from the initial customer interactions and integrate new hypotheses and questions into the research design prior to the conclusion of research activities. This problem is particularly acute when innovation teams are conducting best practices research to identify both broad and narrow customer problems and needs.

Effective customer needs assessment research includes three distinct, iterative waves, each with a specific objective and a unique set of topics (Exhibit 8.8). The objective of the first wave is broad customer and category problem exploration. Specifically, this wave is designed to discover and briefly examine the broad set of customer problems and issues described in the previous section. This would include customers' life issues and the relevant attitudes and behaviors that characterize target customers in the product or service category being examined. At the end of the first wave, platoon members should be able to identify a broad set of consumer needs and need categories and begin to form hypotheses about the factors that drive those frustrations.

Exhibit 8.8 Waves of Customer Needs Assessment Research

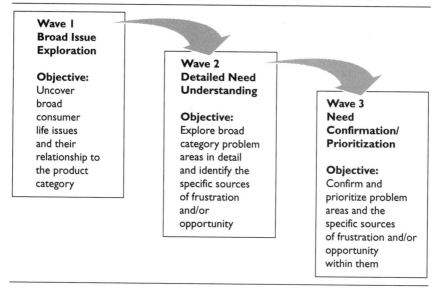

The second wave of customer needs research should focus on help-ing the innovation platoon gain a detailed understanding of the prob-lems and needs identified in wave 1. In short, wave 1 is focused on breadth, while wave 2 is focused on achieving a depth of understand-ing of the first-wave problems. When done well, researchers can dis-cover the "whys" behind customer needs, information that leads to more innovative products and services that solve meaningful prob-lems. By the end of the wave, platoons should be able to answer ques-tions such as:

- What are the specific drivers of the customer need?
- Why does the customer need exist?
- Which benefits are the most important to customers? For which benefits are customers willing to make trade-offs?

Too often, companies identify broad customer needs and need categories without bothering to fully understand the specific details and factors driving those needs. Failing to develop an adequate understanding of customer needs has two negative implications for companies:

- It often leads to products and services with benefits that don't fit tightly with customer needs.
- It leads to products and services with undifferentiated or unsus-tainable positionings.

When companies don't fully understand specific needs and moti-vations, products may end up missing the mark when they are intro-duced in the marketplace. The failures of Apple and AT&T's personal digital assistants (PDAs) resulted from not spending enough time understanding customer needs. Although these companies certainly identified the broad customer need for convenient, electronic orga-nization, they didn't understand specific desired functions and fea-tures and included too many elements to justify their hefty price tags, ultimately overwhelming customers who struggled to use the devices.

In contrast, Palm Computing did a much better job of identifying detailed customer need elements through iterative research. It dis-covered that customers were more interested in a simple tool and, therefore, focused on delivering fewer things very well. Its PDA solution, the Palm Pilot, is an electronic notebook, address book, and calendar that people find familiar and comfortable to use. The Palm Pilot has created a huge new market in which it controls a dominant 70 percent share.

Similarly, a research initiative that does not include enough interactions with customers can lead to the development of undifferentiated products and services. In the first round of customer research, companies hear customers describe broad problems and product dissatisfactions. Companies then often hurry off to develop new products that address those broad problems. Competitors hear the same things and, in most cases, several companies launch me-too products that differ very little from one another. Price then becomes the only basis on which the products compete, and everybody loses.

Companies that go beyond a single wave of research to understand more sophisticated and subtle needs and their elements tend to discover opportunities and new products that are highly unique and more likely to have protectable positioning. In its efforts to develop a differentiated new cooking appliance, General Electric conducted intensive customer research to design a product that would provide "oven quality food in working mom's time," a need the company discovered and explored in depth through iterative research. The oven uses a combination of light waves and microwaves to bake, broil, grill, and roast four to five times faster than a conventional oven without compromising quality.

The final wave of customer research is designed to confirm and prioritize the detailed needs explored in wave 2. The focus is on exposing customers to the previously identified needs and need areas to ensure that they have been described and detailed accurately and to broadly prioritize the needs by separating those that are the most intense from those that are less intense. To facilitate this process, needs should be written in a common format so that customers can compare them quickly and easily. A common needs description format is outlined in Exhibit 8.9.

Determining which problems and needs are the most intense or which offer the greatest potential for breakthrough products and

Exhibit 8.9 Need Description Statement Format

I wish I had a [product or service] that solved my need to [problem or need].

Example: I wish that I had a household cleaning product that solved my need to clean less often with less effort.

services is extremely challenging, regardless of which format they are written in or which research tools are used to test them. But the in-depth understanding of customers and their needs that platoons achieve during the iterative research process adds objectivity to the decision-making process and enables teams to make better decisions about which opportunities to pursue.

Use Platoon Members Across Functions to Conduct Problem Research

Innovation platoons are discussed extensively in Chapter 6, but it should be mentioned here that problem research and other front-end innovation activities need to be undertaken and conducted by employees from a mix of different functional areas to provide the cross section of expertise, perspective, and experience required for breakthrough innovation to occur.

No single functional area is more important than another. The selection of specific functional representatives depends on the type of company and the industry in which it competes. The most common functional areas represented in problem research include marketing, market research, sales, research and development, manufacturing, customer service, and finance. On average, the most successful companies use four to six platoon members in research.

Cross-functional representation in problem research offers two primary benefits to organizations: (1) more well-rounded customer needs and insights, and (2) more accurate translation of customer needs and concept specifications in the later phases of product development. In his book *Thriving on Chaos*, Tom Peters sums up the importance of cross-functional involvement in front-end innovation research: "The single most important reason for delays in development activities is the absence of multifunction representation on development projects from the start."

Individuals from different functions naturally listen for and hear different things in customer problem research. During typical customer research initiatives, marketers consciously or subconsciously listen for insights and data that relate to what customers' particular needs are and how broadly appealing they may be. Product developers listen for potential solutions and ways that needs could be addressed with innovative product and service designs. Only through incorporating insights and thoughts from each of the platoon members does the complete picture of the customer begin to emerge.

Harley-Davidson believes so strongly in the power of cross-functional involvement in front-end innovation that it co-locates platoon members from design engineering, purchasing, manufacturing, and other areas into a single building. The team members are assigned full-time to the innovation initiative. All of the team members participate together in all major activities, including customer problem research and concept design and testing. Earl Werner, Harley's vice president of engineering, explains in a 1998 *Design News* article, "It's crucial to have input and insights from all these areas . . . the more involvement and input we have up front, the better our products will be."

Another reason for using cross-functional teams during customer problem research and throughout the front end of the innovation process is to avoid the mistranslation of insights from one function to another during product development. As Philip Kotler explains in his book *Kotler on Marketing*, "No single function in the company can take total responsibility for product strategy and development. . . . Various departments must participate in developing a product since they will all be involved in supporting it."

Many companies fall prey to what is referred to as the *over-the-wall syndrome*. This problem occurs when one function transfers customer insights and research results over to another function as a product or service moves through the development process. Often, the message picked up by the receiving function may not be the one intended by the sending function. These errors often contribute to misdirection in product design that can lead to innovation failures.

In fact, relying on a single function for problem research can sometimes be as harmful to an organization as not conducting any research at all. Although functions that do not participate in the customer research may be able to identify major customer needs from summary reports and conversations with members of the participating functions, they won't understand the specific factors driving the need or why it is important to customers. This can lead to confusion regarding the specific elements of a problem and the "whys" that characterize customer attitudes and behavior—information that product developers must have to determine which needs should be addressed in the innovation design.

Large innovation projects at Maytag involve almost all functional areas in innovation research. In fact, many of Maytag's platoons even include members from outside of the organization, such as suppliers. The results have been impressive. Maytag has reduced miscommunication and supplier lead time for major innovations by 50 percent. Supplier involvement on platoons has also helped Maytag integrate advanced materials into innovations more quickly and efficiently.

Self-Moderated Research

For most companies, cross-functional participation in customer problem research means that platoon members from different functional areas attend focus groups and in-home interviews and listen to professional moderators talk to customers. While this is definitely a great start, some of the most successful companies go one step further— they actually have platoon members conduct the research with customers themselves.

Most market research managers would cringe at the thought of employees from outside their function talking to customers directly, but we strongly believe that it is the best way to identify breakthrough insights and get the most out of an innovation initiative for two reasons. First, on an in-depth GI system project, platoon members come to know more about customers and their unique problems and needs than anyone else in the company. As a result, they are in the best position to know the right questions to ask and the times when it is appropriate to depart from the "script" to learn something new that could lead to a valuable new finding. With some basic moderator skills training, platoon members become the best interviewers.

Second, the experience of talking with customers face-to-face contributes to a higher level of interest and intensity in exactly what is being said among platoon members than passively listening to a conversation from behind a glass window. Although watching research is certainly better than reading a summary report, interviewing customers personally is the best method of all.

The Power of Problems

The importance of adopting a problem orientation to innovation is critical to achieving consistent success. Corporations that conduct exploratory problem research with customers using a broad mix of research tools and with platoon members from different functions will inevitably discover needs and opportunities that can form the basis for a diverse portfolio of valuable new offerings. The key to discovering these breakthrough insights involves starting broadly—by understanding customers' larger life problems and issues—and then relating those issues to the product or service category being examined through iterative waves of qualitative research.

Along with technology platform research, problem research is one of the primary fuels for generating successful ideas and concepts. A strong problem orientation ensures that ideas and concepts address an identified customer problem or need. Innovations that address real needs provide a source of value to customers and, by doing so, are substantially more likely to be successful in the marketplace. In short, this is the best way for a corporation to ensure that it will produce a consistent stream of innovation winners. Without a strong problem orientation, innovation becomes a hit-or-miss process and success relies more on chance than it should.

CHAPTER 9

PLATFORMS

Successful corporate innovators who want continuous innovation consistently invest in two things: (1) gaining customer insights and (2) developing new technologies or capabilities. Both superior customer insights and practical technological advancements are the primary sources of future innovations.

The role of technology as the "fuel cell" for innovation is instrumental and fundamental. This isn't a quantitative issue—a matter of getting more PCs or some laptops or Palm Pilots. It's about the ability to create new applications, products, and possibilities. That's the key. Technology offers possibilities that previously didn't exist and raises the competitive ante in ways that other improvements, though important, can't match. We use the term *technology* broadly because it can encompass a wide range of elements, such as information technology, computer hardware devices, software, biotechnology, materials, sensory advancements, processes, and intellectual capital.

There are many examples of how a new technology has broken through previous constraints to satisfy latent customer needs. Cellular phone technology is a prime example. Twenty years ago, consumers weren't saying, "I need a portable and wireless phone, so go make me one." In fact, telephones were located in or near virtually every public building imaginable. It was rare for someone in this country not to be able to find a phone. Yet wireless technology opened up the possibility for a whole new behavior to be manifested by consumers. A new set of latent needs was recognized, filled, and gloriously satisfied: safety, security, convenience, privacy, portability, instant accessibility, and connectivity were some of the new benefits that delighted consumers with cellular phones. Moreover, ten years ago, cellular phones were expensive. Today, they are literally free in many cases. This is a great example of how radical technology opens up possibilities and creates new opportunities for companies and consumers.

Clayton Christensen writes in his book, *The Innovator's Dilemma*:

> *Disruptive technologies bring to a market a very different value proposition than has been available previously. Generally, disruptive technologies underperform established products in mainstream markets.*

His key point is that products and services based on disruptive technology usually bring something new to the customer. While they may not replace existing alternatives overnight, their impact can eventually transform a market. Transistors were disruptive to vacuum tubes; fax machines were disruptive to overnight mail delivery; the Internet has become disruptive to retail stores; and health maintenance organizations have been disruptive to the health insurance industry.

Investments in this area provide the potential for companies to discover, create, and apply disruptive technologies in ways that get translated into usable products and services that solve customer problems. For six consecutive years, IBM has filed for more patents than any other company in this country, but its conversion rate of a new technology into a commercialized, profitable new product or service is fairly low. Investing in technology may be step one, but having a process in place that leverages that technology is equally important.

The key is creating a culture that reinforces technology and research and development as investment "banks" rather than cost centers. Future innovations will be sparked and stimulated by technological advancements. Technology is only a tool, but it is enormously useful for fanning the sparks of innovation into full flames.

Creating a Platform Mind-Set

If technology opens up possibilities, then platforms are the way companies use technology to accomplish continuous, rapid innovation. It's how innovation gets done. *Platforms* are underlying technologies and capabilities in which a company invests in order to generate a *portfolio* of different products, applications, or improvements. The old adage in carpentry is "measure twice, cut once." With platforms, the corollary is "invest once, reuse over and over again."

A platform mind-set requires thinking about three things simultaneously:

- A family of multiple products or services
- How that family addresses a variety of customer needs
- What markets or segments of customers are involved

Some platform strategies are thought out well in advance. Others develop due to circumstances: there just isn't enough time or money to develop something new from the ground up, and you have to reuse what you already have. In the late 1970s, Chrysler was facing bankruptcy. Products had quality problems and were relatively undistinguished in the market. Chrysler designers identified a consumer need for a roomier station wagon and dissatisfaction with larger passenger vans. Lacking resources, Chrysler used the widely disliked K-car as a base platform and developed the Dodge Caravan ("car" plus "van"). Caravan created a revolutionary new product category, the minivan, which became widely popular and imitated.

WAYS OF REUSING EXISTING PLATFORMS

The Face-Lift Approach

With this approach, you design a product or service up front then periodically renew it. Companies that use a face-lift approach are basically saying, "If it ain't broke, don't fix it." Often, companies using this approach end up hanging on to their initial design too long. As a result, they are only able to slightly revise their design even in the midst of dramatic changes in customer needs and competition, which ultimately erodes market share.

A leading software company targeting the higher education market tried to hang on too long to its complex, but very robust, mainframe solution. It continued to modify its original design, add on new capabilities, and try to make it all work together. But the emergence of graphic user interfaces, Internet connectivity, and easy-to-support programming languages left this company extremely vulnerable. It couldn't change its original design fast enough to keep up, and the support costs skyrocketed. A face-lift wasn't enough. As a result, a start-up competitor created a new solution from scratch in less than eighteen months that is now threatening to unseat the twenty-year market leader.

The Redesign Approach

With this approach, each design is totally new every time. It's the starting-over-from-scratch approach to innovation. Like a sculpture, each innovation is a "chiseled out" original.

One business-to-business Internet services company is doing just that. Each new service is a "do over," with almost no efficiency gained in subsequent offerings. Unless the company can find a common, reusable platform for service development, its portfolio of offerings will be too limited to be competitive.

The Line Extension/Cloning Approach

In this case, a company designs an initial product or service and then creates knock-offs to access additional customer segments. The idea is that success breeds success. However, if an initial offering is designed for early adopters, success with mainstream offerings depends on the extent to which the mainstream customers and their needs are similar to those of the early adopters. Many companies who use this approach are misled into believing they are taking a platform approach. They aren't. Fundamentally, they create an offering for a particular market then try to make the best of it for the rest of the market.

For example, the cash management division of a major bank signed up two large corporations to help design a new treasury management software solution. The needs of these two early adopter companies were relatively sophisticated and complex. After the solution was completed and launched, the bank found it had overengineered the product relative to most customers' needs. It became too expensive to try to tailor the original design for the rest of the market.

The Platform Approach

This approach involves simultaneously designing a core architecture (or components) and a road map for generating a family of related products or services. With platforms, companies are fundamentally saying "make no small plans." A core technology is developed and incorporated into an offering for the early adopter market. Customization for mainstream market needs is infused into the plan. Offerings can look and feel very different, even though they come off a common platform.

Fundamentally, the platform approach is one of four different technology approaches to innovation (Exhibit 9.1). A well-conceived platform approach can be extremely powerful. Companies that adopt this approach enjoy substantial benefits:

- *Reduced overall development costs.* With a platform approach, upfront development costs may be higher due to increased planning and development work, but long-run costs can be lower due to less redesign of the core architecture for future products and services.
- *Increased ability to reach niche markets.* Markets that would otherwise seem too small to support their own offering are more economical if many of the development costs can be shared.
- *Increased speed to market for subsequent offerings.* With a multigeneration architecture, fewer components need to be modified or redeveloped in subsequent offerings, so the cycle time of subsequent offerings built off the core platform is shorter than when starting over from scratch.
- *Reduced risk of failure.* By targeting multiple niches or markets, a failure in any one area of the market can be offset by success in other areas. Platforms diversify a company's risk.
- *Increased ability to customize/personalize at the point of sale.* Effective platforms support mass customization, an increasingly

Exhibit 9.1 Technology Approaches to Innovation

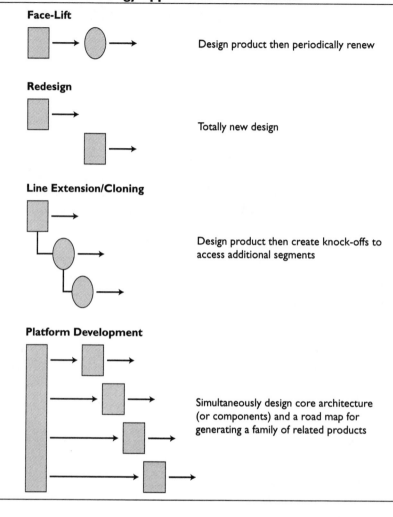

Face-Lift

Design product then periodically renew

Redesign

Totally new design

Line Extension/Cloning

Design product then create knock-offs to access additional segments

Platform Development

Simultaneously design core architecture (or components) and a road map for generating a family of related products

important requirement in many markets. Whether it's the ability to get a made-to-order Toyota Camry delivered in less than a week, a have-it-your-way Whopper at Burger King, or an affinity credit card sponsored by your alma mater or favorite nonprofit organization, platforms can facilitate a level of customization not previously known in the market.

- *Increased profitability.* Ultimately, an effective platform approach should enable a company to reach more customer segments with more tailored offerings for a lower per-offering development cost. The combination of these three factors can have a dramatically positive impact on profits.

One caution is in order: platforms require patience at start-up. Time to market for the first member platform of the family is often longer than other approaches. A platform also can take strange directions if customer needs are not held paramount; specifically, a reengineering–induced emphasis on cost-cutting can result in platform decisions that are inconsistent with what customers need. Finally, the relatively high initial start-up costs of the platform can lead senior managers (especially the financial people) to stick with a platform even when it has exhausted its usefulness. However, it should be noted that these are typical innovation problems. Misreading customer needs, holding on to old ideas that have outlived their usefulness, and failing to beat the competition are typical problems in every business.

For example, in the mid-1980s, Andersen Windows saw a lot of competitors launch a new generation of double-hung (tilt-in) windows for easy cleaning. These windows addressed a strong customer dissatisfaction with the difficulty of cleaning the outside of traditional windows, particularly those located above the first floor. The new tilt-in windows were based on a very different architecture than prior generations. Andersen, the market leader in double-hung windows, had become extremely efficient with its existing platform, which didn't support the tilt-in capability. The company's profits during the late 1980s and early 1990s, as evidenced by record year-end profit-sharing checks to employees, made it difficult to kill the old design and start over. Andersen delayed entry into the tilt-in window market for almost a decade. Its delay enabled several smaller competitors, such as Pella and Marvin, to capture market share and gain significant size and strength. The problem wasn't the approach used but the judgment with respect to customer needs and competition's energy.

While a platform approach is making inroads in many different industries, early adopters of the approach typically have come from industries with the following characteristics: products or services, such as automobile plants and computer chip fabrication, are not otherwise feasible due to high risk and/or high costs, and there is a great need for highly responsive or point-of-sale customization, such as in personal computer architecture, Web personalization, and consulting methodologies. For example, while the Ford Ranger (pickup truck) and Ford Explorer (sport utility vehicle) use the same platform, the final products are highly customized to appeal to the needs of very different customer segments.

Platforms are implemented at three levels: the strategy level, the portfolio level, and the program level (Exhibit 9.2). By setting direction and aligning resources at all three levels, companies make better platform decisions and investments. The *strategy* outlines how platforms will support business objectives. The *portfolio* determines the appropriate mix of efforts and alignment of resources for both short- and long-term objectives. Finally, customer-centered *programs* must be initiated and managed to create value and get results. Across all three levels, a strong focus on the customer distinguishes the best platform approaches from the rest.

Determining Platform Strategies

In the end, platforms are designed to support business objectives, such as revenue growth, differentiation, product life-cycle extension,

Exhibit 9.2 Three Levels of Platform Implementation

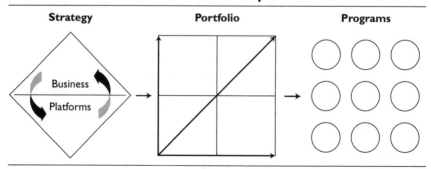

customer segment penetration, market diversification, and earnings growth. How a company uses platforms to support its business objectives is the domain of strategy.

Companies need to create platforms with an objective in mind—one that supports the business strategy. Depending on a company's overall business strategy and sources of competitive advantage, platforms may be developed to pursue one or more of the following five strategies:

- *Multiple niche strategy.* The company creates the ability to address multiple niche markets or customer segments, each with very different needs, that would be too expensive to pursue individually or too small to be worthwhile. Take the Dodge Neon and Chrysler PT Cruiser, for example (Exhibit 9.3). The Dodge Neon is an entry-level sedan targeted to first-time and younger car buyers who need high-quality transportation. The Chrysler PT Cruiser is a hot rod targeted to car enthusiasts who appreciate a car's performance, but it also has

Exhibit 9.3 Multiple Niche Strategy of Dodge Neon and Chrysler PT Cruiser

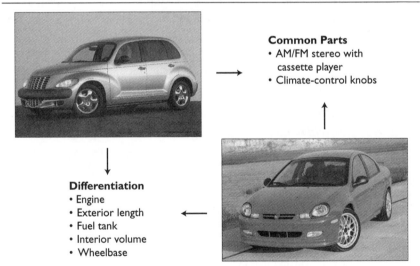

Common Parts
- AM/FM stereo with cassette player
- Climate-control knobs

Differentiation
- Engine
- Exterior length
- Fuel tank
- Interior volume
- Wheelbase

Images courtesy of DaimlerChrysler Corp.

interior characteristics similar to those of a minivan, with more interior space than most full-sized sedans. These two cars serve very different niche markets with different needs. Yet they share some common parts, such as the AM/FM radio with cassette player and climate-control knobs. (Features such as these tend to be shared across all DaimlerChrysler Corp. vehicles.) Differentiation comes in areas such as fuel tank, interior volume, and rear suspension.

Pella Window Company is another example of a company using a multiple niche strategy. Within any product line, the core architecture is similar across all types of residential housing—from lower-end track housing to high-end custom-built homes. Differentiation comes in the design elements—such as paint colors, trim, and hardware—including glass properties such as insulation level and sunlight protection.

- *Single benefit strategy.* The company creates the ability to address multiple markets or categories using a single benefit. With this strategy, a differentiating benefit is applied across multiple markets where customers desire that same benefit. Examples include products such as Lysol, where the antibacterial benefit is spread across a range of markets, including bathroom cleaners, all-purpose cleaners, and air fresheners. Healthy Choice employs this type of platform strategy, taking its know-how in low-fat foods and spreading it across multiple food categories. Procter & Gamble, with its innovative ultra line of formulation and packaging, created a platform across multiple categories that delivers the benefit of lighter and more compact products. In the process, it also took a bite out of its own transportation costs.

- *Scalable benefit strategy.* The company creates the ability to address different customer segments that need the same benefit delivered at different levels. For example, several companies have created a digital subscriber line (DSL) platform that allows customers to choose the speed of Internet access they are willing to pay for. Fundamentally, they can "dial up" or "dial down" their speed of Internet access and pay accordingly. The underlying platform enables a wide range of access speeds to be delivered. CopperCom, a voiceover DSL technology provider, has one-upped the data DSL providers. Its platform also enables small business or residential customers to dial up or down the number of phone lines they need without having to wait for months or incurring substantial provisioning service charges from their local phone company.

Another scalable benefit example is the application of a call center platform to give different callers different levels of service. Using the inbound phone number, a call center platform can identify, classify, and route inbound callers to different places. Higher-use customers can be routed to queues with shorter wait times and more experienced customer service reps. The scalable benefit is speed of service.

- *Multigeography strategy.* The company achieves the ability to address the needs of multiple geographic regions that have some similar relevant characteristic(s). Common characteristics such as socioeconomic status, culture, behavior, time zone, weather, and so on can result in an underlying commonality in customer needs—even in very different geographic regions. If these commonalities are identified and explored, companies can develop platforms that serve multiple geographies. For example, an insecticide company trying to develop multicountry platforms for innovation grouped India, China, and Mexico together. These three countries have similar climates—which translates to similar bugs—and similar socioeconomic status—which translates to a similar ability to pay for solutions. When Citibank originally launched its credit card in Asia Pacific, it set up a centralized call center to support the entire region. One of the key commonalities was time zone.

- *Unknown need strategy.* The company creates the ability to satisfy needs that are currently unknown or difficult to articulate. Trends in demographics, lifestyles, and economic conditions; advances in science; and introductions of new technology can open up possibilities that were previously unknown. Some companies want to strategically invest a portion of their technology efforts to satisfy the business objective of revolutionizing their market or category. They proactively seek to identify and develop new technologies for current and future businesses. Other companies choose not to pursue this strategy at all but prefer to be fast followers or licensers of new technology. The "patch" delivery system for pharmaceuticals is one example of a platform developed out of an undefined need strategy. Customers were unable to articulate the need for an unobtrusive, continuous drug delivery system. Yet the applications are numerous, and this platform has opened up a world of new possibilities.

It is important to determine which of the five platform strategies are needed to fulfill your overall business strategy and objectives. That's why the platform strategy needs to be created and integrated with the business strategy.

Creating a Platform Portfolio

The innovation growth gap, vision, and strategic roles outlined in Chapter 5 determine the extent to which a company needs breakthrough innovation versus incremental innovation. These policy decisions drive the platform portfolio investment goals. The platform portfolio defines the mix, balance, and allocation of resources between existing offerings or business lines and new, as yet undiscovered, innovations.

In *Third Generation R&D*, Roussel, Saad, and Erickson point out three strategic purposes of research and development:

- To defend, support, and expand existing businesses. This includes modifying products; adapting them to meet new requirements; using different materials or processes; and addressing regulatory, legal, or environmental compliance issues.
- To drive new businesses. This involves providing opportunities for new businesses using current or new technologies.
- To broaden/deepen technological capabilities. This may address current or new businesses.

The authors show how the mission of research and development needs to change as the industry/company life cycle matures.

Given the stage of the industry and company maturity, the question for any company is: "What strategic purposes is research and development supporting, and how should resources be allocated to accomplish those purposes?" This is a portfolio decision.

The portfolio determines what percentage of funds and people will be allocated to existing technologies and markets rather than new technologies and markets. Relative to the budget and resource alignment for a balanced portfolio, Exhibit 9.4 presents a model for framing investment opportunities. Four investment areas emerge:

- *Bolstering technology.* Investments that improve performance or cost to current markets
- *Leveraging technology.* Investments that expand the benefits delivered to current markets
- *Synergistic technology.* Investments that use current capabilities to move into new markets or businesses

Exhibit 9.4 Portfolio Investment Model

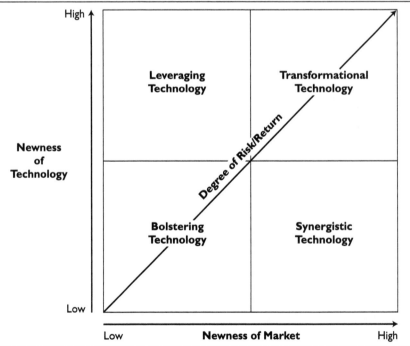

- *Transformational technology*. Investments that provide NTW benefits and/or enable expansion into new businesses.

Research and development often does not have enough resources to meet all the requests it receives. Consequently, a portfolio should ensure that research and development resources are productively focused against the highest potential growth opportunities. A non-profit technology organization analyzed its portfolio only to find over five hundred individual programs under way. No wonder it couldn't make substantial progress on any of them. Resources were spread far too thin. The executive team set out to develop a desired portfolio mix linked to the business strategy. They formed a team to analyze each program against some predefined criteria. Eventually, they eliminated over half of the company's programs.

One element of the portfolio decision is a make versus buy versus partner decision within each of the four investment areas. As *The Economist* recently reprinted from *Red Herring*, a venture-capital monthly:

Innovation used to be about creating 'Transformational technologies' that redefined markets and toppled market leaders—as Intel did with Fairchild and Microsoft did with WordPerfect. Now it is more often concerned with having technologies that target niche markets, or those that are poorly served by the dominant companies. Cisco, Intel, and Microsoft, three technology leaders, all recognize the need to make investments in smaller companies to have access to new, emerging technologies.

Similar to major pharmaceutical companies that invested in small biotech firms in the 1980s as a way to access new discoveries, established companies in many markets today are investing in Internet start-ups to access new opportunities. IBM recently announced an investment fund of $500 million, mostly targeted to the E-business world. Arthur Andersen made a comparable announcement a few weeks later for similar purposes.

Initiating Programs

A $7 billion consumer packaged goods company was passionately committed to using innovation as a core strategy to increase its earnings and beat out competition. Management had put many of the seven Ps in place, secured a charismatic and energetic leader of innovation, adopted a visionary innovation policy, and developed a strategic plan that emphasized more breakthrough innovations. In fact, even the board of directors recommended that more resources be allocated to research and development initiatives that would stimulate totally new technology breakthroughs. To accomplish the overriding objective—developing more breakthrough innovations—the company's research and development group determined their strategy and desired portfolio mix and identified four key technology platforms that represent the pillars or cornerstones of the company's future:

- Microwave packaging technology
- Flavor/taste breakthrough
- Human energy
- Nutrition encapsulation

The selection of these four broad platforms was based on a lot of customer input, management discussion, and trade-off analysis. But, once determined, these platforms were turned into programs that received funding and focus.

What are the two or three platforms that might enable your business to triple within three years? It's this magnitude of outcome that represents a successful breakthrough platform that is commercialized into a stream of derivative products or services.

To determine the appropriate platforms for investment, companies need to plan for platforms within their innovation process. The steps involved are as follows.

1. *Prioritize individual opportunities, target markets, and customer segments and create a product/service family road map.* Determine what products/services and variants will be delivered, at what time,

and to which target customers. This is the road map. For example, if General Motors is considering a "run flat" tire technology for its product lines, the road map might be

- Introduce first into the Cadillac line as a new technology that reinforces Cadillac's repositioning as an innovator.
- Introduce second into high-performance segments by adding unique performance characteristics to the tire. These segments—such as police cruisers, sports cars, and taxicabs— have high practical or psychological needs.
- Develop a scaled-back, lower-cost version, and introduce into the rest of the GM line to appeal to the mainstream market.

2. *Determine the truly differentiating attributes for each product.* The idea is to identify what will drive value for each product or service in the family so the platform can ultimately deliver value. Consider a possible value driver analysis for McDonald's hamburgers. Each sandwich has a few key elements that really drive value perceptions:

Differentiating Attributes	Big Mac	Happy Meal	Adult Sandwiches
Ability to specify condiments	Moderate	Moderate	High
Toy	N/A	High	N/A
Freshness	Moderate	Low	High
Preparation technique	Low	Low	Low
Speed	High	High	High

3. *Explore opportunities to leverage or reuse components.* This is the commonality plan, finding where components can be reused across a product or service line. Using the hamburger example, an examination of a Big Mac shows that most components have high reusability.

Big Mac Components	Comments
2 all-beef patties	Same as used in Happy Meal burgers; fried in same fashion as other burgers and some specialty sandwiches
Special sauce	Trademark component of this sandwich, but not used in any other offering

Lettuce	Must be shredded (unlike whole leaf in other sandwiches); could shred specialty lettuce
Cheese	Same as used in all other sandwiches
Pickles	Same as used in all other sandwiches, but single most-often deleted item on Happy Meal burger
Onions	See "Pickles" above; second most-often deleted item on Happy Meal burger
Sesame seed bun	Trademark component of this sandwich, but not used in any other offering

4. *Iteratively explore trade-offs to create the best marriage of customer value and delivery costs across the product/service family.* In this final step, the company searches for solutions to optimize both value and variety.

Involving Customers and Management

Effective platforms offer a unique or differentiated benefit to customers. Platform development needs to take place in close connection with customer needs, wants, likes, and dislikes.

When considering the application of technology to the design of a new service or product, it's critical to think of both functionality and the user experience (this could mean appearance, fit, or ease of use). Initial and ongoing platform designs need to be heavily influenced by customers. And design is just as important for services as for products. For example, the billing, invoicing, and customer service processes are a big part of designing a successful credit card service.

Effective design techniques include early anthropological observation; that is, observing how people behave, act, and communicate in their home or work environment and understanding why they do what they do. Next, the entire design team should be exposed to the needs and wants of customers. Get the whole team out talking with customers, listening, and watching users. With the right customer input, technologists can apply this knowledge to speed up the development process. Finally, customers should be exposed to partial or complete prototypes early on to enable a rich dialogue and get early feedback.

In addition to early customer involvement, management's ability to influence the outcome of an innovation is much greater up front, in early design phases.

Consequently, management needs to participate on innovation steering committees early on and approve concepts and preliminary business cases. In this way, they can get their issues and concerns addressed early in the process rather than further down the development curve.

Apple is a great example of a company fusing technology advancement with customer wants and needs. In doing so, its stock price increased almost eightfold in less than two years (from $13 per share on January 1, 1998, to over $102 per share in January 2000 after adjusting for splits and dividends). It's clear that Steve Jobs has a passion for technology and conveys how it can make a difference to people.

Apple had lost its pursuit of creativity and innovation. But it returned with the launch of Power Mac G3 in November 1997 and with the multiple-color line of iMACs in July 1998. In personal correspondence, Diane Ryall, the managing director of Apple Computer Australia, commented: "I really believe the G3 . . . has been the single most important factor in getting us back out front. Almost all our machines perform significantly faster than Wintel ones." But is the technology advancement relative to speed and performance the driving customer benefit that has made this product such a success? Or is it technology in concert with the design features, such as the lockable door? Or is it the aesthetics of warm, inviting "fashion" colors rather than the traditional beige and gray? The answer, of course, is all of the above. The key point is not to develop technology for technology's sake but rather to ensure that it will provide a hard-core, functional, economic, or emotional benefit to customers.

The Technology Steering Committee

One of the most important aspects of platforms is sharing knowledge across the corporation. Too often, technology is kept insular within the hallowed halls of research and development, where people wear white coats instead of white shirts and most doors are posted with signs that read "Restricted: Authorized Personnel Only." The barriers (whether real or perceived) need to be penetrated and broken down for all functional managers to better understand, value, and appreciate the role that technology creation plays in breathing possibilities into innovation.

One way to transfer technology knowledge is by forming a technology steering committee consisting of the chief innovation officer, the head of research and development, and several other functional vice presidents (perhaps from marketing, manufacturing, sales, customer service, operations, engineering, systems, or finance), along with either the COO, CEO, or CFO, and at least one divisional or general manager. This seven- to eight-person committee serves as the overall sponsor and champion of technology for the corporation.

At Hewlett-Packard, the interface between research/technology and product development and marketing generates innovation. The H-P laboratories are an applied research division that conducts research in new areas, areas not currently aligned with any business units. This gives freedom to research scientists, increases risk-taking, and provides a scientific knowledge base to be cultivated and expanded. Johnson & Johnson has a Corporate Office of Science & Technology comprising twelve full-time scientists, engineers, and medical doctors. Members of this group spend one-half of their time scouting out new technologies by visiting professors, venture capitalists, and technology providers and the rest of their time on speculative technologies.

The technology steering committee should create opportunities for cross-functional managers to attend workshops and technology conferences, work on technology teams, and become acquainted with competitor technologies. Moreover, this committee should serve as a "resource buster" when problems surface and serve as coach and mentor for all technology teams.

Ultimately, this is the group that creates, monitors, and measures the platform strategy and portfolio and reports quarterly to senior management, providing a scorecard or report card on the state of technology and research and development relative to innovation. The committee ensures platform investments are aligned with business objectives.

Thus, this very critical component of the innovation system sets up the role of technology combined with customer insights to drive out breakthrough innovations. It's the combination that provides incredible synergy and yields powerful results.

CHAPTER 10

PAYBACK METRICS

ew companies actually measure their innovation efforts, and those
that do tend to look at a handful of financial measures at best. In
fact, Kuczmarski & Associates' 1999 study on best practices in innovation revealed that fewer than 50 percent of companies formally
measure innovation on any scale within their organizations and that
fewer than 5 percent measure return on innovation. In today's goal-
oriented culture, where companies establish key performance indicators linked to strategies and then measure progress on a monthly
basis, having so few companies measuring innovation seems shocking. Yet recall from Chapter 2 some of the reasons innovation measurement tends to be overlooked:

- Innovation spans the entire organization.
- Accounting systems do not deal effectively with innovation.
- Innovation does not usually have a specific owner.
- Companies tend to measure only outcomes.
- The results of innovation investments are determined over an
extended time.

Recently, the division president of one company told us that he felt
his organization was successful at innovation. After a few probing
questions, however, it became apparent that he had little data to support this feeling. A few successful innovations seemed to be clouding
his interpretation of the entire picture. Because no measurements
were in place, we had to dig deeper to understand the whole story.

The results were surprising—to him and to others in the company. In looking objectively at the division's performance over the past five years, only two out of fifteen innovations had met their original projections. Overall, innovation accounted for only 15 percent of revenues. And, based on some conservative costing assumptions, innovation had actually generated a negative net contribution to the company's earnings.

What was the root of the problem? After dividing the company's innovation efforts into different categories based on risk, it turned out it was only successful at incremental innovation—low-risk line extensions. Apparently, the company's strong brands, distribution channels, and technical capabilities helped drive success with this type of innovation. The company had launched only one breakthrough initiative, which had yet to deliver any results. The remaining efforts could be classified as medium-risk, new-to-the-company innovations. Closer inspection revealed that these were me-too products launched into markets that had strong established competitors. Without a compelling point of difference or a strong brand or cost advantage, these innovations floundered. They were the real culprits. They represented a sizeable portion of the portfolio but were systematically producing poor results.

Why Measure?

Measurement is critical if a company hopes to improve its innovation effectiveness. Companies can't improve performance if they don't measure it. But innovation measurement is important for reasons beyond performance improvement. It is particularly useful both for analysis of the past and as input to decision making in the future. Specifically, innovation measurement supports six important objectives:

- *Diagnosing underlying reasons for success and failure.* Innovation measurement helps pinpoint opportunities for improvement as well as behaviors to reinforce. Through diagnosis, companies can begin to assess how effective the innovation process is, whether the strategy is working, and whether resources are being appropriately deployed. Fundamentally, innovation measurement provides a critical feedback mechanism to the organization. For example, a software company that served large university libraries found difficulty getting clients to adopt its more leading-edge products. Its buyers, library directors, were conservative. Most directors wanted to see someone else already signed up for a new product before they would sign up. This behavior was dragging down the company's overall return on innovation because adoption rates were so slow. As a solution, the company changed its development process. It started partnering with the more leading-edge universities by bringing them into early stages of the development process. These partner universities then became vocal spokespeople for the new products, providing the badly needed testimonials for the rest of the target market.

- *Benchmarking performance.* Information about competitors' innovation efforts is difficult to get. After all, most companies have trouble getting this information for their own organizations. However, some competitive data can be gleaned by tracking the innovations launched, their success rates, the size of their innovations, advertising spending, and research and development spending (for public companies). A careful analysis of innovations launched by key competitors can help corporations piece together competitors' strategies. In addition, companies can use innovation measurements to benchmark and improve their own performance. Initial metrics set the baseline for comparisons against future performance.

- *Allocating resources.* Innovation metrics can help improve the alignment of innovation resources vis-à-vis goals. By measuring the typical costs and people requirements of past innovation efforts, as well as revenue and profit performance, companies can more effectively allocate resources to achieve their goals. A consumer products company established a $300 million five-year innovation growth gap. Historical measurements suggested a success rate of 70 percent on innovation efforts was achievable, with a typical success representing $20 million in annual revenue by year three. Based on this analysis and some simplifying assumptions, the company realized it would need to nearly double its innovation resource commitment to achieve its aggressive growth goals.

- *Compensating employees.* Chapter 6 outlined four different approaches to rewarding employees for innovation. Each approach requires some form of measurement—for innovation overall, as well as for the efforts of individual platoons. Tying together compensation and innovation heightens the need not only for measurement in general but also for accurate measures that are reported frequently.

- *Informing financial markets.* Once established, innovation measurements enable companies to report expected growth and sources of growth more confidently. Innovation measurements support informing the investment community, shareholders, and employees of expected future performance. Armed with specific information, management can communicate the company's future innovation readiness and earnings potential. And, as previously mentioned, the stock market does value innovation, even though innovation efforts typically extend beyond a ninety-day financial reporting period.

- *Setting future goals.* After measuring innovation efforts, companies have greater confidence and facts to back up their plans. Much of goal setting is top-down, which can provide good direction. But once information exists on how long innovations actually take, how many resources they require, typical success rates, and so on, companies can be more confident of their ability to achieve the stated goals. Innovation measurements help companies evaluate whether their future goals are realistic or beyond stretch goals. A senior vice president of research and development with one of our clients offered the following observation: "Insanity is doing the same things and expecting different results." If historical innovation performance has been subpar, why should anyone expect the future to be dramatically different? They shouldn't—unless the company commits to changing its approaches to innovation.

Innovation must be measured. Without measurement, the wheel eventually falls off the wagon, and the overall innovation system breaks down. With measurement, the innovation system enables a company to continuously improve, reinforce desired behaviors, align goals and resources, communicate expectations, and realistically set future goals.

Measuring the Right Things the Right Way

Measuring innovation seems complicated, but it doesn't need to be. In fact, more often than not, companies that try to establish a system for measuring innovation make it more complicated than necessary. One financial services company we encountered was tracking almost five hundred measures and reporting many of them on a weekly basis. Every Friday, employees would have to give an update on how they were performing against key metrics. These employees ended up spending too much time capturing and reporting data—and not enough time making progress on their innovation initiatives.

Ten Fatal Flaws of Innovation Measurement Systems

A few guidelines may be helpful in recognizing the pitfalls to avoid and the types of measures to consider. In working with a variety of companies to establish and implement innovation measurements, we have identified ten common pitfalls:

1. *Too many metrics.* The overall organization may decide to track many facets of innovation. But individual employees can only deal with a handful of items that are critical to them. Start with a few critical measures and then build from there.
2. *Focused only on results.* Most innovation measurement systems are skewed toward measuring the outcomes of innovation and pay little if any attention to the areas that drive future outcomes. Establish a set of measurements that focuses on interim items as well as outcomes.

3. *Too infrequent.* The default tracking frequency seems to be a company's annual planning cycle and quarterly update cycle. Update innovation measurements frequently enough so the overall portfolio and specific initiatives can be redirected in time for maximum results.

4. *Too focused on dollars.* Related to fatal flaw number 2, companies also tend to focus exclusively on the financial aspects of innovation. While financial measures are one important category, other categories can provide a more insightful view of innovation efforts. Develop a balanced approach that measures financial and nonfinancial items.

5. *Provision of a historical report card rather than prediction.* Companies tend to focus on what has occurred rather than what is likely to happen in the future. Once the credibility of the innovation program has been vindicated by interim measurements of the process, management will gain confidence in the company's ability to predict its future innovation results. Establish measurements around key items that are likely predictors of future performance.

6. *Not linked to business objectives.* Many measurements can be classified as "nice to have" but not required. Use the business objectives and strategies as a filter to be applied against potential innovation measurements. Test each item for its importance relative to the business objectives.

7. *Not integrated with management systems.* Unless integrated with other management systems, innovation measurements will be short-lived. In particular, these measurements require special integration with reward and recognition systems. Otherwise, measuring innovation for its own sake has limited value or appeal.

8. *Too cumbersome to operate.* The quickest way to kill an innovation measurement system is to require employees to put in a lot of effort. The measurements must somehow become part of the course of doing business rather than a set of special activities.

9. *Useful for only a few people.* Anyone participating in innovation should find some of the measurements important. The most common mistake made in this area is focusing measurements on only

one level, that of either the platoon or the overall company, division, or business unit level. Establish measurements that will be relevant to a broad population.

10. ***Used for punishment, not improvement.*** Innovation measurement systems can become a stick for beating up employees. When deadlines are missed, launches fail, or costs are overrun, what happens? How managers use innovation measurements will go a long way toward supporting or breaking down the desired employee behaviors.

Types of Innovation Measurements

Different types of innovation measurements are required for different purposes. Some measurements provide a high-level report card of how the company is doing overall in terms of results. Others can help diagnose what's really going on under the hood of innovation efforts. These measurements focus on more specific items that, if improved, will result in better outcomes.

There are two broad categories of innovation measurements:

- ***Outcome measurements.*** These measurements report how successfully a company is performing in the area of innovation. Potential categories of outcome measures to consider include financial results, customer satisfaction, and success rates.
- ***System measurements.*** These measurements report how well the company's internal innovation systems are working. Since the components of the Guaranteed Innovation system are so critical to innovation success, we have organized the system measurements around each component, or P.

Outcome measurements are similar to tracking the miles per gallon (MPG) performance for your car. With each tank of gas, you can calculate the MPG achieved and compare with the past to determine whether it's going up or down. However, you don't necessarily know why your MPG changes over time or what to do about it. To figure this out, you have to take your car in for some in-depth diagnostics that can tell you what's really going on underneath the hood. Perhaps your MPG is suffering because of a clogged air filter, old spark plugs, or a faulty catalytic converter. Similarly, system measurements tell you why the results of your innovation efforts are increasing or decreasing. They get at the real underlying drivers of performance.

There is no single best set of innovation measures. It depends on the purpose for which they are intended. That's why we don't recommend one set of measures for all companies. Rather, the metric should represent a balanced set of measures relevant for the business and focused on leading indicators of performance as well as areas that need attention.

Outcome Measurements

Companies can measure any number of outcomes resulting from their innovation efforts. Exhibit 10.1 lists five categories of outcome measures. The goal should be to select a few measures from each category that seem most relevant, then establish a baseline of historical performance to compare against future performance. We encourage companies to choose measures from all five categories to provide an appropriate balance.

With some outcome measures, innovation may be only one ingredient affecting them. Consider stock price appreciation. People will suggest that innovation is only one driver of this measure, which is true. Productivity and quality also affect stock price, as do a host of other factors. However, if innovation is a top priority, stock price appreciation is one place innovation effectiveness should show up.

Exhibit 10.1 Categories of Outcome Measures

- Financial measures
- Customer satisfaction measures
- Brand measures
- Success measures
- Portfolio measures

Regardless of which outcome measures are selected, careful thought should be given to three areas:

- **Time horizon.** Most measures can be calculated annually and cumulatively over a three- to five-year period. Annual tracking highlights year-to-year performance changes. Longer-term cumulative tracking provides a more accurate picture of the overall innovation effort, regardless of year-to-year hiccups. Select a time horizon that takes into account typical life cycles for innovations as well as the company's planning horizon.
- **Breakdowns by type of innovation.** For companies that launch a mixed portfolio of innovations, consider tracking key measures for each type of innovation (e.g., new-to-the-world, new-to-the-company, line extensions, etc.) separately. Often, analyzing performance across different types of innovations can help pinpoint strengths and weaknesses.
- **Competitive analysis.** Some outcome measures can be compared with those of competitors, certainly for publicly traded companies. For example, the number of innovations launched, success rates, and some financial measures can be gathered for key competitors. Decide which measures are appropriate for competitive comparison.

Financial Measures

"Show me the money" is a phrase often spoken by skeptical senior managers regarding innovation. Indeed, financial measures are important to track, although some are easier to track than others. Financial measures are by far the most popular innovation measurements. They provide the ultimate proof as to whether a company's innovation efforts are generating adequate returns. The following are five financial innovation measures to consider:

- **Return on innovation.** The total revenues from innovation divided by the total costs associated with innovation. Exhibit 10.2 provides an example of a return on innovation formula used by a product manufacturing company. This measure suffers from the same challenge as average investment—costs are often difficult to track.

Exhibit 10.2 Example Return on Innovation Formula

Cumulative Net Profits Generated from Innovation			
Research costs	+ Development costs	+ Incremental production investments	+ Initial commercialization prelaunch costs

• Market research • Customer research • Concept testing	• Product/service definition • Product/service design • Prototype development • Product/service development	• Tooling • Facilities • Employees	• Market testing • Communications development and media costs

- *Innovation intensity.* The percentage of total revenues, profits, or cash flow coming from innovation. This measure varies wildly by industry. In some industries, companies will totally replace their current product lines within just a few years. It also varies by company within an industry. For example, some companies rely more heavily on acquisitions than internal innovation. Innovation intensity demonstrates how dependent a company is on innovation to drive growth and profits. Interesting information may be found by comparing innovation's revenue impact relative to its profit impact. One company we worked with was generating 20 percent of revenues from innovation, yet only 3 percent of its profits. By digging deeper, we found that a few big failures were really dragging down the overall profitability of innovation.
- *Average investment.* The total cost of innovation divided by the number of innovations launched into the market. It provides insight into the productivity and efficiency of overall innovation efforts. One complication: the investment side of innovation is difficult to track. Specifically, people costs and costs associated with both the existing business as well as innovation can be tricky. For example,

a division of a large consumer services company spends approximately $20 million annually for advertising. However, it spends the bulk of that money advertising its "new news," or new services launched. As part of an effort to maintain a strong brand reputation, the division would spend the $20 million with or without innovation. So, how much should be allocated to innovation? Assumptions made around these types of issues can dramatically impact the outcome.

- *Average time to break even.* The average number of months until an innovation achieves cumulative positive cash flow. This measure brings in the dimension of time, which is critical in today's fast-moving markets. It helps companies assess whether they are being timely in turning innovation investments into profits. Two alternatives exist for when to start the calculation—either at the beginning of the development cycle or at the time of the market launch.

- *Stock price appreciation.* The percent increase or decrease in the company's stock price. Stock price appreciation is typically measured annually and cumulatively over a long time horizon, perhaps a five- to ten-year period. It demonstrates the extent to which the financial community is rewarding a company for its innovation efforts. Innovation often takes time to show tangible results. But over time, the financial community does seem to reward successful innovators.

Customer Satisfaction Measures

The second category of outcome measures is customer satisfaction measures. They provide insight as to whether a company's innovation efforts are valued by customers. Similar to the objections to stock price appreciation, some customer satisfaction measures are impacted by more than just innovation. But over time, customers reward successful innovators with higher satisfaction levels and greater loyalty. The following are four customer satisfaction measures to consider:

- *Innovation satisfaction.* The mean customer satisfaction rating for innovations. It indicates the extent to which innovations are performing up to customers' expectations.

- *Innovation loyalty.* The percent of repeat customers for innovations. For frequently purchased items, innovation loyalty may focus on the number of repeat purchases or time frame before competitive purchase. Innovation loyalty indicates whether innovations are sufficiently solving customers' problems so that customers purchase again.
- *Overall customer satisfaction.* The mean customer satisfaction rating for a company, division, or brand. It indicates the extent to which the company as a whole is performing to customers' expectations.
- *Overall customer loyalty.* The percent of repeat customers for the company, division, or brand. It indicates the extent to which the entire company is sufficiently solving customers' problems to stimulate repeat purchases.

Brand Measures

The third category of outcome measurements is brand measures. They provide insight into whether a company's innovation efforts are positively affecting the brand in terms of overall value and differentiation. Two brand measures to consider are:

- *Brand innovation quotient.* The percent of current and/or potential customers who view the brand as highly innovative. It indicates the extent to which customers perceive the brand as bringing them valuable innovation.
- *Brand differentiation.* The degree to which current and/or potential customers view the brand as significantly different from the competition. It indicates the extent to which customers perceive a noticeable difference in the brand relative to key competitors. Over time, innovation should contribute positively to brand differentiation.

Success Measures

The fourth category of outcome measurements is success rate measures. These provide insight as to whether a company's innovation efforts are meeting objectives and having a lasting impact in the market. Two success rate measures to consider are:

- *Innovation success rate.* The percent of innovations that have met their financial objectives. It provides insight into a company's ability to launch innovations that solve truly meaningful customer problems. One challenge is determining how to attribute the cause of "failure." Did the company set unrealistic objectives, or did the innovation not deliver on a customer need better than competitive alternatives? There has been much debate in the innovation literature about success rates. Recent studies corroborate the findings from Kuczmarski & Associates' innovation best practices research: although there are some variances by industry, the "best" innovators achieve 60 percent to 70 percent success rates.
- *Innovation longevity.* The average time on the market for innovations. Innovation longevity measures success and sustainability. Successful innovations tend to stay on the market longer, and protectable innovations are more sustainable.

Portfolio Measures
The final category of outcome measurements is portfolio measures. They provide insight into whether a company is achieving the desired amount and mix of innovation. Three portfolio measures to consider are:

- *Innovation volume.* The total number of innovations launched in the market. It provides insight into two areas: a company's ability to get innovations to market and its ability to sustain a desired level of innovation over time. A two-year-old business-to-business Internet company set a goal to more than triple its number of services in the market during year three—from thirty services to over one hundred. The company needed to put a tracking mechanism in place at each stage of the innovation process to ensure it could meet its monthly, quarterly, and annual innovation outcome goals.
- *Innovation emphasis.* The percentage of innovations (by number and revenue) commercialized by type of innovation: new-to-the-world, new-to-the-company, line extensions, and improvements. Innovation emphasis is a leading indicator of a company's risk tolerance. It breaks down the company's portfolio to show the relative

emphasis on different innovation types. Frequently this measure reveals a company's over- or underreliance on a particular type of innovation.

- *Research and development innovation emphasis.* The percentage of research and development expenditures devoted to innovation. This demonstrates the extent to which research and development people and dollar resources are being applied to innovation versus maintaining current products, services, and businesses.

Example of Outcome Measures

Exhibits 10.3, 10.4, and 10.5 highlight one company's outcome measurements and overall scorecard for a seven-year period. This company emphasizes financial, success, and portfolio measures with no emphasis on customer satisfaction or brand measures. It focuses on a few key measures, tracks them over time, and reports them in a fairly easy-to-read format.

Exhibit 10.3 Innovation History

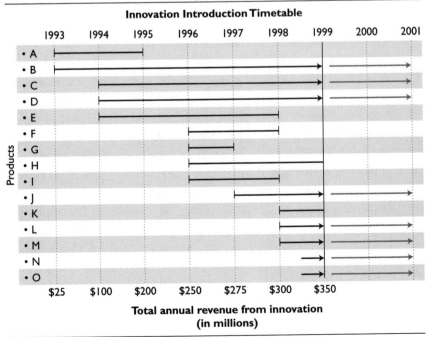

Exhibit 10.4 Breakdown by Type of Innovation

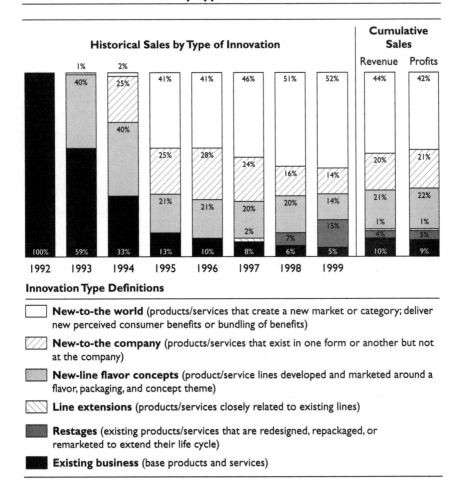

Innovation Type Definitions

☐ **New-to-the world** (products/services that create a new market or category; deliver new perceived consumer benefits or bundling of benefits)

▨ **New-to-the company** (products/services that exist in one form or another but not at the company)

▨ **New-line flavor concepts** (product/service lines developed and marketed around a flavor, packaging, and concept theme)

▧ **Line extensions** (products/services closely related to existing lines)

■ **Restages** (existing products/services that are redesigned, repackaged, or remarketed to extend their life cycle)

■ **Existing business** (base products and services)

Exhibit 10.5 Historical Innovation Scorecard

• Launched:	15
• Still on market:	8
• 2+ years on market:	6
• Met projections:	5
• Cumulative revenues:	$1.5 billion
• % of total revenues:	80%
• Cumulative gross profits:	$900 million
• % of total gross profits:	75%
• Development costs:	$500 million
• Cumulative earnings before interest and taxes:	$100 million

System Measurements

Outcome measurements provide a report card of performance that can be tracked over time, but they incorporate multiple effects. It's difficult to use them to determine what is causing innovation performance to increase or decrease. As a result, outcome measurements are less useful for improving innovation practices. That's where system measurements come in.

System measurements are designed to help companies understand the underlying root causes of success and failure. Rather than waiting until the final results are reported, they provide leading indicators of performance. Similar to the way a pilot uses the plane's navigational system and conversations with air traffic controllers to fine-tune a course while in flight, system measurements help a company fine-tune its innovation efforts in process. Companies like DuPont, Hewlett-Packard, and Dow are well known for having effective system measurements.

Companies should establish system measurements to address each innovation system component. Because system measurements are based exclusively on private, internal information, competitive benchmarking of these measures is extremely difficult.

Regardless of which system measurements are selected, careful thought should be given to three areas:

- *Time horizon.* Most system measures can be calculated monthly, quarterly, annually, and cumulatively over a three- to five-year period. Short-term tracking highlights performance changes. Longer-term cumulative tracking provides a more accurate picture of the overall innovation effort.
- *Breakdowns by type of innovation.* For companies that develop a mixed portfolio of innovations, separate tracking of key measures for each type of innovation (e.g., new-to-the-world, new-to-the-company, line extensions, etc.) should be considered. Often, analyzing performance across different types of innovations can help pinpoint strengths and weaknesses.

• *Level of aggregation.* Some system measures apply to individual platoon initiatives, others to the overall innovation system, and some to both. Determine the level of aggregation most appropriate for each measure.

The goal should be to focus on a few measures within each category. While there are an infinite number of possible measures, we have identified some of the leading candidates for each P of the GI System.

Priority Measures

The first category of system measurements is priority measures. They provide insight into whether a company's actions are consistent with its intention of making innovation a top priority. Three priority measures to consider are:

• *Innovation resource count.* The total number of full-time equivalent people (FTEs) and total budget dollars devoted to innovation. While the innovation resource count may not measure the effectiveness of a company's investments in innovation, it does indicate whether the appropriate amount of FTEs and dollars are being applied to achieve the innovation goals. Rather than polling all employees or filling out time sheets, FTE estimates can be aggregated by innovation platoon leaders. Innovation budget estimates are typically readily available.

• *Executive emphasis.* The percent of executive time being spent on innovation. Although somewhat difficult to measure, the executive emphasis measures whether executives are supporting innovation in the most tangible way—with their time. One approach to determining this measure is asking executive assistants to estimate this percentage.

• *Communication emphasis.* The percent of internal and external company communications that reinforce innovation as a top priority. Communication emphasis measures the extent to which a company's words are aligned with its stated goals. If innovation is truly a priority, then it should be getting sufficient "air time."

Policy Measures

The second category of system measurements is policy measures. They provide insight into how closely the company's innovation strategy is being followed. Two policy measures to consider are:

- *Pipeline portfolio mix.* The total number of innovation initiatives in the pipeline, aggregated by type of initiative (e.g., new-to-the-world, new-to-the-company, line extensions, improvements). The pipeline portfolio mix indicates the alignment between the desired portfolio of innovation and the actual work in progress. This measure can be dissected further—by each stage of the innovation process—to identify potential gaps, bottlenecks, or portfolio imbalances.
- *Total pipeline value.* The total value of innovation initiatives in the pipeline. The total pipeline value provides a leading indicator of whether the current pipeline activity is sufficient to achieve a company's goals. If possible, determine expected values by applying the probability of being launched and the likelihood of success if launched. This measure also can be dissected further—by each stage of the innovation process—to identify potential gaps, bottlenecks, or imbalances.

Platoon Metrics

The third category of system measurements is platoon measures. These measures look closely at the people side of the GI system. Companies can get sophisticated in measuring the effectiveness of their platoons. Many formal team effectiveness surveys already exist (Exhibit 10.6). Companies can select a survey instrument and administer it to platoons at each stage of the process. In so doing, they compile a database of effectiveness scores for future comparison. In addition, they can monitor a particular platoon's effectiveness over time. Beyond platoon effectiveness, two measures to consider are:

- *Platoon turnover.* The total number of platoon members leaving their platoons divided by the total number of innovation participants. Continuity of platoon members is critical to success. Platoon

Exhibit 10.6 Example Team Effectiveness Survey

Five Survey Dimensions	Overall Team Effectiveness Score
I. Mission, Planning, and Goals	High
II. Group Roles	↑ Synergistic Team
III. Group Processes	Effective Group
IV. Group Relationships	Cohesive Group
V. Intergroup Relations	Fragmented Group
	Immature Group
	↓ Low

Source: Team Effectiveness Profile (TEP), Organizational Design and Development, Inc., 1995.

turnover measures the extent to which platoon members and leaders are remaining in place.

- *Average FTEs per platoon.* The total number of innovation FTEs divided by the number of innovation platoons. Often, platoon members get spread too thinly over too many initiatives. This measure ensures each innovation initiative is getting the appropriate level of attention. This measure may vary by stage in the process or by type of initiative.

Problem Orientation Measures

The fourth category of system measurements is problem orientation measures. These measures indicate the extent to which new customer insights are being uncovered, as well as the extent to which current innovation initiatives are linked to customer problems. Two problem orientation measures to consider are:

- *Problem portfolio mix.* The total number of innovation initiatives in the pipeline aggregated by the type of customer problem. The problem portfolio mix performs two important functions. First, it ensures that each initiative in the pipeline is aligned with at least one important customer need. Second, it measures the diversity of customer problems being addressed.
- *Problem category renewal.* The number of new, broad-based customer problem categories identified. The problem category

renewal measure ensures that a company is constantly seeking out new areas of opportunity, not simply mining gold from past research discoveries.

Platform Measures

The fifth category of system measurements is platform measures. These measures indicate the extent to which new technology platforms are being uncovered, as well as the extent to which current technology platforms are being leveraged. Four platform measures to consider are:

- *Platform portfolio mix.* The total number of innovation initiatives in the pipeline aggregated by the type of technology platform. The platform portfolio mix performs two important functions. First, it ensures that each initiative in the pipeline is aligned against an existing technology platform. Those initiatives not reusing an existing technology platform must be identified as requiring either development or acquisition. Second, the platform portfolio mix measures the diversity of platforms being leveraged and the extent to which each platform is being reused.
- *Platform renewal.* The number of new technology platforms under development. The platform renewal measure ensures a company is constantly seeking out new technologies that may address unmet or unsatisfied customer needs.
- *Intellectual property strength.* The number of patents pending (or other measure of intellectual property). The intellectual property strength measures a company's ability to build new, protectable capabilities.
- *Technology transfer ratio.* The percent of patents that are translated into commercialized innovations. The technology transfer ratio measures a company's ability to translate intellectual property into an innovation.

Process Measures

The sixth category of system measurements is process measures. These measures indicate the extent to which the innovation process is effective in screening innovations and efficient in getting innovations to market. Four process measures to consider are:

- *Process pipeline flow.* The total number of innovation initiatives at each stage of the process. The process pipeline flow measure helps ensure the appropriate amount of innovation activity is occurring to achieve company goals. It also helps determine whether the appropriate ratio of activity is occurring at each stage in the process.
- *Start-stop-continue.* The total number of innovation initiatives started, stopped, and continued during a particular period of time. The start-stop-continue measure assesses whether initiatives are being killed—something a lot of companies have difficulty doing—and, at least by inference, how much indecision exists. It also ensures the top of the funnel is being fueled with new initiatives.
- *Speed to market.* The average elapsed time from the start of each initiative until launch. Speed to market can be measured separately for each stage of the process, as well as for different types of initiatives (e.g., new-to-the-world, new-to-the-company, line extensions, improvements). It helps identify potential bottlenecks and measures the overall efficiency of the process.
- *Conformance index.* The percent of innovation initiatives that meet their targeted completion date and budget. The conformance index measures the extent to which innovation initiatives are hitting or overrunning their internal goals. It assesses the accuracy of estimates, as well as uncovers bottlenecks and resource drains.

Getting Started

What is the most important thing to remember in establishing innovation measurements? Demonstrate the value. The key is to show how measuring innovation leads to better results. Show how the information can be used to drive improvement. The best approach is to start small. Pick a few key measures, educate people along the way, and focus on using the information to quickly add value. Following are some rough guidelines for starting an innovation measurement initiative:

1. *Select a few measures in each category.* The number of possible measures can seem overwhelming; yet, this book introduces just a subset of the possible universe. The goal is to create a balanced, manageable, meaningful set of measures. What things are most important to the company? What are the weaknesses today? Where should more time and attention be spent? Look over the categories and the measures outlined here, select a few measures from each category, and create any new ones that might be missing. Keep the number of measures small to start—perhaps just one or two for each of the five outcome measures and six system measures.

2. *Establish initial benchmarks.* Start by establishing a baseline measure. Get the facts. Analyze the past three to five years if data are available. In some cases, the picture is worse than expected. Other times, companies are pleasantly surprised at the strong position they are at. Regardless, you will have a starting point from which to show improvements made and value generated.

3. *Set performance goals.* Set goals and time frames for performance improvement on the key measures. Also, begin setting expectations about how long it may take to change the past. Changes to the innovation system may quickly show up in system measures. However, changes may not have a significant short-term impact on outcome measures.

4. *Establish accountability.* Determine who will be accountable for making sure measures get tracked and reported. This individual will not necessarily do all the measuring, but he or she will ensure it gets done. Someone must take ownership for measuring innovation. Otherwise, it will be neglected.

5. *Create support systems.* Provide user-friendly ways to gather the data. Measuring innovation may require some employees and managers to change their behaviors or perform new tasks. Look for creative ways to lighten the burden. Be prepared to provide the rationale for why measurement will benefit them personally, as well as the training to enable them to do it.

6. *Establish a reporting system.* Set up a periodic reporting system that shows the innovation measures and tracks performance against key goals. For example, some companies post monthly, quarterly,

and annual bulletins that show icons colored green, yellow, or red, demonstrating whether the company is ahead, on target, or behind in terms of achieving its innovation goals.

7. *Close the feedback loop.* Map out who will use the information and how. Make sure that everyone expects the information to result in actions taken.

8. *Develop reinforcers.* Distribute rewards when innovation measures improve. That's the quickest way to bring buy-in to the area of measurement. Provide an upside that encourages people to measure performance and compare results to the past and to goals.

Innovation Measurement—The Big Picture

Measurement is critically important to a healthy innovation system. But what is really important is what gets done with the information. Does it imply needed changes to the innovation process? Should the innovation strategy change? Should resource allocation change? Measurement supplies information that is a vital part of a feedback loop. In the long run, for innovation measurement to be successful it must:

- Become part of the culture
- Be a long-term commitment
- Be viewed as a means, not as an end in itself
- Be focused on continuous feedback to drive improved performance

The ultimate goal should be to have innovation measurement and acting on the information become a natural part of how business gets done.

INNOVATION:
WHAT TO DO TOMORROW MORNING—AND EVERY MORNING THEREAFTER

We ended Chapter 1 with "Corporate America in 2010," a section describing a vision of how companies at the end of the first decade of the new millennium would be consistently and continuously more innovative. Senior executives will be encouraging employees (aka platoon members) to be risk-takers, and people will wake up every morning looking forward to going to work. We fully expect that some CEOs might react to that passage with something like: "OK, nap time's over. Now let's get back to work." Meaning, "Let's make sure productivity is up, profits are up, and our stock price is up—right now." This reaction would be understandable. It's great to speculate about what might happen ten or more years from now. But what should corporate leaders do right now—this afternoon, tomorrow morning—to make their organizations more productive and more profitable and to make their earnings stronger and their stock more valuable?

The Rise of Innovation

The answer to those questions is: innovate. And there is plenty of evidence to prove that corporations have gotten the message. We can walk through the seven Ps for a few examples of how corporate executives are "getting it."

Priority

In 1994, the American Chemical Society established the Award for Team Innovation, an award for excellence by multidisciplinary teams (which are regarded as essential to successful innovation and commercialization). Winners have included teams from Corning, Merck Pharmaceuticals, DuPont, Eli Lily & Co., and (jointly) Genencor International and Procter & Gamble. This award hasn't hit the nightly business news, much less national network news yet. So, why does it matter? Because it is an example of the priorities being set by leaders. In the early days of the Malcolm Baldrige National Quality Awards, the participants were voices in the quality wilderness; as the economic value, not the public relations value, of the processes represented by those awards became obvious, converts were created. The same will happen with innovation. Innovation is being moved up the list of corporate priorities because it represents the next best tool for growth and profitability.

Policy

Closely linked to priority is policy. Policy is sometimes regarded as an abstraction that often falls off employees' radar screens. But few things will get people's attention like the word *free*. Which is the theory Ford Motor Company used in January 2000: it gave all employees—no exceptions—free computers. And to make certain that everyone understood, announcements were made that all Ford employees were being given these free computers because it was Ford policy to increase productivity in all areas of the company for all kinds and levels of skills, whether they involved finance, process, production, or communication. Many companies provide employees the opportunity to buy personal computers at bargain prices, but this was a way to make a bold policy statement in concrete terms that everyone understood. At Ford, computer literacy is clearly part of the policy-level commitment to productive and innovative operations. (To turn a phrase: "At Ford Innovation is Policy 1!")

Platoons

In late 1999, the National Cancer Institute started its Unconventional Innovations Program devoted to the support of peer-reviewed, high-risk, high-impact ideas that could potentially revolutionize cancer treatment. A central operation of the program is the use of multidisciplinary teams with expertise in fields that traditionally have not worked together. Thus, teams with members from such diverse backgrounds as engineering, physics, chemistry, and mathematics are organized to capitalize on the emerging opportunities to translate developments in technology for improved patient care. Breakthrough innovations will depend on the "cross-talk" between and among the sciences, industry, and the academic world. This reflects the special sense of mission that characterizes innovation platoons.

Process

This is where innovative ideas and missions are developed into real-world products and services. Procter & Gamble's Scientific Group based its initial detergent formulations on primary-level research and developed feedback on how each of the new variants performed under different conditions that related to customers who would actually be using the product. This testing was repeated several times and in several phases to focus on the optimum formulation. The products, which were developed by the use of such biotech tools as protein engineering, randomized mutagenesis, and high-throughput screening assays, were part of a screening process based on continuous progress in the generation of new developmental insights. The process was a new marriage of science, product engineering, and consumer-related benefits.

Problem Orientation

Jacques Nasser, the CEO of Ford Motor Company, wants a consumer focus to be at the center of all management and employee activities. He's banking on designers, engineers, marketers, and others doing a much better job of identifying consumer needs, wants, likes, and dislikes. He sends his teams to a Consumer-Insight Center for a day-long course on how to listen to and talk with consumers. Then, small teams are sent out for eight weeks of intense immersion with customers. In this way, design, functionality, comfort, safety, aesthetics, and utility get addressed. Has his strategy worked? In 1999, Ford became the world's most profitable automaker, generating $5.9 billion in net income and achieving a 130 percent increase in stock price since early 1997.

Platforms

The subject of innovation platforms has become a matter of increasing concern and a changing landscape. More and more companies are attempting to organize and formalize the process of developing technical managers, and organizations have begun to recognize the importance of platoonlike working relationships. In 1999, the Industrial Research Institute interviewed seventeen technical managers in five companies—Biogen, Exxon Research & Engineering, IBM Research, Pratt & Whitney, and Wyeth-Ayerst Research—to determine the best predictors of managerial success. Responses were analyzed, synthesized, and categorized to identify and define the key performance requirements.

Payback

Innovation metrics are receiving an increasing amount of attention. For instance, in the spring 2000 issue of *Marketing Management*, Tom Kuczmarski lists more than ten different measures of "R2I" (return on innovation investment). He mentions that more types of measures are possible. As if to prove the point, Clorox measures the annual cost savings ratio (CSR) of its research and development to determine the contributions being made by innovation.

You can pick up the paper every day and see at least a few more examples to supplement those listed here. So, it is clear that corporate managers are attempting to innovate their corporations. However, the key to successful innovation, especially for the large corporation and other organizations at whom this book is directed, lies not in any one of the seven Ps but in the integration of all components described in the previous chapters of this book. Note the emphasis is on the word *integration*.

A National Innovation Agenda

Innovation needs to become the new national strategy. It must be elevated to high-priority status. As a country, the United States needs to embrace innovation and adopt new approaches to doing business differently. And government can become the catalyst for innovation.

To remain successful as individual businesses, as an economy, and as a nation, companies must boldly innovate into the next decade. Understanding how to create a systematic and disciplined approach to innovating the corporation will get them there faster, smarter, and more efficiently. As a total community, U.S. businesses need to come up with new ideas and approaches to make Fortune 1000 companies the leaders and "sculptors" of global innovation.

Americans are extraordinarily influenced by multibillion dollar corporations. Consumers purchase their products every day and use their services each week. When corporate profits are down for an extended time, the stock market is down, the economy weakens, and individual lives are dramatically affected. Since the health and wealth of this nation are directly impacted by large corporations, corporations must be respected for their resources, human potential, economic power, labor benefits, and in particular, the goods and services that everyone consumes and uses on a daily basis.

Large corporations are the mainstay of American business. They have served as the pillars on which the economy has been built. But to continue, they need to become better at creating and instilling a pervasive innovative mind-set. Discipline and a holistic approach to innovation (reflected in the seven Ps) will be key. Corporations need to acknowledge the urgent mandate to turn themselves into effective innovation organisms.

That's why we believe innovation deserves its own national agenda. Government and academia need to hold hands with large corporations in a bond of innovation partnership. Business and government must marry to provide ongoing stimulation and encouragement of innovation. America needs a Declaration of Innovation that encourages leadership and risk-taking and nurtures a new partnership to spur innovation and continue to stimulate growth.

How, as a practical matter, are we going to accomplish this? Here are a few suggestions:

- Academia, government, and corporations should join forces to create new incentives and awards, share research, and exchange knowledge to reinforce the value, importance, and benefit of innovation to corporate America.
- The corporate tax laws should be changed so that research and development spending and capital allocated to innovation will be rewarded, not penalized.
- A National Innovation Team Competition could be created. The top twenty innovation teams from twenty different corporations would win a $500,000 award per team to be shared equally by team members, and another $500,000 would go to the winning corporation to encourage still more innovation.
- A National Venture Capital Fund could be established primarily to foster new technology commercialization. For example, NASA has so much to offer on the innovation front. Its top scientists, amazing research discoveries, scientific expertise, and experimentation should be commercialized more effectively.
- Academic institutions could host innovation workshops and training seminars. The University of Chicago's New Product Lab is an example of a current work in progress that is bridging the gap between academia and corporate America. Corporations sponsor graduate students, who identify and explore new products, services, and business opportunities for academic credit, which concurrently benefits the sponsoring company.
- Establishing a Secretary of Innovation would provide the leadership to evoke a national innovation mind-set. This position could

serve as the focal point for business, government, and academia within this country.

The Business/Government Partnership

There are endless opportunities for innovation-related partnering throughout society. Technology transfer is just one example, but we will focus on it here because it is such a rich source of examples.

Government laboratories at the air force; NASA; the Departments of Agriculture, Energy, Defense, and Commerce; the National Institutes of Health; and others have been investing billions of dollars to advance technology knowledge and know-how to improve national competitiveness. However, the technology is not being transferred from the public sector to the commercial sector as effectively as it might. The reason for this is simple: technology needs to be modified, adjusted, and applied differently from one use, product, or industry to the next. Thus, depending on the company, the application of the technology, and the way it's used, the way in which it is best transferred will differ dramatically. Consequently, cooperative partnering of businesses with government technology-producing agencies should become a core part of a corporation's technology strategy. Medical device companies should be teaming up with NASA, biotechnology companies should be strengthening their partnerships with the National Institutes of Health, and so forth.

Obviously, successful partnerships are those where a win-win situation is created for all involved. Technology transfer can serve as a powerful enabler that leads the commercial development of products and services, which in turn could be purchased by the federal government, possibly for services provided to the general population or to corporations themselves.

As a nation and a society, the United States can find more effective ways of converting its national reseach and development investments into more commercialized applications that benefit everyone. Advocacy of partnership programs—whether high-tech, low-tech, or no-tech—can be a smart addition to the portfolio of national and corporate policies. But, as usual, total commitment from the top is needed to remove the barriers to mutual self-interest.

We need to break down the silos; nowhere is it needed more than for creating this country's innovation future. Tearing down the silos and building bridges and partnerships between and among all functions within a corporation is the first step. Doing the same thing throughout society—across business, government, and academia—is the second. American corporations will become the models of innovation in the first decade of the twenty-first century if, with everyone's passionate support, they become innovation zealots and learn to embrace more risk. If this happens, everyone can make innovation the corporate culture of the future.

BIBLIOGRAPHY

Acland, Holly. "Harnessing Internal Innovation." *Marketing*, 22 July 1999, 27.

Babyak, Richard J. "Better Served." *Appliance Manufacturer*, April 1999, 63.

Brooker, Katrina. "Can Procter & Gamble Change Its Culture, Protect Its Market Share and Find the Next Tide?" *Fortune*, 26 April 1999, 146.

Chamberlain, Gary. "Teamwork Gives Maytag a Jump on Competition." *Purchasing Magazine*, 7 May 1998, 44.

Christenson, Clayton. *The Innovator's Dilemma*. Cambridge, MA: Harvard Business School Press, 1997.

Cooper, Robert G. *Winning at New Products: Accelerating the Process from Idea to Launch*. Reading, MA: Addison-Wesley, 1993.

Cottrill, Ken. "Reinventing Innovation." *Journal of Business Strategy*, March–April 1998, 47.

Eisenhardt, Kathleen M., and Shona L. Brown. "Time Pacing: Competing in Markets That Won't Stand Still." *Harvard Business Review*, March–April 1988, 59–69.

"Fear of the Unknown." *The Economist*, 4 December 1999, 61.

Galvin, Robert. *The Idea of Ideas*. Schaumburg, IL: Motorola University Press, 1991.

Hammer, Michael, and James Champy. *Reengineering the Corporation: A Manifesto for Business Revolution*. New York: Harper Business, 1994.

Hartmann, Lynn. "The Agenda: Total Team Work." *Fast Company*, 1 April 1998, 148.

Kotler, Philip. *Kotler on Marketing: How to Create, Win, and Dominate Markets.* New York: Free Press, 1999.

Kuczmarski & Associates, K&A Winning New Products & Services Best Practices Study, 1999, Chicago, IL.

Kuczmarski, Susan Smith, and Thomas D. Kuczmarski. *Values-Based Leadership.* Upper Saddle River, NJ: Prentice Hall, 1995.

Kuczmarski, Thomas D. *Innovation: Leadership Strategies for the Competitive Edge.* Lincolnwood, IL: NTC Business Books, 1996.

———. *Managing New Products: The Power of Innovation.* Chicago: Book Ends Publishing, 1992.

———. *Managing New Products: Using the MAP System to Accelerate Growth.* Chicago: Book Ends Publishing/The Innovation Press, 2000.

———. "Measuring Your Return on Innovation." *Marketing Management,* spring 2000, 25.

Lipman-Blumen, Jean, and Harold J. Leavitt. *Hot Groups: Seeding Them, Feeding Them, and Using Them to Ignite Your Organization.* New York: Oxford University Press, 1999.

Lucenko, Kristina. "Implementing Innovation." *Across the Board,* January 1999, 55.

Macli, Charles. Review of: *What Were They Thinking: Lessons I've Learned from over 80,000 New Products, Innovations, and Idiocies,* by Robert McMath and Thom Forbes. *The Globe and Mail,* 14 March 1998, D15.

Matheson, David, and Jim Matheson. *The Smart Organization: Creating Value Through Strategic R&D.* Boston: Harvard Business School Press, 1998.

McKibben, Gordon. *Cutting Edge: Gillette's Journey to Global Leadership.* Cambridge, MA: Harvard Business School Press, 1997.

McLuhan, Robert. "Careful Research Continues to Pay." *Marketing,* 15 April 1999, 31.

Middlebrooks, Arthur, and Craig Terrill. *Market Leadership Strategies for Service Companies: Creating Growth, Profits, and Customer Loyalty.* Lincolnwood, IL: NTC Business Books, 2000.

Minhan, Tim. "Harley-Davidson Revs Up Development Process." *Design News,* 18 May 1998, 518.

Nussbaum, Bruce. "A Decade of Design: How Great Products Can Boost the Bottom Line." *Business Week,* 29 November 1999, 85–119.

Peters, Tom. *Thriving on Chaos: Handbook for a Management Revolution.* New York: HarperCollins, 1991.

Roussel, Philip A., Kamal N. Saad, and Tamara J. Erickson. *Third Generation R&D: Managing the Link to Corporate Strategy.* Boston: Harvard Business School Press, 1991.

Sanders, Elizabeth. "Converging Perspectives: Product Development Research for the 1990s." *Design Management Journal,* fall 1992.

Schilling, Melissa A., and Charles W. Hill. "Managing the New Product Development Process: Strategic Imperatives." *Academy of Management Executive,* August 1998, 67.

Scott, George M. "Top Priority Management Concerns About New Product Development." *Academy of Management Executive,* August 1999, 77.

Sheridan, John H. "Nurturing Successful Innovation: Tips to Foster Actual Product Development from Great Ideas." *Industry Week,* 18 May 1998, 16.

Smith, Gregory R., William C. Herbein, and Robert C. Morris. "Front-End Innovation at AlliedSignal and Alcoa." *Research Technology Management,* November 1999, 15.

Swaddling, Jeffrey D., and Mark W. Zobel. "Beating the Odds." *Marketing Management,* winter/spring 1996, 21–33.

Valery, Nicholas. "Innovation in Industry." *The Economist,* 20 February 1999, 25.

Wilcox, Stephen B. "Trust, but Verify." *Appliance Manufacturer,* January 1998, 8.

Willoughby, Jack. "Adverse Reaction: Hammered Hard by Scandals, McKesson's Shares Could Be Bargain." *Barron's,* 21 August 1999, 19.

INDEX

ABOUT THE AUTHORS

Tom Kuczmarski is a nationally recognized expert in new product and service development and innovation. For more than two decades, he has been developing new products, services, and businesses for more than one hundred companies. He has also helped scores of companies enhance their culture to foster an innovation mind-set. Beginning as a new products manager in 1975, he has advanced state-of-the-art thinking as well as the practices of innovation strategy and execution throughout the country. His research, writings, books, speeches, seminars, teaching, and practical consulting position have made him one of the top five leading experts in his field.

Mr. Kuczmarski is regularly quoted in newspapers and periodicals, including the *Wall Street Journal*, *Fortune*, and *Newsweek*, and he speaks on the topic of innovation around the world. An adjunct professor at Northwestern University's Kellogg School of Management for the past eighteen years, Mr. Kuczmarski holds master's degrees in business and international affairs from Columbia University. In addition, he is the author of three books on leading and managing innovation, *Managing New Products*, *Values-Based Leadership*, and *Innovation*.

Arthur Middlebrooks specializes in helping service and high-technology companies grow profitably through new product and service development, differentiation, and effective marketing strategies. He has worked extensively with service companies from a variety of industries, including energy, telecommunications, financial services, insurance, Internet services, software, professional services, and environmental services.

He has been published in the *PDMA Handbook of New Product Development, Management Review*, and *Sales and Marketing Management* and has co-authored a book devoted to service companies titled *Market Leadership Strategies for Service Companies*. He is an adjunct professor at the University of Chicago Graduate School of Business, teaching new product and service development as well as services marketing. Prior to joining DigitalWork.com as director of new service development, he did new product development consulting for Kuczmarski & Associates and strategy consulting for Andersen Consulting.

Mr. Middlebrooks received an MBA from the University of Chicago Graduate School of Business and a B.S. from Duke University. He is a member of the Beta Gamma Sigma and Phi Beta Kappa honor societies.

Jeff Swaddling is an engagement manager with Prophet Brand Strategy, where he specializes in developing innovation and marketing strategies and processes and applying exploratory qualitative research techniques to help companies create new concepts and brand extension opportunities. Specifically, he focuses on the early stages of innovation, including strategy formulation, problem identification, idea generation, and concept development, along with the cultural implications of adopting innovation within an organization.

Mr. Swaddling has led dozens of new product and service projects for companies such as Tribune, Pella, and S.C. Johnson & Son. He is a frequent guest lecturer on new product development and innovation at top business schools, including the Kellogg Graduate School of Management and the University of Chicago Graduate School of Management. He has also published articles in the American Marketing Association's *Marketing Management* journal.